THE WESTERN EXPERIENCE
1750 TO THE PRESENT
A Reader

Compiled by

Mark S. Micale
Department of History
University of Illinois, Champaign-Urbana

 McGraw-Hill Primis
Custom Publishing

Boston   Burr Ridge, IL   Dubuque, IA   Madison, WI   New York   San Francisco   St. Louis
Bangkok   Bogotá   Caracas   Lisbon   London   Madrid
Mexico City   Milan   New Delhi   Seoul   Singapore   Sydney   Taipei   Toronto

McGraw-Hill Higher Education

A Division of The McGraw-Hill Companies

THE WESTERN EXPERIENCE
1750 to the Present
A Reader

McGraw-Hill's Primis Custom Publishing consists of products that are produced from camera-ready copy. Peer review, class testing, and accuracy are primarily the responsibility of the author(s).

2 3 4 5 6 7 8 9 0 QSR QSR 0 9 8 7 6 5

ISBN 0-07-466261-9

Sponsoring Editor: Dee Renfrow
Production Editor: Sue Culbertson
Cover Design: Fairfax Hutter
Printer/Binder: Quebecor World

TABLE OF CONTENTS

FRONTISPICE DE L'ENCYCLOPEDIE.

Charles-Nicolas Cochin, Frontispiece to the Diderot *Encyclopedia*, volume 1 (1751). Beinecke Rare Book and Manuscript Library, Yale University.

2

Immanuel Kant

WHAT IS ENLIGHTENMENT?

Immanuel Kant (1724–1804) was born, lived, and died in Königsberg, eastern Prussia, but wandered much more widely in his mind. A rationalist and disciple of Christian von Wolff, he set himself the task of working out the philosophical implications of Newtonian physics. Appointed to the chair of logic and metaphysics at the University of Königsberg in 1770, he began work on his great system of critical thought. His trilogy, Critique of Pure Reason *(1781),* Critique of Practical Reason *(1788), and* Critique of Judgment *(1790), provided the foundations for reliable human knowledge. In addition, he penned popular shorter essays that explained aspects of his thought. One of the most famous of these appears here. Publication of his last great work,* Religion in the Bounds of Reason *(1793), earned the censure of the Prussian government. Alone and silent, he died a decade later.*

Enlightenment is man's emergence from his self-imposed nonage. Nonage is the inability to use one's own understanding without another's guidance. This nonage is self-imposed if its cause lies not in lack of understanding but in indecision and lack of courage to use one's own mind without another's guidance. *Dare to know!* "Have the courage to use your own understanding," is therefore the motto of the enlightenment.

Laziness and cowardice are the reasons why such a large part of mankind gladly remain minors all their lives, long after nature has freed them from external guidance. They are the reasons why it is so easy for others to set themselves up as guardians. It is so comfortable to be a minor. If I have a book that thinks for me, a pastor who acts as my conscience, a physician who prescribes my diet, and so on — then I have no need to exert myself. I have no need to think, if only I can pay; others will take care of that disagreeable business for me. Those guardians who have kindly taken supervision upon themselves see to it that the overwhelming majority of mankind — among them the entire fair sex — should consider the step to maturity not only as hard, but as extremely dangerous. First, these guardians make their domestic cattle stupid and carefully prevent the docile creatures from taking a single step without the leading-strings to which they have fastened them. Then they show them the danger that would threaten

Immanuel Kant, "What Is Enlightenment?" in Peter Gay, ed., "*The Enlightenment; A Comprehensive Anthology* (New York, Simon and Schuster, 1973), pp. 383-389.

them if they should try to walk by themselves. Now, this danger is really not very great; after stumbling a few times they would, at last, learn to walk. However, examples of such failures intimidate and generally discourage all further attempts.

Thus it is very difficult for the individual to work himself out of the nonage which has become almost second nature to him. He has even grown to like it and is at first really incapable of using his own understanding, because he has never been permitted to try it. Dogmas and formulas, these mechanical tools designed for reasonable use—or rather abuse—of his natural gifts, are the fetters of an everlasting nonage. The man who casts them off would make an uncertain leap over the narrowest ditch, because he is not used to such free movement. That is why there are only a few men who walk firmly, and who have emerged from nonage by cultivating their own minds.

It is more nearly possible, however, for the public to enlighten itself; indeed, if it is only given freedom, enlightenment is almost inevitable. There will always be a few independent thinkers, even among the self-appointed guardians of the multitude. Once such men have thrown off the yoke of nonage, they will spread about them the spirit of a reasonable appreciation of man's value and of his duty to think for himself. It is especially to be noted that the public which was earlier brought under the yoke by these men afterward forces these very guardians to remain in submission, if it is so incited by some of its guardians who are themselves incapable of any enlightenment. That shows how pernicious it is to implant prejudices: they will eventually revenge themselves upon their authors or their authors' descendants. Therefore, a public can achieve enlightenment only slowly. A revolution may bring about the end of a personal despotism or of avaricious and tyrannical oppression, but never a true reform of modes of thought. New prejudices will serve, in place of the old, as guidelines for the unthinking multitude.

This enlightenment requires nothing but *freedom*—and the most innocent of all that may be called "freedom": freedom to make public use of one's reason in all matters. Now I hear the cry from all sides: "Do not argue!" The officer says: "Do not argue—drill!" The tax collector: "Do not argue—pay!" The pastor: "Do not argue—believe!" Only one ruler in the world says: "Argue as much as you please, and about what you please, but obey!" We find restrictions on freedom everywhere. But which restriction is harmful to enlightenment? Which restriction is innocent, and which advances enlightenment? I reply: the public use of one's reason must be free at all times, and this alone can bring enlightenment to mankind.

On the other hand, the private use of reason may frequently be narrowly restricted without especially hindering the progress of enlightenment. By "public use of one's reason" I mean that use which a man, as *scholar*, makes of it before the reading public. I call "private use" that use which a man makes of his reason in a civic post that has been entrusted to him. In some affairs affecting the interest of the community a certain governmental mechanism is necessary in which some members of the community remain passive. This creates an artificial unanimity which will serve the fulfillment of public objectives, or at least keep these objectives from being destroyed. Here arguing is not permitted: one must obey. Insofar as a part of this machine considers himself at the same time a member of a universal community—a world society of citizens—(let us say that he thinks of himself as a scholar rationally addressing his public through his writings) he may indeed argue, and the affairs with which he is associated in part as a passive member will not suffer. Thus, it would be very unfortunate if an officer on duty and under orders from his superiors should want to criticize the appropriateness or utility of his orders. He must obey. But as a scholar he could not rightfully be prevented from taking notice of the mistakes in the military service and from submitting his views to his public for its judgment. The citizen cannot refuse to pay the taxes levied upon him; indeed, impertinent censure of such taxes could be punished as a scandal that might cause general disobedience. Nevertheless, this man does not violate the duties of a citizen if, as a scholar, he publicly expresses his objections to the impropriety or possible injustice of such levies. A pastor too is bound to preach to his congregation in accord with the doctrines of the church which he serves, for he was ordained on that condition. But as a scholar he has full freedom, indeed the obligation, to communicate to his public all his carefully examined and constructive thoughts concerning errors in that doctrine and his proposals concerning improvement of religious dogma and church institutions. This is nothing that could burden his conscience. For what he teaches in pursuance of his office as representative of the church, he represents as something which he is not free to teach as he sees it. He speaks as one who is employed to speak in the name and under the orders of another. He will say: "Our church teaches this or that; these are the proofs which it employs." Thus he will benefit his congregation as much as possible by presenting doctrines to which he may not subscribe with full conviction. He can commit himself to teach them because it is not completely impossible that they may contain hidden truth. In any event, he has found nothing in the doctrines that contradicts the heart of religion. For if he believed that such contradictions existed he would not be able to administer his office with a clear conscience. He would have to resign it. Therefore the use which a scholar makes of his reason before the congregation that employs him is only a private use, for, no matter how sizable, this is only a domestic audience. In view of this he, as preacher, is not free and ought not to be free, since he is carrying out the orders of others. On the other hand, as the scholar who speaks to his own public (the world) through his writings, the minister in the public use of his reason enjoys unlimited freedom to use his own reason and to speak for himself. That the spiritual guardians of the people should themselves be treated as minors is an absurdity which would result in perpetuating absurdities.

But should a society of ministers, say a Church Council,... have the right to commit itself by oath to a certain unalterable doctrine, in order to secure perpetual guardianship over all its members and through them over the people? I say that this is quite impossible. Such a contract, concluded to keep all further enlightenment from humanity, is simply null and void even if it should be confirmed by the sovereign power, by parliaments, and by the most solemn treaties. An epoch cannot conclude a pact that will commit succeeding ages, prevent them from increasing their significant insights, purging themselves of errors, and generally progressing in enlightenment. That would be a crime against human nature, whose proper destiny lies precisely in such progress. Therefore, succeeding ages are fully entitled to repudiate such decisions as unauthorized and outrageous. The touchstone of all those decisions that may be made into law for a people lies in this question: Could a people impose such a law upon itself? Now, it might be possible to introduce a certain order for a definite short period of time in expectation of a better order. But while this provisional order continues, each citizen (above all, each pastor acting as a scholar) should be left free to publish his criticisms of the faults of existing institutions. This should continue until public understanding of these matters has gone so far that, by uniting the voices of many (although not necessarily all) scholars, reform proposals could be brought before the sovereign to protect those congregations which had decided according to their best lights upon an altered religious order, without, however, hindering those who want to remain true to the old institutions. But to agree to a perpetual religious constitution which is not to be publicly questioned by anyone would be, as it were, to annihilate a period of time in the progress of man's improvement. This must be absolutely forbidden.

A man may postpone his own enlightenment, but only for a limited period of time. And to give up enlightenment altogether, either for oneself or one's descendants, is to violate and to trample upon the sacred rights of man. What a people may not decide for itself may even less be decided for it by a monarch, for his reputation as a ruler consists precisely in the way in which he unites the will of the whole people within his own. If he only sees to it that all true or supposed improvement remains in step with the civic order, he can for the rest leave his subjects alone to do what they find necessary for the salvation of their souls. Salvation is none of his business; it *is* his business to prevent one man from forcibly keeping another from determining and promoting his salvation to the best of his ability. Indeed, it would be prejudicial to his majesty if he meddled in these matters and supervised the writings in which his subjects seek to bring their views into the open, even when he does this from his own highest insight, because then he exposes himself to the reproach: *Caesar non est supra grammaticos.*[1] It is worse when he debases his sovereign power so far as to support the spiritual despotism of a few tyrants in his state over the rest of his subjects.

When we ask, Are we now living in an enlightened age? the answer is, No, but we live in an age of enlightenment. As matters now stand it is still far from true that men are already capable of using their own reason in religious matters confidently and correctly without external guidance. Still, we have some obvious indications that the field of working toward the goal of religious truth is now being opened. What is more, the hindrances against general enlightenment or the emergence from self-imposed nonage are gradually diminishing. In this respect this is the age of the enlightenment and the century of Frederick.

A prince ought not to deem it beneath his dignity to state that he considers it his duty not to dictate anything to his subjects in religious matters, but to leave them complete freedom. If he repudiates the arrogant word *tolerant*, he is himself enlightened; he deserves to be praised by a grateful world and posterity as that man who was the first to liberate mankind from dependence, at least on the government, and let everybody use his own reason in matters of conscience. Under his reign, honorable pastors, acting as scholars and regardless of the duties of their office, can freely and

---

[1] Caesar is not above grammarians.

openly publish their ideas to the world for inspection, although they deviate here and there from accepted doctrine. This is even more true of every other person not restrained by any oath of office. This spirit of freedom is spreading beyond the boundaries of Prussia, even where it has to struggle against the external hindrances established by a government that fails to grasp its true interest. Frederick's Prussia is a shining example that freedom need not cause the least worry concerning public order or the unity of the community. When one does not deliberately attempt to keep men in barbarism, they will gradually work out of that condition by themselves.

I have emphasized the main point of the enlightenment—man's emergence from his self-imposed nonage—primarily in religious matters, because our rulers have no interest in playing the guardian to their subjects in the arts and sciences. Above all, nonage in religion is not only the most harmful but the most dishonorable. But the disposition of a sovereign ruler who favors freedom in the arts and sciences goes even further: he knows that there is no danger in permitting his subjects to make public use of their reason and to publish their ideas concerning a better constitution, as well as candid criticism of existing basic laws. We already have a striking example [of such freedom], and no monarch can match the one whom we venerate.

But only the man who is himself enlightened, who is not afraid of shadows, and who commands at the same time a well-disciplined and numerous army as guarantor of public peace—only he can say what a free state cannot dare to say: "Argue as much as you like, and about what you like, but obey!" Thus we observe here as elsewhere in human affairs, in which almost everything is paradoxical, a surprising and unexpected course of events: a large degree of civic freedom appears to be of advantage to the intellectual freedom of the people, yet at the same time it establishes insurmountable barriers. A lesser degree of civic freedom, however, creates room to let that free spirit expand to the limits of its capacity. Nature, then, has carefully cultivated the seed within the hard core—namely, the urge for and the vocation of free thought. And this free thought gradually reacts back on the modes of thought of the people, and men become more and more capable of acting in freedom. At last free thought acts even on the fundamentals of government, and the state finds it agreeable to treat man, who is now more than a machine, in accord with his dignity.

3

Thomas Jefferson

THE DECLARATION OF INDEPENDENCE

This is the basic document of American democracy. It was written by Thomas Jefferson (1743–1826) at the direction of the Second Continental Congress, meeting in Philadelphia between 10 June and 4 July 1776. On the latter date it was adopted by the Congress and sent to the state legislatures.

THE UNANIMOUS DECLARATION OF THE
THIRTEEN UNITED STATES OF AMERICA,

When in the Course of human events, it becomes necessary for one people to dissolve the political bands which have connected them with another, and to assume among the Powers of the earth, the separate and equal station to which the Laws of Nature and of Nature's God entitle them, a decent respect to the opinions of mankind requires that they should declare the causes which impel them to the separation.

We hold these truths to be self-evident, that all men are created equal, that they are endowed by their Creator with certain unalienable Rights, that among these are Life, Liberty and the pursuit of Happiness. That to secure these rights, Governments are instituted among Men, deriving their just powers from the consent of the governed, That whenever any Form of Government becomes destructive of these ends, it is the Right of the People to alter or to abolish it, and to institute new Government, laying its foundation on such principles and organizing its powers in such form, as to them shall seem most likely to effect their Safety and Happiness. Prudence, indeed, will dictate that Governments long established should not be changed for light and transient causes; and accordingly all experience hath shown, that mankind are more disposed to suffer, while evils are sufferable, than to right themselves by abolishing the forms to which they are accustomed. But when a long train of abuses and usurpations, pursuing invariably the same Object evinces a design to reduce them under absolute Despotism, it is their right, it is their duty, to throw off such Government, and to provide new Guards for their future security.—Such has been the patient sufferance of these Colonies; and such is

Thomas Jefferson, "Declaration of Independence" (1776) in Howard Preston, ed., *Documents Illustrative of American History* (New York, G. P. Putnam, 1893), 210–215; reproduced in Mark S. Kishlansky, ed., *Sources of the West: Readings in Western Civilization* (New York, Longman, 2001), 96–98.

now the necessity which constrains them to alter their former Systems of Government. The history of the present King of Great Britain is a history of repeated injuries and usurpations, all having in direct object the establishment of an absolute Tyranny over these States. To prove this, let Facts be submitted to a candid world.

He has refused his Assent to Laws, the most wholesome and necessary for the public good.

He has forbidden his Governors to pass Laws of immediate and pressing importance, unless suspended in their operation till his Assent should be obtained; and when so suspended, he has utterly neglected to attend to them.

He has refused to pass other Laws for the accommodation of large districts of people, unless those people would relinquish the right of Representation in the Legislature, a right inestimable to them and formidable to tyrants only.

He has called together legislative bodies at places unusual, uncomfortable, and distant from the depository of their Public Records, for the sole purpose of fatiguing them into compliance with his measures.

He has dissolved Representative Houses repeatedly, for opposing with manly firmness his invasions on the rights of the people.

He has refused for a long time, after such dissolutions, to cause others to be elected; whereby the Legislative Powers, incapable of Annihilation, have returned to the People at large for their exercise; the State remaining in the mean time exposed to all the dangers of invasion from without, and convulsions within.

He has endeavoured to prevent the population of these States; for that purpose obstructing the Laws of Naturalization of Foreigners; refusing to pass others to encourage their migration hither, and raising the conditions of new Appropriations of Lands.

He has obstructed the Administration of Justice, by refusing his Assent to Laws for establishing Judiciary Powers.

He has made Judges dependent on his Will alone, for the tenure of their offices, and the amount and payment of their salaries.

He has erected a multitude of New Offices, and sent hither swarms of Officers to harass our People, and eat out their substance.

He has kept among us, in times of peace, Standing Armies without the Consent of our legislature.

He has affected to render the Military independent of and superior to the Civil Power.

He has combined with others to subject us to a jurisdiction foreign to our constitution, and unacknowledged by our laws; giving his Assent to their acts of pretended legislation:

For quartering large bodies of armed troops among us:

For protecting them, by a mock Trial, from Punishment for any Murders which they should commit on the Inhabitants of these States:

For cutting off our Trade with all parts of the world:

For imposing taxes on us without our Consent:

For depriving us in many cases, of the benefits of Trial by Jury:

For transporting us beyond Seas to be tried for pretended offences:

For abolishing the free System of English Laws in a neighbouring Province, establishing therein an Arbitrary government, and enlarging its Boundaries so as to render it at once an example and fit instrument for introducing the same absolute rule into these Colonies:

For taking away our Charters, abolishing our most valuable Laws, and altering fundamentally the Forms of our Governments:

For suspending our own Legislature, and declaring themselves invested with Power to legislate for us in all cases whatsoever.

He has abdicated Government here, by declaring us out of his Protection and waging War against us.

He has plundered our seas, ravaged our Coasts, burnt our towns, and destroyed the lives of our people.

He is at this time transporting large armies of foreign mercenaries to compleat the works of death, desolation and tyranny, already begun with circumstances of Cruelty & perfidy scarcely paralleled in the most barbarous ages, and totally unworthy the Head of a civilized nation.

He has constrained our fellow Citizens taken Captive on the high Seas to bear Arms against their Country, to become the executioners of their friends and Brethren, or to fall themselves by their Hands.

He has excited domestic insurrections amongst us, and has endeavoured to bring on the inhabitants of our frontiers, the merciless Indian Savages, whose known rule of warfare, is an undistinguished destruction of all ages, sexes and conditions.

In every stage of these Oppressions We have Petitioned for Redress in the most humble terms: Our repeated Petitions have been answered only by repeated injury. A Prince, whose character is thus marked by every act which may define a Tyrant, is unfit to be the ruler of a free People.

Nor have We been wanting in attention to our Brittish brethren. We have warned them from time to time of attempts by their legislature to extend an unwarrantable jurisdiction over us. We have reminded them of the circumstances of our emigration and settlement here. We have appealed to their native justice and magnanimity, and we have conjured them by the ties of our common kindred to disavow these usurpations, which, would inevitably interrupt our connections and correspondence. They too have been deaf to the voice of justice and of consanguinity. We must, therefore, acquiesce in the necessity, which denounces our Separation, and hold them, as we hold the rest of mankind, Enemies in War, in Peace Friends.

We, therefore, the Representatives of the United States of America, in General Congress, Assembled, appealing to the Supreme Judge of the world for the rectitude of our intentions, do, in the Name, and by Authority of the good People of these Colonies, solemnly publish and declare, That these United Colonies are, and of Right ought to be Free and Independent States; that they are Absolved from all Allegiance to the British Crown, and that all political connection between them and the State of Great Britain, is and ought to be totally dissolved; and that as Free and Independent States, they have full Power to levy War, conclude Peace, contract Alliances, establish Commerce, and to do all other Acts and Things which Independent States may of right do. And for the support of this Declaration, with a firm reliance on the Protection of Divine Providence, we mutually pledge to each other our Lives, our Fortunes and our sacred Honor.

John Hancock.

New Hampshire
JOSIAH BARTLETT,
WM. WHIPPLE,
MATTHEW THORNTON.

Massachusetts-Bay
SAML. ADAMS,
JOHN ADAMS,
ROBT. TREAT PAINE,
ELBRIDGE GERRY.

Rhode Island
STEP. HOPKINS,
WILLIAM ELLERY.

Connecticut
ROGER SHERMAN,
SAM'EL HUNTINGTON,
WM. WILLIAMS,
OLIVER WOLCOTT.

Georgia
BUTTON GWINNETT,
LYMAN HALL,
GEO. WALTON.

Maryland
SAMUEL CHASE,
WM. PACA,
THOS. STONE,
CHARLES CARROLL of
Carrollton.

Virginia
GEORGE WYTHE,
RICHARD HENRY LEE,
TH. JEFFERSON,
BENJA. HARRISON,
THS. NELSON, JR.,
FRANCIS LIGHTFOOT LEE,
CARTER BRAXTON.

New York
WM. FLOYD,
PHIL. LIVINGSTON,
FRANS. LEWIS,
LEWIS MORRIS.

Pennsylvania
ROBT. MORRIS,
BENJAMIN RUSH,
BENJA. FRANKLIN,
JOHN MORTON,
GEO. CLYMER,
JAS. SMITH,
GEO. TAYLOR,
JAMES WILSON,
GEO. ROSS.

Delaware
CAESAR RODNEY,
GEO. READ,
THO. M'KEAN.

North Carolina
WM. HOOPER,
JOSEPH HEWES,
JOHN PENN.

South Carolina
EDWARD RUTLEDGE,
THOS. HEYWARD, JUNR.,
THOMAS LYNCH, JUNR.,
ARTHUR MIDDLETON.

New Jersey
RICHD. STOCKTON,
JNO. WITHERSPOON,
FRAS. HOPKINSON,
JOHN HART,
ABRA. CLARK.

4

DECLARATION OF THE RIGHTS OF MAN AND CITIZEN

The following is the text of the Declaration of the Rights of Man and the Citizen adopted on August 26, 1789:

The representatives of the French people, constituted as a National Assembly, considering that ignorance, disregard or contempt of the rights of man are the sole causes of public misfortunes and governmental corruption, have resolved to set forth a solemn declaration of the natural, inalienable and sacred rights of man: in order that this declaration, by being constantly present to all members of the social body, may keep them at all times aware of their rights and duties; that the acts of both the legislative and executive powers, by being liable at every moment to comparison with the aim of all political institutions, may be the more fully respected; and that demands of the citizens, by being founded henceforward on simple and incontestable principles, may always redound to the maintenance of the constitution and the general welfare.

The Assembly consequently recognizes and declares, in the presence and under the auspices of the Supreme Being, the following rights of man and the citizen:

I. Men are born and remain free and equal in rights. Social distinctions may be based only on common utility.

II. The aim of all political association is to preserve the natural and imprescriptible rights of man. These rights are liberty, property, security and resistance to oppression.

III. The principle of all sovereignty rests essentially in the nation. No body and no individual may exercise authority which does not emanate from the nation expressly.

IV. Liberty consists in the ability to do whatever does not harm another; hence the exercise of the natural rights of each man has no limits except those which assure to other members of society the enjoyment of the same rights. These limits can only be determined by law.

V. Law may rightfully prohibit only those actions which are injurious to society. No hindrance should be put in the way of anything not prohibited by law, nor may any man be forced to do what the law does not require.

"Declaration of the Rights of Man and Citizen" (1789) from Georges Lefebvre, *The Coming of the French Revolution* (Princeton University Press, 1947), Appendix, 221–223; also available in John Hall, *A Documentary Survey of the French Revolution* (Prentice-Hall, Upper Saddle River, NJ, 1951).

VI. Law is the expression of the general will. All citizens have the right to take part, in person or by their representatives, in its formation. It must be the same for all whether it protects or penalizes. All citizens being equal in its eyes are equally admissible to all public dignities, offices and employments, according to their capacity, and with no other distinction than that of their virtues and talents.

VII. No man may be indicted, arrested or detained except in cases determined by law ant according to the forms which it has prescribed. Those who instigate, expedite, execute or cause to be executed arbitrary orders should be punished; but any citizen summoned or seized by virtue of the law should obey instantly, and renders himself guilty by resistance.

VIII. Only strictly necessary punishments may be established by law, and no one may be punished except by virtue of a law established and promulgated before the time of the offense, and legally put into force.

IX. Every man being presumed innocent until judged guilty, if it is deemed indispensable to keep him under arrest, all rigor not necessary to secure his person should be severely repressed by law.

X. No one may be disturbed for his opinions, even in religion, provided that their manifestation does not trouble public order as established by law.

XI. Free communication of thought and opinion is one of the most precious of the rights of man. Every citizen may therefore speak, write and print freely, on his own responsibility for abuse of this liberty in cases determined by law.

XII. Preservation of the rights of man and the citizen requires the existence of public forces. These forces are therefore instituted for the advantage of all, not for the private benefit of those to whom they are entrusted.

XIII. For maintenance of public forces and for expenses of administration common taxation is necessary. It should be apportioned equally among all citizens according to their capacity to pay.

XIV. All citizens have the right, by themselves or through their representatives, to have demonstrated to them the necessity of public taxes, to consent to them freely, to follow the use made of the proceeds and to determine the shares to be paid, the means of assessment and collection and the duration.

XV. Society has the right to hold accountable every public agent of administration.

XVI. Any society in which the guarantee of rights is not assured or the separation of powers not determined has no constitution.

XVII. Property being an inviolable and sacred right, no one may be deprived of it except for an obvious requirement of public necessity, certified by law, and then on condition of a just compensation in advance.

5

REVOLUTIONARY AND NAPOLEONIC EUROPE: 1789–1815

May 4, 1789—Opening of the Estates General at Versailles.

June 20, 1789—Taking of the "Tennis Court Oath" by members of the Third Estate.

July 14, 1789—Storming of the Bastille provoked by the dismissal of Necker.

August 4, 1789—Nobles surrender feudal privileges at night session of the National Assembly.

October 5–6, 1789—Parisian women march to Versailles and return with royal family.

1789–1791—Period of National and Legislative Assemblies working at a national constitution balancing central and local, legislative and royal powers.

July, 1790—Civil Constitution of the Clergy stripping the Church of special privileges and placing it under governmental control.

June, 1791—Attempted flight of the king and royal family from Paris to Varennes.

April, 1792—French declaration of war against Austria; first of the revolutionary wars.

August, 1792—Paris crowd seizes Louis XVI and family at Tuileries Palace and demands royal trial.

1793–1794—Period of the "Republic of Virtue" and "Reign of Terror" under Robespierre and the Committee of Public Safety.

January 21, 1793—Execution of Louis XVI.

March, 1793—"White Terror" or provincial counterrevolutions, especially strong in the department of the Vendée, against Jacobin extremism in Paris.

June, 1793—Jacobin suppression of moderate Girondist leaders.

October 16, 1793—Execution of Marie-Antoinette.

November, 1793—Adoption of "Republic of Virture" cultural forms: revolutionary calendar, Cult of the Supreme Being, etc.

July, 1794 — "Thermidorean Reaction:" Robespierre shouted down by the National Convention of the "9th of Termidor" and guillotined the next day.

1795–1799 — Period of the Directory: balanced constitutional government based on moderate coalition; constant power challenges from left and right.

September, 1795 — General Bonaparte called to Paris to put down royalist plot against the Directory.

1796–1797 — Series of victories in Italy by Bonaparte over Austria.

November 9, 1799 — The "18th of Brumaire:" Coup d'état of Bonaparte and the Abbé Sieyès against the Directory; plebiscite establishes Bonaparte as First Consul.

1801 — Concordat with the Pope.

1802–1805 — Years of key legal, financial and educational reforms of Napoleon; Code Napoleon (1804).

1803 — Beethoven composes Third ("Eroica") Symphony.

December, 1804 — Papal Coronation of Napoleon in Notre Dame.

1804–1814 — Period of the French Imperium; Napoleon as Emperor.

October 21, 1805 — Battle of Trafalgar: Admiral Nelson destroys French fleet.

December, 1805 — Battle of Austerlitz: sweeping victory for the French against Austrian and Russian troops; first seizure of Vienna.

1806 — Dissolution of the Holy Roman Empire; victory against the Prussians at the Battle of Jena; establishment of the "Continental System" of commercial blocade against England.

1808 — Goethe's *Faust*.

1809 — Napoleon divorces Josephine and marries Hapsburg princess in search of Napoleonic heir.

1810 — Napoleon at zenith of Continental power with national annexations and satellite states; Britain alone remains resistant.

June, 1812–December, 1812 — Napoleon's Russian campaign: victory at Borodino; Russian scorched earth policy and burning of Moscow; winter retreat of French troops from Moscow with severe losses.

1813 — Battle of Leipzig: victory of European coalition against French troops.

April, 1814 — Combined European forces occupy Paris: surrender of Napoleon and exile to the island of Elba; recall of the Bourbon Pretender, Louis XVIII.

September, 1814 — The Congress of Vienna: Castlereagh, Talleyrand, Metternich, and Alexander I inaugurate the congress system and balance-of-power diplomacy; establishment of the Quadruple Alliance.

March to June, 1815 — The "One Hundred Days" of Napoleon.

June 18, 1815 — Final defeat of Napoleonic forces by Duke of Wellington at Waterloo; Napoleon exiled to island of St. Helena.

6

Edmund Burke

REFLECTIONS ON THE REVOLUTION IN FRANCE (1790)

The revolution in France had been under way for little more than a year when the veteran parliamentarian and author wrote this lengthy pamphlet in the form of a letter to a Frenchman.

Dear Sir,

...Though I do most heartily wish that France may be animated by a spirit of rational liberty, and that I think you bound, in all honest policy, to provide a permanent body, in which that spirit may reside, and an effectual organ, by which it may act, it is my misfortune to entertain great doubts concerning several material points in your late transactions....

The circumstances are what render every civil and political scheme beneficial or noxious to mankind. Abstractedly speaking, government, as well as liberty, is good; yet could I, in common sense, ten years ago, have felicitated France on her enjoyment of a government (for she then had a government) without enquiry what the nature of that government was, or how it was administered? Can I now congratulate the same nation upon its freedom? Is it because liberty in the abstract may be classed amongst the blessings of mankind, that I am seriously to felicitate a madman, who has escaped from the protecting restraint and wholesome darkness of his cell, on his restoration to the enjoyment of light and liberty? Am I to congratulate an highwayman and murderer, who has broke prison, upon the recovery of his natural rights?...

I must be tolerably sure, before I venture publicly to congratulate men upon a blessing, that they have really received one. Flattery corrupts both the receiver and the giver; and adulation is not of more service to the people than to kings. I should therefore suspend my congratulations on the new liberty of France, until I was informed how it had been combined with government; with public force; with the discipline and

---

Edmund Burke, *Reflections on the Revolution in France* (1790), excerpt from Walter Arnstein, ed., *The Past Speaks: Sources and Problems in British History* (Lexington, Mass., D. C. Heath, 1981), volume 2: 130–138. Reproduced from Burke's *Reflections* (Doubleday Dolphin edition, Garden City, NY, 1961), 17, 19–21, 27, 29–30, 33–34, 38–43, 45–46, 57–65, 71–75, 89–92, 101–105, 110, 137–139, 167, 236–237, 264.

obedience of armies; with the collection of an effective and well-distributed revenue; with morality and religion; with the solidity of property; with peace and order; with civil and social manners. All these (in their way) are good things too; and, without them, liberty is not a benefit whilst it lasts, and is not likely to continue long. The effect of liberty to individuals is, that they may do what they please: We ought to see what it will please them to do, before we risque congratulations, which may be soon turned into complaints....

It looks to me as if I were in a great crisis, not of the affairs of France alone, but of all Europe, perhaps of more than Europe. All circumstances taken together, the French revolution is the most astonishing that has hitherto happened in the world....

[Dr. Richard Price of the Revolution Society] proceeds dogmatically to assert, that by the principles of the Revolution [of 1688] the people of England have acquired three fundamental rights, all which, with him, compose one system, and lie together in one short sentence; namely, that we have acquired a right

1. "To choose our own governors."
2. "To cashier them for misconduct."
3. "To frame a government for ourselves."

...Unquestionably there was at the Revolution, in the person of King William, a small and a temporary deviation from the strict order of a regular hereditary succession; but it is against all genuine principles of jurisprudence to draw a principle from a law made in a special case, and regarding an individual person....

The two houses, in the act of King William, did not thank God that they had found a fair opportunity to assert a right to choose their own governors, much less to make an election the *only lawful* title to the crown. Their having been in a condition to avoid the very appearance of it, as much as possible, was by them considered as a providential escape. They threw a politic, well-wrought veil over every circumstance tending to weaken the rights, which in the meliorated order of succession they meant to perpetuate; or which might furnish a precedent for any future departure from what they had then settled for ever.

A state without the means of some change is without the means of its conservation. Without such means it might even risque the loss of that part of the constitution which it wished the most religiously to preserve. The two principles of conservation and correction operated strongly at the two critical periods of the Restoration [of 1660] and Revolution [of 1688], when England found itself without a king. At both those periods the nation had lost the bond of union in their antient edifice; they did not, however, dissolve the whole fabric.... It was still a line of hereditary descent; still an hereditary descent in the same blood, though an hereditary descent qualified with Protestantism. When the legislature altered the direction, but kept the principle, they showed that they held it inviolable....

The second claim of the Revolution Society is "a right of cashiering their governors for *misconduct*."...

No government could stand a moment, if it could be blown down with any thing so loose and indefinite as an opinion of "*misconduct*." They who led at the Revolution, grounded the virtual abdication of King James upon no such light and uncertain principle. They charged him with nothing less than a design, confirmed by a multitude of illegal overt acts, to *subvert the Protestant church and state,* and their *fundamental,* unquestionable laws and liberties: they charged him with having broken the *original contract* between king and people. This was more than *misconduct....*

By the statute of the 1ˢᵗ of King William, sess. 2d, called *"the act for declaring the rights and liberties of the subject, and for settling the succession of the crown,"* they enacted, that the ministers should serve the crown on the terms of that declaration. They secured soon after the *frequent meetings of parliament,* by which the whole government would be under the constant inspection and active controul of the popular representative and of the magnates of the kingdom....

Kings, in one sense, are undoubtedly the servants of the people, because their power has no other rational end than that of the general advantage; but it is not true that they are, in the ordinary sense (by our constitution, at least) any thing like servants; the essence of whose situation is to obey the commands of some other, and to be removeable at pleasure. But the king of Great Britain obeys no other person; all other persons are individually, and collectively too, under him, and owe to him a legal obedience....

The ceremony of cashiering kings, of which these gentlemen talk so much at their ease, can rarely, if ever, be performed without force. It then becomes a case of war, and not of constitution.... The question of dethroning, or, if these gentlemen like the phrase better, "cashiering kings," will always be, as it has always been, an extraordinary question of state, and wholly out of the law; a question (like all other questions of state) of dispositions, and of means, and of probable consequences, rather than of positive rights....

The third head of right, asserted by [Dr. Price and the Revolution Society], namely, the "right to form a government for ourselves," has, at least as little countenance from any thing done at the Revolution [of 1688], either in precedent or principle, as the two first of their claims. The Revolution was made to preserve our *antient* indisputable laws and liberties, and that *antient* constitution of government which is our only security for law and liberty.... The very idea of the fabrication of a new government, is enough to fill us with disgust and horror. We wished at the period of the Revolution, and do now wish, to derive all we possess as *an inheritance from our forefathers....*

You will observe, that from Magna Charta [in 1215] to the Declaration of Right [in 1689], it has been the uniform policy of our constitution to claim and assert our liberties, as an *entailed inheritance* derived to us from our forefathers, and to be transmitted to our posterity; as an estate specially belonging to the people of this kingdom without any reference whatever to any other more general or prior right. By this means our constitution preserves an unity in so great a diversity of its parts. We have an inheritable crown; an inheritable peerage; and an house of commons and a people inheriting privileges, franchises, and liberties from a long line of ancestors.

This policy appears to me to be the result of profound reflection; or rather the happy effect of following nature, which is wisdom without reflection, and above it. A spirit of innovation is generally the result of a selfish temper and confined views. People will not look forward to posterity, who never look backward to their ancestors. Besides, the people of England well know, that the idea of inheritance furnishes a sure principle of conservation, and a sure principle of transmission; without at all excluding a principle of improvement. It leaves acquisition free; but it secures what it acquires....

In what we improve we are never wholly new; in what we retain we are never wholly obsolete. By adhering in this manner and on those principles to our forefathers, we are guided not by the superstition of antiquarians, but by the spirit of philosophic analogy. In this choice of inheritance we have given to our frame of polity the image of a relation in blood; binding up the constitution of our country with our dearest domestic ties; adopting our fundamental laws into the bosom of our family affections; keeping inseparable, and cherishing with the warmth of all their combined and mutually reflected charities, our state, our hearths, our sepulchres, and our altars.

You [in France] had all these advantages in your antient [Estates of the Realm]; but you chose to act as if you had never been moulded into civil society, and had every thing to begin anew. You began ill, because you began by despising every thing that belonged to you. You set up your trade without a capital. If the last generations of your country appeared without much lustre in your eyes, you might have passed them by, and derived your claims from a more early race of ancestors....

[But] your National Assembly...has no fundamental law, no strict convention, no respected usage to restrain it. Instead of finding themselves obliged to conform to a fixed constitution, they have a power to make a constitution which shall conform to their designs.... But—*"fools rush in where angels fear to tread."* In such a state of unbounded power, for undefined and undefinable purposes, the evil of a moral and almost physical inaptitude of the man to the function must be the greatest we can conceive to happen in the management of human affairs....

Turbulent, discontented men of quality, in proportion as they are puffed up with personal pride and arrogance, generally despise their own order. One of the first symptoms they discover of a selfish and mischievous ambition, is a profligate disregard of a dignity which they partake with others. To be attached to the subdivision, to love the little platoon we belong to in society, is the first principle (the germ as it were) of public affections. It is the first link in the series by which we proceed towards a love to our country and to mankind....

Every person in your country, in a situation to be actuated by a principle of honour, is disgraced and degraded, and can entertain no sensation of life, except in a mortified and humiliated indignation. But this generation will quickly pass away. The next generation of the nobility will resemble the artificers and clowns, and money-jobbers, usurers, and Jews, who will be always their fellows, sometimes their masters. Believe me, Sir, those who attempt to level, never equalize. In all societies, consisting of various descriptions of citizens, some description must be uppermost. The levellers therefore only change and pervert the natural order of things; they load the edifice of society, by setting up in the air what the solidity of the structure requires to be on the ground. The associations of taylors and carpenters, of which the republic (of Paris, for instance) is composed, cannot be equal to the situation, into which, by the worst of usurpations, an usurpation on the prerogatives of nature, you attempt to force them.

The chancellor of France at the opening of the states, said, in a tone of oratorial flourish, that all occupations were honourable. If he meant only, that no honest employment was disgraceful, he would not have gone beyond the truth. But in asserting, that any thing is honourable, we imply some distinction in its favour. The occupation of an hair-dresser, or of a working tallow-chandler, cannot be a matter of honour to any person—to say nothing of a number of other more servile employments. Such descriptions of men ought not to suffer oppression from the state; but the state suffers oppression, if such as they; either individually or collectively, are permitted to rule. In this you think you are combating prejudice, but you are at war with nature.

You do not imagine, that I wish to confine power, authority, and distinction to blood, and names, and titles. No, Sir. There is no qualification for government, but virtue and wisdom, actual or presumptive. Wherever they are actually found, they have, in whatever state, condition, profession or trade, the passport of Heaven to human place and honour. Woe to the country which would madly and impiously reject the service of the talents and virtues, civil, military, or religious, that are given to grace and to serve it; and would condemn to obscurity every thing formed to diffuse lustre and glory around a state. Woe to that country too, that passing into the opposite extreme, considers a low education, a mean contracted view of things, a sordid mercenary occupation, as a preferable title to command. Every thing ought to be open; but not indifferently to every man. No rotation; no appointment by lot; no mode of election operating in the spirit of sortition or rotation, can be generally good in a government conversant in extensive objects. Because they have no tendency, direct or indirect, to select the man with a view to the duty, or to accommodate the one to the other, I do not hesitate to say, that the road to eminence and power, from obscure condition, ought not to be made too easy, nor a thing too much of course. If rare merit be the rarest of all rare things, it ought to pass through some sort of probation. The temple of honour ought to be seated on an eminence. If it be open through virtue, let it be remembered too, that virtue is never tried but by some difficulty, and some struggle.

Nothing is a due and adequate representation of a state, that does not represent its ability, as well as its property.... The characteristic essence of property, formed out of the combined principles of its acquisition and conservation, is to be *unequal*. The great masses therefore which excite envy, and tempt rapacity, must be put out of the possibility of danger.... The plunder of the few would indeed give but a share inconceivably small in the distribution to the many. But the many are not capable of making this calculation; and those who lead them to rapine, never intend this distribution.

The power of perpetuating our property in our families is one of the most valuable and interesting circumstances belonging to it, and that which tends the most to the perpetuation of society itself. It makes our weakness subservient to our virtue; it grafts benevolence even upon avarice. The possessors of family wealth, and of the distinction which attends hereditary possession (as most concerned in it) are the natural securities for this transmission....

It is said, that twenty-four millions ought to prevail over two hundred thousand. True; if the constitution of a kingdom be a problem of arithmetic. This sort of discourse does well enough with the lamp-post for its second: to men who *may* reason calmly, it is ridiculous. The will of the many, and their interest, must very often differ; and great will be the difference when they make an evil choice. A government of five hundred country attornies and obscure curates is not good for twenty-four millions of men, though it were chosen by eight and forty millions; nor is it the better for being guided by a dozen of persons of quality, who have betrayed their trust in order to obtain that power. At present, you seem in every thing to have strayed out of the high road of nature. The property of France does not govern it. Of course property is destroyed, and rational liberty has no existence. All you have got for the present is a paper circulation, and stock-jobbing constitution: and as to the future, do you seriously think that the territory of France, upon the republican system of eighty-three independent municipalities (to say nothing of the parts that compose them) can ever be governed as one body, or can ever be set in motion by the impulse of one mind?

Far am I from denying in theory; full as far is my heart from withholding in practice (if I were of power to give or to withhold) the *real* rights of men.... They have a right to justice; as between their fellows, whether their fellows are in politic function or in ordinary occupation. They have a right to the fruits of their industry; and to the means of making their industry fruitful. They have a right to the acquisitions of their parents; to the nourishment and improvement of their offspring; to instruction in life, and to consolation in death. Whatever each man can separately do, without trespassing upon others, he has a right to do for himself; and he has a right to a fair portion of all which society, with all its combinations of skill and force can do in his favour. In this partnership all men have equal rights; but not to equal things. He that has but five shillings in the partnership, has as good a right to it, as he that has five hundred pound has to his larger proportion. But he has not a right to an equal dividend in the product of the joint stock; and as to the share of power authority, and direction which each individual ought to have in the management of the state, that I must deny to be amongst the direct original rights of man in civil society; for I have in my contemplation the civil social man, and no other. It is a thing to be settled by convention.

If civil society be the offspring of convention, that convention must be its law. That convention must limit and modify all the descriptions of constitution which are formed under it.... Government is a contrivance of human wisdom to provide for human *wants*. Men have a right that these wants should be provided for by this wisdom. Among these wants is to be reckoned the want, out of civil society, of a sufficient restraint upon their passions. Society requires not only that the passions of individuals should be subjected, but that even in the mass and body as well as in the individuals, the inclinations of men should frequently be thwarted, their will controlled, and their passions brought into subjection. This can only be done *by a power out of themselves*; and not, in the exercise of its function, subject to that will and to those passions which it is its office to bridle and subdue. In this sense the restraints on men, as well as their liberties, are to be reckoned among their rights.... What is the use of discussing a man's abstract right to food or to medicine? The question is upon the method of procuring and administering them. In that deliberation I shall always advise to call in the aid of the farmer and the physician, rather than the professor of metaphysics.

The science of constructing a commonwealth, or renovating it, or reforming it, is, like every other experimental science, not to be taught *à priori*. Nor is it a short experience that can instruct us in that practical science; because the real effects of moral causes are not always immediate; but that which in the first instance is prejudicial may be excellent in its remoter operation; and its excellence may arise even from the ill effects it produces in the beginning.... The science of government [is] a matter which requires experience, and even more experience than any person can gain in his whole life, however sagacious and observing he may be, it is with infinite caution that any man ought to venture upon pulling down an edifice which has answered in any tolerable degree for ages the common purposes of society, or on building it up again, without having models and patterns of approved utility before his eyes....

The pretended rights of these theorists are all extremes; and in proportion as they are metaphysically true, they are morally and politically false. The rights of men are in a sort of *middle*, incapable of definition, but not impossible to be discerned. The rights of men in governments are their advantages; and these are often in balances between differences of good; in compromises sometimes between good and evil, and sometimes, between evil and evil....

It is now sixteen or seventeen years since I saw the queen of France, then the dauphiness, at Versailles; and surely never lighted on this orb, which she hardly seemed to touch, a more delightful vision. I saw her just above the horizon, decorating and cheering the elevated sphere she just began to move in,—glittering like the morning-star, full of life, and splendor, and joy. Oh! what a revolution! and what an heart must I have, to contemplate without emotion that elevation and that fall! Little did I dream when she added titles of veneration to those of enthusiastic, distant, respectful love, that she should ever be obliged to carry the sharp antidote against disgrace concealed in that bosom; little did I dream that I should live to see such disasters fallen upon her in a nation of gallant men, in a nation of men of honour and of cavaliers. I thought ten thousand swords must have leaped from their scabbards to avenge even a look that threatened her with insult.—But the age of chivalry is gone.—That of sophisters, oeconomists, and calculators, has succeeded; and the glory of Europe is extinguished for ever. Never, never more, shall we behold that generous loyalty to rank and sex, that proud submission, that dignified obedience, that subordination of the heart, which kept alive, even in servitude itself, the spirit of an exalted freedom....

But now all is to be changed. All the pleasing illusions, which made power gentle, and obedience liberal, which harmonized the different shades of life, and which, by a bland assimilation, incorporated into politics the sentiments which beautify and soften private society, are to be dissolved by this new conquering empire of light and reason. All the decent drapery of life is to be rudely torn off....

On this scheme of things, a king is but a man; a queen is but a woman; a woman is but an animal; and an animal not of the highest order. All homage paid to the sex in general as such, and without distinct views, is to be regarded as romance and folly. Regicide, and parricide, and sacrilege, are but fictions of superstition, corrupting jurisprudence by destroying its simplicity. The murder of a king or a queen, or a bishop, or a father, are only common homicide; and if the people are by any chance, or in any way gainers by it, a sort of homicide much the most pardonable, and into which we ought not to make too severe a scrutiny.

On the scheme of this barbarous philosophy, which is the offspring of cold hearts and muddy understandings, and which is as void of solid wisdom, as it is destitute of all taste and elegance, laws are to be supported only by their own terrors, and by the concern, which each individual may find in them, from his own private speculations, or can spare to them from his own private interests....

But power, of some kind or other, will survive the shock in which manners and opinions perish; and it will find other and worse means for its support.... Kings will be tyrants from policy when subjects are rebels from principle....

Nothing is more certain, than that our manners, our civilization, and all the good things which are connected with manners, and with civilization, have, in this European world of ours, depended for ages upon two principles; and were indeed the result of both combined; I mean the spirit of a gentleman, and the spirit of religion. The nobility and the clergy, the one by profession, the other by patronage, kept learning in existence, even in the midst of arms and confusions, and whilst governments were rather in their causes than formed. Learning paid back what it received to nobility and to priesthood; and paid it with usury, by enlarging their ideas, and by furnishing their minds. Happy if they had all continued to know their indissoluble union, and their proper place!...

We are not the converts of Rousseau; we are not the disciples of Voltaire; Helvetius has made no progress amongst us. Atheists are not our preachers; madmen are not our lawgivers. We know that *we* have made no discoveries; and we think that no discoveries are to be made, in morality; nor many in the great principles of government, nor in the ideas of liberty, which were understood long before we were born, altogether as well as they will be after the grave has heaped its mould upon our presumption, and the silent tomb shall have imposed its law on our pert loquacity....

Your literary men, and your politicians...conceive, very systematically, that all things which give perpetuity are mischievous, and therefore they are at inexpiable war with all establishments. They think that government may vary like modes of dress, and with as little ill effect; that there needs no principle of attachment, except a sense of present conveniency, to any constitution of the state. They always speak as if they were of opinion that there is a singular species of compact between them and their magistrates, which binds the magistrate, but which has nothing reciprocal in it, but that the majesty of the people has a right to dissolve it without any reason, but its will....

Formerly your affairs were your own concern only. We felt for them as men; but we kept aloof from them, because we were not citizens of France. But when we see the model held up to ourselves, we must feel as Englishmen, and feeling, we must provide as Englishmen. Your affairs, in spite of us, are made a part of our interest; so far at least as to keep at a distance your panacea, or your plague. If it be a panacea, we do not want it. We know the consequences of unnecessary physic. If it be a plague; it is such a plague, that the precautions of the most severe quarantine ought to be established against it....

We know, and what is better we feel inwardly, that religion is the basis of civil society, and the source of all good and of all comfort. In England we are so convinced of this, that there is no rust of superstition, with which the accumulated absurdity of the human mind might have crusted it over in the course of ages, that ninety-nine in an hundred of the people of England would not prefer to impiety....

We know, and it is our pride to know, that man is by his constitution a religious animal; that atheism is against, not only our reason but our instincts; and that it cannot prevail long. But if, in the moment of riot, and in a drunken delirium from the hot spirit drawn out of the alembick of hell, which in France is now so furiously boiling, we should uncover our nakedness by throwing off that Christian religion which has hitherto been our boast and comfort, and one great source of civilization amongst us, and among many other nations, we are apprehensive (being well aware that the mind will not endure a void) that some uncouth, pernicious, and degrading superstition, might take place of it.

Instead of quarrelling with establishments, as some do, who have made a philosophy and a religion of their hostility to such institutions, we cleave closely to them. We are resolved to keep an established church, an established monarchy, an established aristocracy, and an established democracy, each in the degree it exists, and in no greater....

Society is indeed a contract. Subordinate contracts for objects of mere occasional interest may be dissolved at pleasure—but the state ought not to be considered as nothing better than a partnership agreement in a trade of pepper and coffee, callico or tobacco, or some other such low concern, to be taken up for a little temporary interest, and to be dissolved by the fancy of the parties. It is to be looked on with other reverence; because it is not a partnership in things subservient only to the gross animal existence of a temporary and perishable nature. It is a partnership in all science; a partnership in all art; a partnership in every virtue, and in all perfection. As the ends of such a partnership cannot be obtained in many generations, it becomes a partnership not only between those who are living, but between those who are living, those who are dead, and those who are to be born. Each contract of each particular state is but a clause in the great primaeval contract of eternal society, linking the lower with the higher natures, connecting the visible and invisible world, according to a fixed compact sanctioned by the inviolable oath which holds all physical and all moral natures, each in their appointed place....

When all the fraud, impostures, violences, rapines, burnings, murders, confiscations, compulsory paper currencies, and every description of tyranny and cruelty employed to bring about and to uphold this revolution, have their natural effect, that is, to shock the moral sentiments of all virtuous and sober minds, the abettors of this philosophic system immediately strain their throats in a declamation against the old monarchical government of France.... Have these gentlemen never heard, in the whole circle of the worlds of theory and practice, of any thing between the despotism of the monarch and the despotism of the multitude? Have they never heard of a monarchy directed by laws, controlled and balanced by the great hereditary wealth and hereditary dignity of a nation; and both again controlled by a judicious check from the reason and feeling of the people at large acting by a suitable and permanent organ? Is it then impossible that a man may be found who, without criminal ill intention, or pitiable absurdity, shall prefer such a mixed and tempered government to either of the extremes....

I do not know under what description to class the present ruling authority in France. It affects to be a pure democracy, though I think it in a direct train of becoming shortly a mischievous and ignoble oligarchy. But for the present I admit it to be a contrivance of the nature and effect of what it pretends to. I reprobate no form of government merely upon abstract principles. There may be situations in which the purely democratic form will become necessary. There may be some (very few, and very particularly circumstanced) where it would be clearly desireable. This I do not take to be the case of France, or of any other great country. Until now, we have seen no examples of considerable democracies. The antients were better acquainted with them. Not being wholly unread in the authors, who had seen the most of those constitutions, and who best understood them, I cannot help concurring with their opinion, that an absolute democracy, no more than absolute monarchy, is to be reckoned among the legitimate forms of government. They think it rather the corruption and degeneracy, than the sound constitution of a republic.... Of this I am certain, that in a democracy, the majority of the citizens is capable of exercising the most cruel oppressions upon the minority whenever strong divisions prevail in that kind of polity, as they often must; and that oppression of the minority will extend to far greater numbers, and will be carried on with much greater fury, than can almost ever be apprehended from the dominion of a single sceptre....

I see the confiscators begin with bishops, and chapters, and monasteries; but I do not see them end there. I see the princes of the blood, who, by the oldest usages of that kingdom, held large landed estates, (hardly with the compliment of a debate) deprived of their possessions, and in lieu of their stable independent property, reduced to the hope of some precarious, charitable pension, at the pleasure of an assembly, which of course will pay little regard to the rights of pensioners at pleasure, when it despises those of legal proprietors. Flushed with the insolence of their first inglorious victories, and pressed by the distresses caused by their lust of unhallowed lucre, disappointed but not discouraged, they have at length ventured completely to subvert all property of all descriptions throughout the extent of a great kingdom. They have compelled all men, in all transactions of commerce, in the disposal of lands, in civil dealing, and through the whole communion of life, to accept as perfect payment and good and lawful tender, the symbols of their speculations on a projected sale of their plunder. What vestiges of liberty or property have they left? The tenant-right of a cabbage-garden, a year's interest in a hovel, the good-will of an ale-house or a baker's shop, the very shadow of a constructive property, are more ceremoniously treated in our parliament than with you the oldest and most valuable landed possessions in the hands of the most respectable personages, or than the whole body of the monies and commercial interest of your country. We entertain an high opinion of the legislative authority; but we have never dreamt that parliaments had any right whatever to violate property, to overrule prescription, or to force a currency of their own fiction in the place of that which is real, and recognized by the law of nations. But you, who began with refusing to submit to the most moderate restraints have ended by establishing an unheard of despotism....

[The] relation of your army to the crown will, if I am not greatly mistaken, become a serious dilemma in your politics.... In the weakness of one kind of authority, and in the fluctuation of all, the officers of an army will remain for some time mutinous and full of faction, until some popular general, who understands the art of conciliating the soldiery, and who possesses the true spirit of command, shall draw the eyes of all men upon himself. Armies will obey him on his personal account. There is no other way of securing military obedience in this state of things. But the moment in which that event shall happen, the person who really commands the army is your master; ...the master of your assembly, the master of your whole republic....

The improvements of the National Assembly are superficial, their errors fundamental.... Whatever they are, I wish my countrymen rather to recommend to our neighbours the example of the British constitution, than to take models from them for the improvement of our own....

7

Walter E. Houghton

THE VICTORIAN FRAME OF MIND 1830–1870

Chapter 1
CHARACTER OF THE AGE

In 1858 a Victorian critic, searching for an epithet to describe "the remarkable period in which our own lot is cast," did not call it the age of democracy or industry or science, nor of earnestness or optimism. The one distinguishing fact about the time was "that we are living in *an age of transition*."[1] This is the basic and almost universal conception of the period.[2] And it is peculiarly Victorian. For although all ages are ages of transition, never before had men thought of their own time as an era of change *from* the past *to* the future. Indeed, in England that idea and the Victorian period began together. When John Stuart Mill in 1831 found transition to be the leading characteristic of the time—"mankind have outgrown old institutions and old doctrines, and have not yet acquired new ones"—he noted that this had become obvious to the more discerning only "a few years ago," and that now "it forces itself upon the most inobservant."[3]

To Mill and the Victorians the past which they had outgrown was not the Romantic period and not even the eighteenth century. It was the Middle Ages. They recognized, of

---

[1] "The Progress and Spirit of Physical Science," *Edinburgh Review, 108* (1858), 71. The writer (who was kindly identified for me by Professor R. D. Altick) was Sir Henry Holland. The article was reprinted in his *Essays on Scientific and Other Subjects Contributed to the Edinburgh and Quarterly Reviews*, London, 1862.

[2] The specific words "transition" or "transitional" are used by Prince Albert, Matthew Arnold, Baldwin Brown, Carlyle, Disraeli, Frederic Harrison, Bulwer Lytton, W. H. Mallock, Harriet Martineau, John Mill, John Morley, William Morris, Herbert Spencer, Hugh Stowell, J. A. Symonds, Tennyson, and no doubt many others.

[3] *The Spirit of the Age*, p. 6, and cf. p. 1. Here and throughout the present work the particular edition used for cited and quoted works, if not identified in the note, will be found in the Bibliography.

Walter E. Houghton, *The Victorian Frame of Mind, 1830–1870* (New Haven, Yale University Press, 1957), chapter 1: "The Character of the Age," 1–23.

course, that there were differences between themselves and their immediate predecessors, but from their perspective it was the medieval tradition from which they had irrevocably broken—Christian orthodoxy under the rule of the church and civil government under the rule of king and nobility; the social structure of fixed classes, each with its recognized rights and duties; and the economic organization of village agriculture and town guilds. That was "the old European system of dominant ideas and facts" which Arnold saw dissolving in the nineteenth century.[4] But the process had begun much earlier, starting with the Renaissance and the Reformation, gaining momentum, quietly but steadily, through the next two centuries of philosophic rationalism and expanding business, until it finally broke into the open when the French Revolution of 1789 proclaimed the democratic Rights of Man and the atheistical worship of the Goddess of Reason. That was the first overt manifestation, in Mill's opinion, that Europe was in a state of transition.[5] But it was not realized at the time, not in England. There it was not until the rising agitation for a reform bill (finally successful in 1832), the passage of Catholic Emancipation, the attack on the Church by Whig Liberals and Benthamite agnostics together with the outbreak of the 1830 revolutions abroad, that men suddenly realized they were living in an age of radical change.[6] Then they began to say that "old opinions, feelings—ancestral customs and institutions are crumbling away, and both the spiritual and temporal worlds are darkened by the shadow of change."[7]

For "old" and "ancestral" we may read "medieval" or "feudal." When Arnold observed that many people thought it possible to keep a good deal of "the past," his next sentence defined the term: the extremists, indeed, hoped "to retain or restore the whole system of the Middle Ages."[8] "Until quite recently," wrote Baldwin Brown in his important lectures of 1869–70, *The Revolution of the Last Quarter of a Century*, "...our modes of thought and speech, our habits of action, our forms of procedure in things social and political, were still feudal."[9] To Carlyle and Ruskin and Thomas Arnold, the period is one of decaying or dying feudalism.[10] This was not an abstract idea. Victorians like Thackeray who had grown up in the 1820's felt they had lived in two distinct worlds:

---

[4] "Heine," *Essays in Criticism, First Series*, pp. 186–7.

[5] *The Spirit of the Age*, p. 67. Cf. Carlyle, "Signs of the Times," *Essays*, 2, 82.

[6] See Mill, "The Claims of Labour," *Dissertations and Discussions*, 2, 188; and George Eliot, *Felix Holt*, 1, chap. 3, pp. 66–7.

[7] Edward Bulwer Lytton, *England and the English*, p. 281. But this passage may have been written by Mill: see his *Autobiography*, chap. 6, p. 168.

[8] "Democracy" (1861), *Mixed Essays*, p. 22. Robert Vaughan began *The Age of Great Cities* (1843) with a section "On the Conflict between Feudalism and Civilization in Modern Society" in which he noticed (pp. 5–6) a reactionary movement that would "diminish everything commercial and civic, so as to place the military and the feudal in its old undisturbed ascendancy" and would "restore the power of the Christian priesthood in much of the form and greatness which distinguished it during the middle age."

[9] *First Principles of Ecclesiastical Truth*, p. 273. The lectures are on pp. 209–364. For their date see p. vii.

[10] Thomas Arnold and Carlyle are quoted below, p. 4; for Ruskin, see *The Crown of Wild Olive, Works, 18*, Lecture 4, p. 494. Cf. Dowden, quoted below, note 14.

It was only yesterday; but what a gulf between now and then! *Then* was the old world. Stage-coaches, more or less swift, riding-horses, pack-horses, highwaymen, knights in armour, Norman invaders, Roman legions, Druids, Ancient Britons painted blue, and so forth—all these belong to the old period. I will concede a halt in the midst of it, and allow that gunpowder and printing tended to modernise the world. But your railroad starts the new era, and we of a certain age belong to the new time and the old one. We are of the time of chivalry as well as the Black Prince of Sir Walter Manny. We are of the age of steam.[11]

From a mere glance at the title page of Carlyle's *Past and Present*, any Victorian might have guessed that the book was a comparison of the Middle Ages with the nineteenth century.

By definition an age of transition in which change is revolutionary has a dual aspect: destruction and reconstruction. As the old order of doctrines and institutions is being attacked or modified or discarded, at one point and then another, a new order is being proposed or inaugurated. Both tendencies were apparent by 1830. After his description of the breakup of timeworn landmarks, Bulwer Lytton continued: "The age then is one of *destruction*!... Miserable would be our lot were it not also an age of preparation for reconstructing."[12] Twenty years later at the center of the Victorian period, what new construction had emerged? Or rather—for this is the important question for getting at the temper of the age—what did men think distinguished their time most significantly from the past? What did they think was peculiarly Victorian about "the state of society and of the human mind?"[13]

1. The State of Society

By the late nineteenth century it was clear that the feudal and agrarian order of the past had been replaced by a democratic and industrial society.[14] The emergence of democracy meant not only the transference of political power from the aristocracy to the people, mainly by the successive Reform Bills of 1832, 1867, and 1884 but also the arrival of what is often called a democratic society. The latter, indeed, was so striking that Mill once called the distinguishing feature of modern institutions and of modern life itself the fact "that human beings are no longer born to their place in life...but are free to employ their faculties, and such favourable chances as offer, to achieve the lot which may appear to them most desirable."[15] This breakdown of the old conception of status owed something to democratic ideas about the rights of man, but its primary cause was

---

[11] "De Juventute" (1860), published in the *Roundabout Papers, Works*, 12, 232. For the tendency to idealize the prerailroad world of the early century, see Kathleen Tillotson, *Novels of the Eighteen-Forties*, pp. 102-9, where Thackeray's essay is quoted.

[12] *England and the English*, p. 281; but see note 7. Cf. Carlyle, *Sartor Resartus*, Bk. III, chap. 7, p. 244.

[13] These are Mill's categories in *The Spirit of the Age*, pp. 2, 6.

[14] Cf. Dowden, "Victorian Literature" (1887), *Transcripts and Studies* (London, 1896), p. 159: "Society, founded on the old feudal doctrines, has gone to wreck in the storms that have blown over Europe during the last hundred years. A new industrial and democratic period has been inaugurated."

[15] *The Subjection of Women*, chap. 1, p. 445. Cf. Brown, *First Principles*, pp. 274–9.

economic. The development of commerce, drawing men off from the land and opening new and independent careers to talent, had been the main instrument in dissolving the feudal nexus of society.[16] In politics, too, the Industrial Revolution underlay the democratic revolution. What Thomas Arnold had in mind when he remarked, on seeing the first train pass through the Rugby countryside, that "feudality is gone for ever,"[17] is made explicit by a passage in *Sartor Resartus*, written on the eve of the Reform Bill of 1832: "Cannot the dullest hear Steam-Engines clanking around him? Has he not seen the Scottish Brassmith's IDEA (and this but a mechanical one) travelling on fire-wings round the Cape, and across two Oceans; and stronger than any other Enchanter's Familiar, on all hands unweariedly fetching and carrying: at home, not only weaving Cloth; but rapidly enough overturning the whole old system of Society; and, for Feudalism and Preservation of the Game, preparing us, by indirect but sure methods, Industrialism and the Government of the Wisest?"[18]

Whether wisest or not, the bankers and manufacturers who rose to political power through the revolutionary legislation of 1828–1835—the repeal of the Test and Corporation Acts, the Municipal Reform Act, and above all, the Reform Bill—owed their victory to the financial and psychological power they acquired from the Industrial Revolution. Both factors are seen in Disraeli's analysis of the capitalist mind in *Coningsby*. Mr. Millbank is discussing the English peerage: "I have yet to learn they are richer than we are, better informed, wiser, or more distinguished for public or private virtue. Is it not monstrous, then, that a small number of men, several of whom take the titles of Duke and Earl from towns in this very neighbourhood, towns which they never saw, which never heard of them, which they did not form, or build, or establish,—I say, is it not monstrous that individuals so circumstanced should be invested with the highest of conceivable privileges, the privilege of making laws?"[19] Those are the social forces, wealth and outraged pride, which demanded the Reform Bill. And once the middle class attained political as well as financial eminence, their social influence became decisive. The Victorian frame of mind is largely composed of their characteristic modes of thought and feeling.

But far more striking at the time than democracy was the tremendous industrial development that came with the use of new machines for manufacturing and communication.[20] The great inventions date from the later eighteenth century; and in the early decades of the nineteenth the introduction of more canals, macadam roads, railways, and steamboats hastened the growth of large-scale production by making

---

[16] Brown, pp. 280–1, and cf. Mill, "Democracy in America," *Dissertations*, 2, 62–71.

[17] A. P. Stanley, *Life of Thomas Arnold*, appendix D, p. 723 n., with the journal entry for August 4, 1839.

[18] Bk. II, chap. 4, p. 118. The Scottish Brassmith is James Watt.

[19] *Works*, 12, chap. 26, p. 225. Cf. Brougham's speech in the House of Lords advocating the Reform Bill, quoted in A. V. Dicey, *Lectures on the Relation of Law and Public Opinion in England*, pp. 184–5.

[20] Cf. T. H. Huxley, "The Progress of Science, 1837–1887," *Method and Results*, p. 42: "The most obvious and the most distinctive feature of the History of Civilisation, during the last fifty years, is the wonderful increase of industrial production by the application of machinery, the improvement of old technical processes and the invention of new ones, accompanied by an even more remarkable development of old and new means of locomotion and intercommunication."

possible a vast expansion of commerce. This development revolutionized the economic life of England. The old system of fixed regulations, which paralleled that in fixed social relations, was abandoned for the new principle of laissez-faire, on which the manufacturer bought his materials in the cheapest market and sold them in the highest, and hired his labor wherever he liked, for as long as he pleased, at the lowest wages he could pay. In Southey's *Colloquies on the Progress and Prospects of Society* (1829) and Macaulay's fighting review of it (1830), the world of big business and unlimited competition was debated by the old conservatism and the new liberalism.

To live in this dynamic, free-wheeling society was to feel the enormous pressure of work, far beyond anything known before. When new and more distant sources of supply and demand were constantly being opened up by the railroad and the steamship, the battle for new markets became intense. To neglect them could mean ruin. So could failure to take advantage of the latest invention or adapt one's business methods to the most recent developments. Disraeli's Coningsby is startled to learn from Mr. Head, who is building a new mill at Staleybridge, that Manchester is already gone by. "If you want to see life," he says, "go to Staley-bridge or Bolton. There's high-pressure." Only the Manchester Bank has kept up with the times: "That's a noble institution, full of commercial enterprise; understands the age, sir; high-pressure to the backbone."[21] The masters had to work almost as long hours as their hands—the Messrs. Carson, for example, who did not become acquainted with their agreeable daughters until their mill was burned down: "There were happy family evenings now that the men of business had time for domestic enjoyments."[22] The same pressure was felt in the professions. "The eminent lawyer, the physician in full practice, the minister, and the politician who aspires to be a minister—even the literary workman, or the eager man of science—are one and all condemned to an amount and continued severity of exertion of which our grandfathers knew little."[23] That was due as much to the social system as to business conditions. When class lines broke down and it became possible as never before to rise in the world by one's own strenuous efforts, the struggle for success was complemented by the struggle for rank.[24] Even apart from personal ambitions, the very existence of hundreds of objects, once unknown or within the reach of few, now made widely available and therefore desirable, increased the size of one's expenses and the load of his work.[25] Moreover, the growing wealth of the wealthy advanced the style of living in the middle and upper classes to a point where the Victorian had to struggle for things his father had been able to ignore. George Eliot remarked that £3,000 a year had seemed wealth to provincial families in 1830, "innocent of future gold-fields, and of that gorgeous plutocracy which has so nobly exalted the necessities of genteel life."[26]

---

[21] *Works, 12*, chap. 24, p. 210. The date is 1844.

[22] Mrs. Gaskell, *Mary Barton* (first ed., 1848; London, 1911), chap. 6, p. 67.

[23] W. R. Greg, "Life at High Pressure" (1875), *Literary and Social Judgments, 2*, 272.

[24] This is discussed below, Chap. 8.

[25] Cf. Mark Pattison, "The Age of Reason," *Fortnightly Review, 27* (1877), 357: "To live at all is a struggle; to keep within reach of the material advantages which it is the boast of our century to have provided is a competition in which only the strong can succeed—the many fail."

[26] *Middlemarch, 1*, Bk. I, chap. 1, p. 6; and cf. Greg, p. 278.

Not only the tempo of work but the tempo of living had increased with striking impact, so much so that one observer thought that "the most salient characteristic of life in this latter portion of the 19th century is its SPEED."[27] Until the Victorian period the rate of locomotion and communication had remained almost what it had been for centuries. The horse and the sailing vessel were still the fastest things on earth. But within a few years the speed of travel by land increased from twelve to fifty miles an hour on the new railroads (over 400 per cent) and the new steamships were doing fifteen knots "with wonderful regularity, in spite of wind and tide."[28] But it was less the mechanical speed of the new inventions than the speed of living they produced which impressed the Victorians. Faster locomotion, of goods and letters and people, simply increased the number of things one crowded into a day, and the rush from one to another. Once upon a time "people did not run about the town or the land as we do." They traveled less often, did not hurry to catch trains, wrote one letter a morning instead of ten. Now "we are whirled about, and hooted around, and rung up as if we were all parcels, booking clerks, or office boys."[29] It seems far more modern than Victorian. But if the speed of life has increased in the twentieth century, the sense of speed has declined, for what has become commonplace today was then a startling novelty. Our great-grandfathers may have had more leisure than we do but it seemed less. Even more than ourselves they felt they were living "without leisure and without pause—a life of *haste*—above all a life of excitement, such as haste inevitably involves— a life filled so full…that we have no time to reflect where we have been and whither we intend to go…still less what is the value, and the purpose, and *the price* of what we have seen, and done, and visited."[30]

This sense of faster and more crowded living had its intellectual as well as its mechanical basis. The spread of education coupled with the enormous expansion of knowledge and the corresponding increase of publication, books and periodicals and newspapers, gave "every man…a hundred means of rational occupation and amusement which were closed to his grandfather,"[31] and led George Eliot, in a threnody on the death of leisure ("gone where the spinning-wheels are gone, and the pack-horses, and the slow wagons, and the pedlers, who brought bargains to the door on sunny afternoons") to say that "even idleness is eager now,—eager for amusement; prone to excursion-trains, art-museums, periodical literature, and exciting novels; prone even to scientific theorizing, and cursory peeps through microscopes."[32] By the sixties Frances Cobbe was comparing her own generation with that of 1800–30 in words which sound

---

[27] Greg, p. 263.

[28] Ibid., p. 264, quoted from Greg's earlier *Enigmas of Life*, pp. 38–9. Cf. Frederic Harrison, "A Few Words about the Nineteenth Century," *The Choice of Books*, pp. 421–2.

[29] Frederic Harrison, *Autobiographic Memoirs*, 1, 12, 18–19. Though he was writing in the 1880's, he was comparing conditions in his later life with those of his youth (he was born in 1831).

[30] Greg, p. 268.

[31] Kingsley, "Great Cities and Their Influence for Good and Evil" (1857), *Sanitary and Social Essays*, p. 203.

[32] *Adam Bede*, 2, chap. 28, p. 339. In editions where the chapters are numbered consecutively this is chap. 52.

exactly like someone today comparing the generation of 1950 with that of 1850: "That constant sense of being driven—not precisely like 'dumb' cattle, but cattle who must read, write, and talk more in twenty-four hours than twenty-four hours will permit, can never have been known to them."[33]

2. The State of the Human Mind

The radical transition in the human mind was less apparent at first than that in society, but sensitive observers were soon aware that the traditional framework of thought was breaking down. By 1838 Thomas Arnold had noticed a new "atmosphere of unrest and paradox hanging around many of our ablest young men of the present day." He was speaking not merely of religious doubts but "of questions as to great points in moral and intellectual matters; where things which have been settled for centuries seem to be again brought into discussion."[34] This is the atmosphere reflected in the early essays of Macaulay and Carlyle, in *Sartor Resartus* and Mill's *Spirit of the Age*, and the novels of Sterling and Maurice. All of them, written between 1825 and 1834, show that the old certitudes are certain no longer and that a reconstruction of thought is now a prime necessity. "The Old has passed away," wrote Carlyle in 1831, "but, alas, the New appears not in its stead; the Time is still in pangs of travail with the New."[35] There was, of course, more destruction to come, for the old was by no means gone (traditional Christianity, indeed, under Wesleyan and presently Tractarian influence was reviving). And there had been earlier efforts to bring forth the new, most notably by Bentham and Coleridge, the respective heirs of the French *philosophes* and the German transcendentalists, "the two great seminal minds of England in their age."[36] But *the New* had not yet appeared by the thirties. All that was then clear to the intellectuals was that their task was precisely what Carlyle found attempted in the two books he had under review in the essay "Characteristics": "Both these Philosophies are of the Dogmatic or Constructive sort: each in its way is...an endeavour to bring the Phenomena of man's Universe once more under some theoretic Scheme...they strive after a result which shall be positive; their aim is not to question, but to establish."[37]

That is the starting point. What was the situation a generation later? What corresponds in the intellectual world to the establishment of bourgeois industrial society? The answer is—nothing. In 1850 the age is still one "of fusion and transition.... Old formula, old opinions, hoary systems are being thrown into the smelting-pan; they are fusing—they must be cast anew: who can tell under what new shapes...they will come forth from the moulds?" In the seventies men are still searching—"amid that

---

[33] "The Nineteenth Century," *Fraser's Magazine, 69* (1864), 482 (for the attribution of this article to Frances Cobbe see the Bibliography, below). Cf. Brown *First Principles*, pp. 222–3, inviting his hearers in 1869 to compare "the rate at which you are living,...the rate of thought, feeling, and energy—in these as compared with those quiet and comfortable times" in the first decades of the century.

[34] Stanley, *Life of Arnold*, p. 484, from a letter dated October 5, 1838. The next sentence justifies my insertion of "merely."

[35] "Characteristics," *Essays, 3,* 32.

[36] Mill, "Bentham," *Dissertations, 1,* 331.

[37] *Essays, 3,* 33.

break-up of traditional and conventional notions respecting our life, its conduct, and its sanctions, which is undeniably befalling our age,—for some clear light and some sure stay." By the eighties "the disintegration of opinion is so rapid that wise men and foolish are equally ignorant where the close of this waning century will find us."[38] Though the Victorians never ceased to look forward to a new period of firm convictions and established beliefs, they had to live in the meantime between two worlds, one dead or dying, one struggling but powerless to be born, in an age of doubt.[39]

The phrase is ambiguous—and at first glance dubious. When one thinks of Macaulay, Spencer, and Huxley, or of Browning, even of Mill and Ruskin, let alone thousands of pious Evangelicals and Anglicans, one is ready to deny it. Indeed, it was still common until very recently to draw a radical contrast between the Victorians and ourselves. One modern critic thought that "a spirit of certitude, wonderful to us who live in an age which has taken the note of interrogation as its emblem, impregnated the great Victorians." Another has claimed that it was only after 1900 that "the old certainties were certainties no longer," and "everything was held to be open to question"; and that "the Victorians seemed to themselves to be living in a house built on unshakable foundations and established in perpetuity...the Home, the Constitution, the Empire, the Christian religion—each of these...was accepted as a final revelation."[40] From such assumptions we could predict the reversal, under the powerful incitement of nostalgia, of the anti-Victorian movement represented by Lytton Strachey:

> If, after the first World War, we were all debunking the nineteenth century, after the second we are deferring to it, and even yearning nostalgically after it: *tendentesque manus ripae ulterioris amore.* In our own unpleasant century we are mostly displaced persons, and many feel tempted to take flight into the nineteenth as into a promised land...In that distant mountain country, all that we now lack seems present in abundance: not only peace, prosperity, plenty and freedom, but faith, purpose and buoyancy.[41]

Though this contrast of the Victorian period with our own has its element of truth, the tendency to invest the past with the virtues one finds lacking in the present has led to a serious misconception. The fact is, while moral values were firm until about 1870,

---

[38] The three quotations are by Hugh Stowell, "The Age We Live In," in *Exeter Hall Lectures,* 6 (London, 1850–51), 45–6; Matthew Arnold, "Bishop Butler and the Zeit-Geist," *Last Essays on Church and Religion,* p. 287; and J. A. Froude, preface to *Short Studies,* 4, v–vi.

[39] See Arnold, "Stanzas from the Grande Chartreuse" (1855), lines 85–8. After Bulwer Lytton in *England and the English* refers (p. 281) to living in an age of transition, he adds in apposition, "an age of disquietude and doubt." Cf. Winwood Reade, *The Martyrdom of Man* (first published in 1872), p. 540: "We are now in the dreary desert that separates two ages of belief." Mill's important statement is quoted below, p. 30.

[40] The two critics are D. Willoughby in *The Great Victorians,* ed. H. J. Massingham and Hugh Massingham (Garden City, N.Y., 1932), p. 242 and A. C. Ward, *Twentieth-Century Literature. The Age of Interrogation, 1901–1925* (London, 1930), pp. 2, 4.

[41] Basil Willey, *Nineteenth Century Studies,* p. 52.

all intellectual theories, including those of morality, were insecure. What John Morley said of the fifties and sixties applies to the entire period, though with greater intensity and wider repercussions as the years passed: "It was the age of science, new knowledge, searching criticism, followed by multiplied doubts and shaken beliefs."[42] The very effort to resolve the situation made it worse. New solutions raised new controversies, which raised new questions. "Intellectually," wrote J. A. Froude—with religion in mind, but his remark has broader relevance—"the controversies to which I had listened had unsettled me. Difficulties had been suggested which I need not have heard of, but out of which some road or other had now to be looked for."[43] But which road? The choice was baffling. "None of the ways in which...mental regeneration is sought," Mill recognized in 1842, "Bible Societies, Tract Societies, Puseyism, Socialism, Chartism, Benthamism, etc.—will *do*, though doubtless they have all some elements of truth and good in them"; with the result that he was finding it very hard to make up his mind "as to the course which must be taken by the present great transitional movement of opinion and society."[44]

The range of discussion reflected by Mill's list is significant. It was not only in religion that one faced a series of alternatives: is there a God or is there not, and if so, is he a person or an impersonal force? Is there a heaven and a hell? or a heaven but no hell? or neither? If there *is* a true religion, is it Theism or Christianity? And what is Christianity? Roman Catholicism or Protestantism? Is it Church or Chapel? High Church? Broad Church? Low Church? Similar questions, if not so pressing or so widespread, invaded ethical theory and the conception of man: have we free-will or are we human automatons? and if we have the power of moral choice, what is its basis? a God-given voice of conscience? or rational calculation deciding which of two actions will promote the greatest happiness of the greatest number? Is man a man or simply a higher ape? Even the political-economic order of bourgeois capitalism, if an established fact of the outer environment in 1850, held no unquestioned supremacy in the world of ideas. The sanctity and blessings of private property, laissez-faire, and unlimited competition were challenged, in one aspect or another, by Owen and Mill, Carlyle and Ruskin, the Chartists and the Christian Socialists. The abortive "communism" of 1848 in France further opened Victorian eyes to the possibility that the old political economy

---

[42] *Recollections*, 1, 100. The view of the period I am advocating—not that doubt existed, which has long been recognized, but that it was an "age of doubt" rather than of certitude—emerged, here and there, in *Ideas and Beliefs of the Victorians* (1949): see pp. 19, 23–5, 71–7, 423; and in 1953 Gaylord C. LeRoy published a book on Victorian writers called *Perplexed Prophets*. But as recently as June 19, 1953, a critic in the *Times Literary Supplement* (p. 397) wrote of the era: "We may envy the unquestioning firmness of its faith, whether the object of that faith was religion, or science, or humanity."

[43] "The Oxford Counter-Reformation," *Short Studies*, 4, 311–12. On p. 252 Froude notices that the Oxford Tracts, designed to check the advance of liberalism and atheism, "provoked doubts, in those whom they failed to persuade, about Christianity itself." Also cf. "The Age We Live In," *Fraser's Magazine*, 24 (1841), 5: "The very truths which have come forth have produced doubts...and the very lights that have shone in one quarter have only dazzled in others, and this dazzle too often has ended in darkness."

[44] From a letter to R. B. Fox printed in Caroline Fox, *Memories of Old Friends*, ed. H. N. Pym (Philadelphia, 1882), pp. 393–4.

was limited and temporary. And the provisional character of middle-class government, suggested by the Chartist agitation of the forties, was confirmed by the Reform Bill of 1867. By 1870 the uncertain future seemed to belong to the unpredictable populace.

It was not, however, the mere existence of competing philosophies which called all in doubt. It was also the prevailing atmosphere. As one prophet after another stepped forward with his program of reconstruction, the hubbub of contending theories, gaining in number as the century advanced, and spreading out from the intellectuals to the large audience of the periodicals, created a climate of opinion in which, quite apart from any specific doubts, the habit of doubt was unconsciously bred. One had an uneasy feeling, perhaps only half-conscious, that his beliefs were no longer quite secure. Nor should we forget the complementary effect of the vast increase of knowledge, scientific and historical, that almost inundated the Victorians and left them often baffled by the sheer number and complexity of its implications. The yeasty state of mind which Kingsley ascribed to the young men of 1851 was not only one in which "the various stereotyped systems which they have received by tradition [are] breaking up under them like ice in a thaw"; it was also one in which "a thousand facts and notions, which they know not how to classify, [are] pouring in on them like a flood."[45] Three years later Mill's diary for January 13, 1854, contains what is perhaps the best single statement on Victorian doubt:

> "Scarcely any one, in the more educated classes, seems to have any opinions, or to place any real faith in those which he professes to have.... It requires in these times much more intellect to marshal so much greater a stock of ideas and observations. This has not yet been done, or has been done only by very few: and hence the multitude of thoughts only breeds increase of uncertainty. Those who should be the guides of the rest, see too many sides to every question. They hear so much said, or find that so much can be said, about everything, that they feel no assurance of the truth of anything.[46]

Without contrary evidence, who would be surprised if the passage were dated 1954?

This evidence—and much more could be given—suggests that continuity rather than contrast is the conclusion to be drawn from comparing the Victorians with ourselves. And yet, if both periods can be called ages of doubt, it is certainly with a difference. Neither the kind of doubt nor the strength of its hold was the same in 1850 as it is today.

In the four decades under inspection, doubt never reached the point of positive or terminal skepticism. It never involved a denial of the mind as a valid instrument of truth. No mid-Victorian ever described his age as Dobrée described the 1930's, "All the previous ages...had something they could take for granted....We can be sure of nothing; our civilization is threatened, even the simplest things we live by....In our present

---

[45] "Epilogue" to *Yeast*, p. 312. Cf. Harrison, "A Few Words about the Nineteenth Century," pp. 437, 442; and Matthew Arnold, *Letters of Arnold to Clough*, p. 130: "Yes—*congestion of the brain* is what we suffer from—I always feel it and say it—and cry for air like my own Empedocles."
[46] *Letters*, 2, 359.

confusion our only hope is to be scrupulously honest with ourselves, so honest as to doubt our own minds and the conclusions they arrive at. Most of us have ceased to believe, except provisionally, in truths, and we feel that what is important is not so much truth as the way our minds move towards truths."[47] Though the seeds of that radical doubt were planted by the 1870's, as we shall see in a moment, they did not grow up until the dissolving influences of modern sociology, anthropology, and psychology had done their work, and mined the old confidence with relativism and rationalization.[48] The Victorians might be, and often were, uncertain about what theory to accept or what faculty of the mind to rely on; but it never occurred to them to doubt their capacity to arrive at truth. When Mill thought of his age as one of intellectual anarchy, his reaction to such a condition was quite different from ours. He could see it as a momentary and necessary stage in a process of growth: "So long as this intellectual anarchy shall endure, we may be warranted in believing that we are in a fair way to become wiser than our forefathers; but...we have not yet advanced beyond the unsettled state, in which the mind is, when it has recently found itself out in a grievous error, and has not yet satisfied itself of the truth."[49] Not yet but soon! "If your opinions, or mine, are right," he told Sterling, "they will in time be unanimously adopted by the instructed classes."[50] It is this faith in the existence of ultimate truths in religion and ethics, in politics, economics, and aesthetics (as well as in the natural sciences), and in the capacity of the human mind to discover them, by some form of reason or of intuition, which unites the partisans of every school. That, one is tempted to say, is the one intellectual certitude in Victorian England. But it is a great one, for on such a foundation the universe can be held together: it can remain rational. That is why Chesterton could claim that the Victorian period was "orderly compared with what came after." (But not, he added, "compared with the centuries that came before.")[51] On that foundation it was still possible, as it no longer is, to find comfort in the thought

> That, though I perish, Truth is so:
> That, howsoe'er I stray and range,
> Whate'er I do, Thou dost not change.[52]

It was still possible to adopt this or that theory of Church or State with full confidence that it might well be true—though not that it *was*.

---

[47] *Modern Prose Style* (Oxford, 1934), p. 220.
[48] Cf. W. H. Auden, writing on these modern studies in *Poets of the English Language*, ed. W. H. Auden and N. H. Pearson (5 vols. New York, 1950), 5, xxii-xxiii: "Their exhibition of the mind's capacity for self-deception, of the unconscious effect upon its thinking of social status and sex, their demonstration that the customs and beliefs of other peoples could not be dismissed as merely savage, irrational, and quaint but must be accepted as rival civilizations complete in themselves, cast doubts on the finality of any truth."
[49] *The Spirit of the Age*, pp. 12-13.
[50] *Letters*, 1, 6. Cf. *The Spirit of the Age*, p. 33.
[51] *The Autobiography of G. K. Chesterton* (New York, 1936), p. 20.
[52] Arthur Hugh Clough, "It fortifies my soul to know," *Poems*, p. 75.

But less possible after 1870. For about that time a number of things converged to suggest the relativity of knowledge and the subjective character of thought. This radical change, bounding the mid-Victorian temper, is documented in the popular work of Walter Pater.

The historical method, as it was formulated under the influences of Romantic and scientific conceptions of development, meant the study of social phenomena of all kinds, institutions, customs, beliefs, as the natural product of a given time and place; with the result that the type of question one put to the past underwent a crucial change. One no longer asked, What do I think of this? is it good? is it true? For once everything was thought relative, good or true only for a particular society at a particular stage in its cultural evolution, the right questions became: How shall I account for it? Why did men believe that it was good or true?[53]

> In the intellectual as in the organic world the given product, its normal or abnormal characteristics, are determined, as people say, by the "environment." The business of the young scholar therefore, in reading Plato, is not to take his side in a controversy, to adopt or refute Plato's opinions...still less, to furnish himself with arguments on behalf of some theory or conviction of his own. His duty is rather to follow intelligently, *but with strict indifference*, the mental process there, as he might witness a game of skill.... To put Plato into his natural place, as a result from antecedent and contemporary movements of Greek speculation, of Greek life generally: such is the proper aim of the historic, that is to say, of the really critical study of him.[54]

The phrase I have italicized adds the final touch: nothing could be less Victorian. Though recognized earlier, the awareness that the historical attitude could issue in skepticism did not reach general consciousness, I think, until after 1870 when it came to be debated in the periodicals by men like John Morley, Edward Dowden, and Henry Sidgwick.[55]

At the same time the scientific view that all things, material and human, were in constant flux, changing under the inevitable influences of many and complex factors, could make all truths seem relative only to a particular moment. In the opening paragraphs of the "Coleridge" (1866) and the "Conclusion" to *The Renaissance* (1873), Pater revived the skepticism of Hume and reduced all knowledge to a series of "impressions unstable, flickering, inconsistent," each of which "is the impression of the individual in his isolation, each mind keeping as a solitary prisoner its own dream of a

---

[53] See Morley, *Recollections*, 1, 71-2, and Wilfrid Ward, "The Time-Spirit of the Nineteenth Century," *Edinburgh Review*, 194 (1901), 92–131, reprinted in his *Problems and Persons*, London, 1903.

[54] Pater, *Plato and Platonism* (New York, 1901), p. 6. The italics are mine.

[55] Morley, *On Compromise*, pp. 18–21; Dowden, *Studies in Literature*, pp. 106–9; Sidgwick "The Historical Method," *Mind*, 11 (1886), 213–15.

world."[56] On such assumptions the intellectual life was ridiculous. Only the aesthetic life of delicate perceptions and sensitive response had any importance. Not that philosophy or "speculative culture" was ruled out. It still had value for the human spirit—but only "to rouse, to startle it into sharp and eager observation." By suggesting "points of view" it could "help us to gather up what might otherwise pass unregarded by us."[57]

To turn back from Pater to Arnold is to return to the Victorian world. For Arnold threw his whole weight against relativism. Not, it is true, with reference to historical or scientific theories, but to the liberal dogma of individualism and its assertion of private judgment, which in society as a whole was the major force that undermined the belief in absolute truths. By 1864 Arnold was aware of a "baneful notion that there is no such thing as a high, correct standard in intellectual matters; that every one may as well take his own way."[58] To the contemporary boast that every Englishman could believe what he liked, what was true for him, Arnold kept asking whether it was not important that what people were free to believe should be worth believing; whether, in short, the anarchy of individualism should not be checked by the authority of Culture, with its inherent power of discovering truth. For Culture, "bent on seeing things as they are," can dissipate delusions like the worship of freedom for its own sake, and fix "standards of perfection that are real!"[59] What is meant here by things as they are or standards that are real is the very absolutes which Plato affirmed and Pater denied. "To see things as they are" is "to draw towards a knowledge of the universal order which seems to be intended and aimed at in the world...to learn, in short, the will of God"; and this insight comes from the use of right reason, meaning intuitive judgment, by a man of wide learning and flexible intelligence. Indeed, Arnold cites Plato by name as explicitly denying to the mere man of virtue the Greek instinct for what he (Plato) calls "the true, firm, intelligible law of things." "He reserves it for the lover of pure knowledge, of seeing things as they really are,—the φιλομαθής."[60]

The contrast of Pater with Arnold is pointed by their respective conceptions of the "modern spirit." To Pater, of course, it is the relative spirit, which considers that "truth itself is but a possibility, realisable not as a general conclusion, but rather as the elusive

[56] *Appreciations*, pp. 65–7, and *The Renaissance*, pp. 246–9. The quotation is on p. 248. The "Conclusion" was first written in 1868. On Pater's skepticism, see Helen H. Young, *The Writings of Walter Pater. A Reflection of British Philosophical Opinion from 1860 to 1890* (1933), chap. 3, esp. pp. 27–9, and Milton Millhauser, "Walter Pater and the Flux," *Journal of Aesthetics and Art Criticism*, 11 (1952–53), 214–23. Cf. Karl Pearson, *The Grammar of Science* (1892), where the same skeptical conclusions were systematically advanced. That book and its impact are discussed in *The Education of Henry Adams*, chap. 31.
[57] *Renaissance*, pp. 249, 251.
[58] "The Literary Influence of Academies," *Essays in Criticism, First Series*, p. 66.
[59] *Culture and Anarchy*, chap. 1, p. 51. Cf. Lionel Trilling, *The New Yorker Magazine* (June 18, 1949), p. 74, where—with Arnold plainly in his mind—he spoke of George Orwell's "commitment to intellect" as "fortified by an old-fashioned faith that the truth can be got at, that we can, if we actually want to, see the object as it really is."
[60] *Culture and Anarchy*, chaps. 1, 4, 5, pp. 46, 134, 147. Arnold was also indebted to Cicero and the Stoic theory of natural law: see the essay cited in note 58, p. 54. It is true that Arnold sometimes uses "things as they are" to mean as they "objectively exist" or "as they are in fact," in contrast with how they appear to a prejudiced mind.

effect of a particular personal experience"; and which "must needs content itself with suspension of judgment, at the end of the intellectual journey, to the very last asking: *Que scais-je?* Who knows?"[61] For Arnold the modern spirit is the awareness that traditional beliefs and institutions are no longer adequate to embody contemporary life; and the representatives of the modern spirit, "the would-be remodellers of the old traditional European order," are "the invokers of reason against custom." For them the end of the intellectual journey is not doubt but reconstruction.[62]

Pater and Arnold face each other across the gulf between two basic conceptions of the human mind that opened up between 1865 and 1875. By 1877, at the house party given by W. H. Mallock where "culture, faith, and philosophy" are discussed in a new "Republic," the Paters have become a society, still small but destined to rise to fame, or notoriety, in the nineties. Mr. Herbert, who speaks for the mid-Victorians (he is Ruskin) berates the younger generation because, in the face of conflicting opinions, they persuade themselves "that neither opinion is of much moment—that the question cannot be decided absolutely—that it should not be decided absolutely."[63] This is as true of morality as of everything else. "There is no recognised rule of life anywhere," comments Mr. Leslie. "Every one who does right at all only does what is right in his own eyes. All society, it seems, is going to pieces." To which another guest replies:

> "I," said Mr. Rose, "look upon social dissolution as the true condition of the most perfect life. For the centre of life is the individual, and it is only through dissolution that the individual can re-emerge. All the warrings of endless doubts, all the questionings of matter and of spirit, which I have myself known, I value only because, remembering the weariness of them, I take a profounder and more exquisite pleasure in the colour of a crocus, the pulsations of a chord of music, or a picture of Sandro Botticelli's."[64]

Mr. Rose, I need hardly say, is Pater—a caricature of Pater. A decade later Canon Liddon, who like Arnold and Ruskin was a mid-Victorian, observed that "a morbidly active imagination which cannot acquiesce in the idea of fixed and unalterable truth" had become a malady of modern society.[65]

> Though the Victorians were certain that truth existed and the mind could discover it, they found themselves involved in two forms of doubt: either what

---

[61] *Plato*, pp. 156–7. As the quotation suggests, Pater found the beginning of the modern, relative spirit in Montaigne.

[62] "Heine," *Essays in Criticism, First Series*, pp. 185, 189–90. Though I develop it somewhat differently, this contrast between Pater and Arnold was suggested to me by Graham Hough, *The Last Romantics*, pp. 134–41.

[63] W. H. Mallock, *The New Republic, or, Culture, Faith, and Philosophy in an English Country House*, p. 279.

[64] Pages 54–5.

[65] Quoted by R. H. Hutton, *Aspects of Religious and Scientific Thought*, p. 17. For a similar account of "the intellectual revolution of our time," which he sees beginning somewhat later, viz. "about 1890," see H. Stuart Hughes, *An Essay for Our Times* (New York, 1950), pp. 15–17. For an extended discussion of the Victorian faith in absolute and universal laws, see below, Chap. 6, sec. 2.

is sometimes called negative skepticism, when the judgment is suspended between alternate conclusions, one of which is considered true; or the affirmation of a belief which they only half believed—and half doubted. Both types of insecurity are present in the important passage from Mill's diary quoted earlier: "Scarcely any one, in the more educated classes seems to have any opinions [because he sees "too many sides to every question"] or to place any real faith in those which he professes to have."[66]

When Alfred North Whitehead spoke of the nineteenth century as being disturbed by the conflicting claims of incompatible doctrines, he pointed out that Cardinal Newman in his *Apologia pro Vita Sua* found it a peculiarity of Pusey, the great Anglican ecclesiastic, that "he was haunted by no intellectual perplexities." "In this respect," Whitehead continued, "Pusey recalls Milton, Pope, Wordsworth, as in contrast with Tennyson, Clough, Matthew Arnold, and Newman himself."[67] A letter of George Eliot's, written in 1839, gives a characteristic illustration of this new state of mind, and with reference to a topic which for Newman was especially baffling:

> I think no one feels more difficulty in coming to a decision on controverted matters than myself…. The other day Montaigne's motto came to my mind (it is mentioned by Pascal) as an appropriate one for me,—"Que sais-je?"—beneath a pair of balances, though, by the by, it is an ambiguous one, and may be taken in a sense that I desire to reprobate…. I use it in a limited sense as a representation of my oscillating judgment. On no subject do I veer to all points of the compass more frequently than on the nature of the visible Church. I am powerfully attracted in a certain direction, but when I am about to settle there, counter-assertions shake me from my position.[68]

Nothing could better describe the negative skepticism of the time, including, as it does, the rejection of the positive skepticism which Pater drew from the same passage in Montaigne.[69] It was not, of course, limited to religion. In the forties Disraeli found society "in the midst of a convulsion in which the very principles of our political and social systems are called in question," and created a hero in its image—"confused, perplexed," his mind "a chaos"; but his spirit sustained "by a profound, however vague, conviction, that there are still great truths, if we could but work them out."[70] In the same years, worried because the condition-of-England problem was "shaking many old

---

[66] Reference in note 46, above. In discussions of the period, both contemporary and modern, the word "doubt" is sometimes used to mean religious unbelief. In this book I restrict it to the two definitions just given, which apply to all areas of thought, but especially religious thought, and use "religious skepticism," "unbelief," "agnosticism," or "atheism" for outright disbelief in a divine reality.

[67] *Science and the Modern World*, p. 120.

[68] J. W. Cross, *George Eliot's Life as Related in Her Letters and Journals*, 1, 41, letter to Miss Lewis, May 20, 1839.

[69] For the Victorian view of Montaigne, see John Sterling's essay in the *Westminster Review*, 29 (1838), 321–52, reprinted in his *Essays and Tales*, 1, 129–87.

[70] *Coningsby*, in *Works*, 12, chap. 23, pp. 196–7.

beliefs, and leading him whither he knew not," Tom Brown at Oxford plunged into works on political economy, then consulted an Anglo-Catholic friend about High Church teaching on social questions, and finally read *Past and Present*—and so filled his head "full of a set of contradictory notions and beliefs." By the time he graduated, reading and discussion had combined to drag him into "perplexities, and doubts, and dreams, and struggles."[71] The Victorian plight was summed up by Clough in a poem which deals with still another area of doubt, the nature of man: *Is* he a human automaton?

> Oh say it, all who think it,
> Look straight, and never blink it!
> If it is so, let it be so,
> And we will all agree so;
> But the plot has counterplot,
> It may be, and yet be not.[72]

It must not be supposed, however, that the normal state of the Victorian mind was one of indecision or suspended judgment. The confidence in reason or intuition and the powerful will to believe made doubt itself unstable. It came and went. Individuals passed through it. Mill confessed in 1833 that "I am often in a state almost of scepticism, and have no theory of Human Life at all, or seem to have conflicting theories, or a theory which does not amount to a belief"; but he added at once, "This is only a *recent* state, and, as I well know, a passing one, and my convictions will be firmer."[73] Passing but recurrent. What he says of his own transition (from his early Benthamism through doubt to his later liberalism) applies in general to all the mid-Victorian intellectuals. For reasons we shall have to consider, Carlyle, Newman, Disraeli, Froude, Eliot, Arnold — none was any more content than Mill to remain "confused and unsettled."[74] All like him succeeded in weaving new ideas and old dogmas into a fresh pattern of thought.

Not until the sixties does a settled state of baffled judgment and a mind empty of beliefs begin to appear. It was then, when the *Origin of Species* and *Essays and Reviews* intensified the difficulties of decision, especially in religion, while at the same time positive skepticism was emerging, that Frances Cobbe was struck by a new disposition "to accept as a finality that condition of hesitation and uncertainty which in the nature of things should be one of transition."[75] Such a condition, as we might expect, is habitual

---

[71] Thomas Hughes, *Tom Brown at Oxford* (which describes the university when Hughes was there from 1842 to 1845), chaps. 35 and 50, pp. 415–19, 572.

[72] *Poems*, p. 44, from an untitled poem beginning, "Is it true, ye gods, who treat us."

[73] *Letters*, 1, 48–9.

[74] *Autobiography*, chap. 5, pp. 132–3. For the "reasons," see below, Chap. 4, sec. 2, on the will to believe.

[75] *Fraser's Magazine*, 69 (1864), 491. A few years later Henry Sidgwick (*Henry Sidgwick: A Memoir*, p. 158) detected signs that "an age of general indecisiveness" seemed to be commencing; and Symonds (Horatio F. Brown, *John Addington Symonds*, pp. 316–17) referred to "the *habitual* condition of scepticism" in which the soul is denuded of "moral ideas and fixed principles," and went on to say that nowadays a man "is *always* saying like Montaigne: 'Ni comme ceci, ni comme cela, ni même autrement'; or again, 'Peut-être oui, peut-être non, peut-être ni l'un ni l'autre.'" The italics are mine.

in the society of Mallock's *New Republic*, where "nobody knows what to believe, and most people believe nothing,"[76] but it did not exist a generation earlier. It had only afflicted individuals for shorter or longer intervals. Most of the time the Victorian mind contained beliefs and not doubts—but the beliefs were shaky.[77]

What *is* constantly present, therefore, is the fear or suspicion, or simply the vague uneasy feeling, that one was not sure he believed what he believed. I do not mean that no one had any strong beliefs. The traditional morality was firmly held by almost everyone until the seventies and by a vast majority until after World War I; and there were certainly many people whose religious or political convictions remained unshaken. But the more one studies the period, the more certain he is that most Victorians were aptly described by Mill himself in *The Spirit of the Age*: "The men of the present day rather incline to an opinion than embrace it; few...have full confidence in their own convictions"; or, in a variant phrase, people "have no strong or deep-rooted convictions at all."[78] How could it have been otherwise in a period of dissolving creeds and clashing theories? If one's formal doubts were sooner or later discarded for one creed or another, the taint of doubt remained. A prayer attributed to the Victorians is a witty distortion of the truth: "O God—if there is a God—save my soul—if I have a soul." Like Spencer in later life (and the example is significant, since no one could seem more certain or dogmatic), one clung to his dogmas, old or new or a mixture of both, "but without confident faith."[79] Or like Tennyson. In the representative poem of the age, the key words are "trust," "hope," "guess":

> Behold, we know not anything;
>   I can but trust that good shall fall
>   At last—far off—at last, to all.

> I trust I have not wasted breath:
>   I think we are not wholly brain,
>   Magnetic mockeries.

> The Power in darkness whom we guess.[80]

---

[76] Page 50. Cf. Harrison, *Autobiographic Memoirs*, 1, 24 in 1882, Beatrice Webb; *My Apprenticeship*, p. 165, in 1884 (and cf. pp. 49–50); Mark Rutherford, *Mark Rutherford's Deliverance*, pp. 28, 75–6, in 1885.

[77] This was particularly true of religious beliefs; and in calling the period one of doubt, I do not mean to imply that it was one of religious skepticism. On the contrary, Christian faith was characteristic of the frame of mind. If most Victorians had reservations about one or more theological doctrines, they instinctively looked for the hand of God in the events of life; interpreted success as the reward for virtue, or suffering as the punishment for sin. They thought of death quite literally as a reunion with the loved ones who had gone ahead. The churches were crowded; Bibles (on chains!) were placed in railroad stations; sermons outsold novels. But here, too, as in other areas, belief was shaky.

[78] *The Spirit of the Age*, pp. 12, 13. These remarks were made in 1831, but the quotation from his diary given above (p. 13) shows that he would have thought them entirely applicable in 1854.

[79] Beatrice Webb, *My Apprenticeship*, p. 32.

[80] *In Memoriam* (1850), secs. 54, 120, 124.

In Memoriam is not a poem of belief or of unbelief. It is a poem of doubt, that is, of doubtful beliefs. In our generation, Kingsley noted, "few of us deeply believe anything."[81]

The two outstanding features of their world which most impressed the Victorians are now before us. No one could escape them. No one could take them, as we can take them now, with the indifference or the neutrality adopted toward the customary. Everyone in all classes to some degree felt their impact. We might well expect, therefore, that the major Victorian attitudes would have been mainly determined by the powerful influence (as much from the reaction they provoked as from their positive effect) of these two things, one or both of which are implicit in every reference to "the age of transition" — bourgeois industrial society and widespread doubt about the nature of man, society, and the universe. In the analysis that follows this is the central thread in a pattern planned to include, in due relation to it, other important influences, especially that of the so-called Puritan or Evangelical revival.[82]

At the threshold stand two emotional attitudes, in the broad sense of pleasure-pain responses, which were bound to occur in a period of conscious and radical change, and which were nourished by many of the same social and intellectual developments. The Victorians reacted to their age with hope and dismay, optimism and anxiety.

---

[81] *Letters and Memories,* 1, 113 (unabridged ed., 1, 141).

[82] Elie Halévy's well-known thesis (a typical statement is in the "Conclusion" to his *England in 1815*) that Victorian culture was the child of Evangelicalism and Industrialism has been widely adopted; indeed, this has been the only general key to the period. Valuable as it is, I think it gives too much importance in the total picture to the Puritan revival, however central that was for a few attitudes, mainly moral earnestness (though even there other factors must be reckoned with, as we shall see in Chap. 10); and it ignores the widespread and demonstrable influence of doubt upon the Victorian frame of mind.

8

GENESIS

The creation of the world

1 In the beginning of creation, when God made heaven and earth,[1] the earth was without form and void, with darkness over the face of the abyss, and a mighty wind that swept[2] over the surface of the waters. God said, 'Let there be light', and there was light; and God saw that the light was good, and he separated light from darkness. He called the light day, and the darkness night. So evening came, and morning came, the first day.

God said, 'Let there be a vault between the waters, to separate water from water.' So God made the vault, and separated the water under the vault from the water above it, and so it was; and God called the vault heaven. Evening came, and morning came, a second day.

God said, 'Let the waters under heaven be gathered into one place, so that dry land may appear'; and so it was. God called the dry land earth, and the gathering of the waters he called seas; and God saw that it was good. Then God said, 'Let the earth produce fresh growth, let there be on the earth plants bearing seed, fruit-trees bearing fruit each with seed according to its kind.' So it was; the earth yielded fresh growth, plants bearing seed according to their kind and trees bearing fruit each with seed according to its kind; and God saw that it was good. Evening came, and morning came, a third day.

God said, 'Let there be lights in the vault of heaven to separate day from night, and let them serve as signs both for festivals and for seasons and years. Let them also shine in the vault of heaven to give light on earth.' So it was; God made the two great lights, the greater to govern the day and the lesser to govern the night; and with them he made the stars. God put these lights in the vault of heaven to give light on earth, to govern day and night, and to separate light from darkness; and God saw that it was good. Evening came, and morning came, a fourth day.

God said, 'Let the waters teem with countless living creatures, and let birds fly above the earth across the vault of heaven.' God then created the great sea-monsters and

---

[1] *Or* In the beginning God created heaven and earth.
[2] *Or* and the spirit of God hovering.

"Genesis," *The Holy Bible*, new revised standard version, New York and Oxford, Oxford University Press, 1989, 1–2.

all living creatures that move and swarm in the waters, according to their kind, and every kind of bird; and God saw that it was good. So he blessed them and said, 'Be fruitful and increase, fill the waters of the seas; and let the birds increase on land.' Evening came, and morning came, a fifth day.

God said, 'Let the earth bring forth living creatures, according to their kind: cattle, reptiles, and wild animals, all according to their kind.' So it was; God made wild animals, cattle, and all reptiles, each according to its kind; and he saw that it was good. Then God said, 'Let us make man in our image and likeness to rule the fish in the sea, the birds of heaven, the cattle, all wild animals on earth, and all reptiles that crawl upon the earth.' So God created man in his own image; in the image of God he created him; male and female he created them. God blessed them and said to them, 'Be fruitful and increase, fill the earth and subdue it, rule over the fish in the sea, the birds of heaven, and every living thing that moves upon the earth.' God also said, 'I give you all plants that bear seed everywhere on earth, and every tree bearing fruit which yields seed: they shall be yours for food. All green plants I give for food to the wild animals, to all the birds of heaven, and to all reptiles on earth, every living creature.' So it was; and God saw all that he had made, and it was very good. Evening came, and morning came, a sixth day.

2   Thus heaven and earth were completed with all their mighty throng. On the sixth day God completed all the work he had been doing, and on the seventh day he ceased from all his work. God blessed the seventh day and made it holy, because on that day he ceased from all the work he had set himself to do.

This is the story of the making of heaven and earth when they were created.

1.1-2.4: The creation account, composed by priests. Order evolves from chaos by divine command, followed by God's resting, in example, on the Sabbath. 1) That *creation* arose out of nothing—that is, not out of materials at hand—became the usual understanding of this verse; see 2 Macc.7.28. 2) *Abyss*: in Ancient Near Eastern thought, the sea, personified as a dragon, fathered the great sea serpents. *Wind*: in non-Hebrew epics, the wind-god was the creator. Here, however, sea and wind are portrayed as creations, subject to God. 5) *Evening… morning*: day began at sundown and hence the order given here. 6) *Vault*: a solid dome (Job 37.18), retaining the upper waters whence the rains come (Gen.7.11-12). 14) *Lights*: Israel's neighbors regarded the celestial bodies as deities (see Deut.4.19). Here, they are mere results of God's creation. 20) *Living creatures*: hence, the worship of animals as gods, by Israel's neighbors, was foolish. 26) The plural *us* (3.22; 11.7) may be a majestic plural, or else refer to the minor divine beings thought to surround God, like courtiers of a human king (1 Kgs.22.19-22; Job 1.6). *Image*: most often used to denote a physical thing, its meaning here is not precisely stated. 28: To *subdue* the earth is to be free from nature's tyranny and from idolizing mere objects.

9

Charles Darwin

THE DESCENT OF MAN (1871)†

Introduction

The nature of the following work will be best understood by a brief account of how it came to be written. During many years I collected notes on the origin or descent of man, without any intention of publishing on the subject, but rather with the determination not to publish, as I thought that I should thus only add to the prejudices against my views. It seemed to me sufficient to indicate, in the first edition of my 'Origin of Species,' that by this work "light would be thrown on the origin of man and his history;" and this implies that man must be included with other organic beings in any general conclusion respecting his manner of appearance on this earth. Now the case wears a wholly different aspect. When a naturalist like Carl Vogt ventures to say in his address as President of the National Institution of Geneva (1869), "personne, en Europe au moins, n'ose plus soutenir la création indépendante et de toutes pièces, des espèces," it is manifest that at least a large number of naturalists must admit that species are the modified descendants of other species; and this especially holds good with the younger and rising naturalists. The greater number accept the agency of natural selection; though some urge, whether with justice the future must decide, that I have greatly overrated its importance. Of the older and honoured chiefs in natural science, many unfortunately are still opposed to evolution in every form.

In consequence of the views now adopted by most naturalists, and which will ultimately, as in every other case, be followed by others who are not scientific, I have bean led to put together my notes, so as to see how far the general conclusions arrived at in my former works were applicable to man. This seemed all the more desirable, as I had never deliberately applied these views to a species taken singly. When we confine our attention to any one form, we are deprived of the weighty arguments derived from the nature of the affinities which connect together whole groups of organisms—their geographical distribution in past and present times, and their geological succession. The

†The present text is excerpted from the second edition (1874), an extensive revision which contains a note by T. H. Huxley on the brains of humans and apes.

Charles Darwin, *The Descent of Man* (1871), selections from Philip Appleman, *Darwin: A Norton Critical Reader*, second edition (W. W. Norton, 1979), 132–154, 176–208.

homological structure, embryological development, and rudimentary organs of a species remain to be considered, whether it be man or any other animal, to which our attention may be directed; but these great classes of facts afford, as it appears to me, ample and conclusive evidence in favour of the principle of gradual evolution. The strong support derived from the other arguments should, however, always be kept before the mind.

The sole object of this work is to consider, firstly, whether man, like every other species, is descended from some pre-existing form; secondly, the manner of his development; and thirdly, the value of the differences between the so-called races of man. As I shall confine myself to these points, it will not be necessary to describe in detail the differences between the several races—an enormous subject which has been fully discussed in many valuable works. The high antiquity of man has recently been demonstrated by the labours of a host of eminent men, beginning with M. Boucher de Perthes; and this is the indispensable basis for understanding his origin. I shall, therefore, take this conclusion for granted, and may refer my readers to the admirable treatises of Sir Charles Lyell, Sir John Lubbock, and others. Nor shall I have occasion to do more than to allude to the amount of difference between man and the anthropomorphous apes; for Prof. Huxley, in the opinion of most competent judges, has conclusively shewn that in every visible character man differs less from the higher apes, than these do from the lower members of the same order of Primates.

This work contains hardly any original facts in regard to man; but as the conclusions at which I arrived, after drawing up a rough draft, appeared to me interesting, I thought that they might interest others. It has often and confidently been asserted, that man's origin can never be known: but ignorance more frequently begets confidence than does knowledge: it is those who know little, and not those who know much, who so positively assert that this or that problem will never be solved by science. The conclusion that man is the co-descendant with other species of some ancient, lower, and extinct form, is not in any degree new. Lamarck long ago came to this conclusion, which has lately been maintained by several eminent naturalists and philosophers; for instance, by Wallace, Huxley, Lyell, Vogt, Lubbock, Büchner, Rolle, &c.,[1] and especially by Häckel. This last naturalist, besides his great work, 'Generelle Morphologie' (1866), has recently (1868, with a second edit. in 1870), published his 'Natürliche Schöpfungsgeschichte,' in which he fully discusses the genealogy of man. If this work had appeared before my essay had been written, I should probably never have completed it. Almost all the conclusions at which I have arrived I find confirmed by this

---

[1] As the works of the first-named authors are so well known, I need not give the titles; but as those of the latter are less well known in England, I will give them:—'Sechs Vorlesungen über die Darwin'sche Theorie:' zweite Auflage, 1868, von Dr. L. Büchner; translated into French under the title 'Conférences sur la Théorie Darwinienne,' 1869. 'Der Mensch, im Lichte der Darwin'sche Lehre,' 1865, von Dr. F. Rolle. I will not attempt to give references to all the authors who have taken the same side of the question. Thus G. Canestrini has published ('Annuario della Soc. d. Nat.,' Modena, 1867, p. 81) a very curious paper on rudimentary characters, as bearing on the origin of man. Another work has (1869) been published by Dr. Francesco Barrago, bearing in Italian the title of "Man, made in the image of God, was also made in the image of the ape."

naturalist, whose knowledge on many points is much fuller than mine. Wherever I have added any fact or view from Prof. Häckel's writings, I give his authority in the text; other statements I leave as they originally stood in my manuscript, occasionally giving in the foot-notes references to his works, as a confirmation of the more doubtful or interesting points.

During many years it has seemed to me highly probable that sexual selection has played an important part in differentiating the races of man; but in my 'Origin of Species' (first edition, p. 199) I contented myself by merely alluding to this belief. When I came to apply this view to man, I found it indispensable to treat the whole subject in full detail.[2] Consequently the second part of the present work, treating of sexual selection, has extended to an inordinate length, compared with the first part; but this could not be avoided.

I had intended adding to the present volumes an essay on the expression of the various emotions by man and the lower animals. My attention was called to this subject many years ago by Sir Charles Bell's admirable work. This illustrious anatomist maintains that man is endowed with certain muscles solely for the sake of expressing his emotions. As this view is obviously opposed to the belief that man is descended from some other and lower form, it was necessary for me to consider it. I likewise wished to ascertain how far the emotions are expressed in the same manner by the different races of man. But owing to the length of the present work, I have thought it better to reserve my essay for separate publication.

Chapter 1
The Evidence of the Descent of Man from Some Lower Form

Nature of the evidence bearing on the origin of man — Homologous structures in man and the lower animals — Miscellaneous points of correspondence — Development — Rudimentary structures, muscles, sense-organs, hair, bones, reproductive organs, &c. — The bearing of these three great classes of facts on the origin of man.

He who wishes to decide whether man is the modified descendant of some pre-existing form, would probably first enquire whether man varies, however slightly, in bodily structure and in mental faculties; and if so, whether the variations are transmitted to his offspring in accordance with the laws which prevail with the lower animals. Again, are the variations the result, as far as our ignorance permits us to judge, of the same general causes, and are they governed by the same general laws, as in the case of other organisms; for instance, by correlation, the inherited effects of use and disuse, &c.? Is man subject to similar malconformations, the result of arrested development, of reduplication of parts, &c., and does he display in any of his anomalies reversion to some former and ancient type of structure? It might also naturally be

---

[2] Prof. Häckel was the only author who, at the time when this work first appeared, had discussed the subject of sexual selection, and had seen its full importance, since the publication of the 'Origin'; and this he did in a very able manner in his various works.

enquired whether man, like so many other animals, has given rise to varieties and sub-races, differing but slightly from each other, or to races differing so much that they must be classed as doubtful species? How are such races distributed over the world; and how, when crossed, do they react on each other in the first and succeeding generations? And so with many other points.

The enquirer would next come to the important point, whether man tends to increase at so rapid a rate, as to lead to occasional severe struggles for existence; and consequently to beneficial variations, whether in body or mind, being preserved, and injurious ones eliminated. Do the races or species of men, whichever term may be applied, encroach on and replace one another, so that some finally become extinct? We shall see that all these questions, as indeed is obvious in respect to most of them, must be answered in the affirmative, in the same manner as with the lower animals. But the several considerations just referred to may be conveniently deferred for a time: and we will first see how far the bodily structure of man shows traces, more or less plain, of his descent from some lower form. In succeeding chapters the mental powers of man, in comparison with those of the lower animals, will be considered.

The Bodily Structure of Man

It is notorious that man is constructed on the same general type or model as other mammals. All the bones in his skeleton can be compared with corresponding bones in a monkey, bat, or seal. So it is with his muscles, nerves, blood-vessels and internal viscera. The brain, the most important of all the organs, follows the same law, as shewn by Huxley and other anatomists. Bischoff,[3] who is a hostile witness, admits that every chief fissure and fold in the brain of man has its analogy in that of the orang; but he adds that at no period of development do their brains perfectly agree; nor could perfect agreement by expected, for otherwise their mental powers would have been the same. Vulpian[4] remarks: "Les différences réelles qui existent entre l'encéphale de l'homme et celui des singes supérieurs, sont bien minimes. Il ne faut pas se faire d'illusions à cet égard. L'homme est bien plus près des singes anthropomorphes par les caractères anatomiques de son cerveau que ceux-ci ne le sont non seulement des autres mammifères, mais même de certains quadrumanes, des guenons et des macaques." But it would be superfluous here to give further details on the correspondence between man and the higher mammals in the structure of the brain and all other parts of the body.

It may, however, be worth while to specify a few points, not directly or obviously connected with structure, by which this correspondence or relationship is well shewn.

---

[3] 'Grosshirnwindungen des Menschen,' 1868, s. 96. The conclusions of this author, as well as those of Gratiolet and Aeby, concerning the brain, will be discussed by Prof. Huxley in the Appendix alluded to in the Preface to this edition.
[4] 'Leç. sur la Phys.' 1866, p. 890, as quoted by M. Dally, 'L'Ordre des Primates et le Transformisme,' 1868, p. 29.

Man is liable to receive from the lower animals, and to communicate to them, certain diseases, as hydrophobia, variola, the glanders, syphilis, cholera, herpes, &c.;[5] and this fact proves the close similarity[6] of their tissues and blood, both in minute structure and composition, far more plainly than does their comparison under the best microscope, or by the aid of the best chemical analysis. Monkeys are liable to many of the same non-contagious diseases as we are; thus Rengger,[7] who carefully observed for a long time the *Cebus Azaræ* in its native land, found it liable to catarrh, with the usual symptoms, and which, when often recurrent, led to consumption. These monkeys suffered also from apoplexy, inflammation of the bowels, and cataract in the eye. The younger ones when shedding their milk-teeth often died from fever. Medicines produced the same effect on them as on us. Many kinds of monkeys have a strong taste for tea, coffee, and spirituous liquors: they will also, as I have myself seen, smoke tobacco with pleasure.[8] Brehm asserts that the natives of north-eastern Africa catch the wild baboons by exposing vessels with strong beer, by which they are made drunk. He has seen some of these animals, which he kept in confinement, in this state; and he gives a laughable account of their behaviour and strange grimaces. On the following morning they were very cross and dismal; they held their aching heads with both hands, and wore a most pitiable expression: when beer or wine was offered them, they turned away with disgust, but relished the juices of lemons.[9] An American monkey, an Ateles, after getting drunk on brandy, would never touch it again, and thus was wiser than many men. These trifling facts prove how similar the nerves of taste must be in monkeys and man, and how similarly their whole nervous system is affected.

Man is infested with internal parasites, sometimes causing fatal effects; and is plagued by external parasites, all of which belong to the same genera or families as those infesting other mammals, and in the case of scabies to the same species.[10] Man is subject, like other mammals, birds, and even insects,[11] to that mysterious law, which causes certain normal processes, such as gestation, as well as the maturation and duration of various diseases, to follow lunar periods. His wounds are repaired by the

---

[5] Dr. W. Lauder Lindsay has treated this subject at some length in the 'Journal of Mental Science,' July 1871; and in the 'Edinburgh Veterinary Review,' July 1858.

[6] A Reviewer has criticised ('British Quarterly Review,' Oct. 1st, 1871, p. 472) what I have here said with much severity and contempt; but as I do not use the term identity, I cannot see that I am greatly in error. There appears to me a strong analogy between the same infection or contagion producing the same result, or one closely similar, in two distinct animals, and the testing of two distinct fluids by the same chemical reagent.

[7] 'Naturgeschichte der Säugethiere von Paraguay,' 1830, s. 50.

[8] The same tastes are common to some animals much lower in the scale. Mr. A. Nicols informs me that he kept in Queensland, in Australia, three individuals of the *Phaseolarctus cinereus*; and that, without having been taught in any way, they acquired a strong taste for rum, and for smoking tobacco.

[9] Brehm, 'Thierleben,' B. i. 1864, s. 75, 86. On the Ateles, s. 105. For other analogous statements, see s. 25, 107.

[10] Dr. W. Lauder Lindsay, 'Edinburgh Vet. Review,' July 1858, p. 13.

[11] With respect to insects see Dr. Laycock, "On a General Law of Vital Periodicity," 'British Association,' 1842. Dr. Macculloch, 'Silliman's North American Journal of Science,' vol. xvii. p. 305, has seen a dog suffering from tertian ague. Hereafter I shall return to this subject.

same process of healing; and the stumps left after the amputation of his limbs, especially during an embryonic period, occasionally possess some power of regeneration, as in the lowest animals.[12]

The whole process of that most important function, the reproduction of the species, is strikingly the same in all mammals, from the first act of courtship by the male,[13] to the birth and nurturing of the young. Monkeys are born in almost as helpless a condition as our own infants; and in certain genera the young differ fully as much in appearance from the adults, as do our children from their full-grown parents.[14] It has been urged by some writers, as an important distinction, that with man the young arrive at maturity at a much later age than with any other animal: but if we look to the races of mankind which inhabit tropical countries the difference is not great, for the orang is believed not to be adult till the age of from ten to fifteen years.[15] Man differs from woman in size, bodily strength, hairiness, &c., as well as in mind, in the same manner as do the two sexes of many mammals. So that the correspondence in general structure, in the minute structure of the tissues, in chemical composition and in constitution, between man and the higher animals, especially the anthropomorphous apes, is extremely close.

Embryonic Development

Man is developed from an ovule, about the 125th of an inch in diameter, which differs in no respect from the ovules of other animals. The embryo itself at a very early period can hardly be distinguished from that of other members of the vertebrate kingdom. At this period the arteries run in arch-like branches, as if to carry the blood to branchiæ which are not present in the higher vertebrate, though the slits on the sides of the neck still remain (*f, g,* fig. 1), marking their former position. At a somewhat later period, when the extremities are developed, "the feet of lizards and mammals," as the illustrious Von Baer remarks, "the wings and feet of birds, no less than the hands and feet of man, all arise from the same fundamental form." It is, says Prof. Huxley,[16] quite in the later stages of development that the young human being presents marked differences from the young ape, while the latter departs as much from the dog in its

---

[12] I have given the evidence on this head in my 'Variation of Animals and Plants under Domestication,' vol. ii. p. 15, and more could be added.

[13] Mares e diversis generibus Quadrumanorum sine dubio dignoscunt feminas humanas a maribus. Primum, credo, odoratu, postea aspectu. Mr. Youatt, qui diu in Hortis Zoologicis (Bestiariis) medicus animalium erat, vir in rebus observandis cautus et sagax, hoc mihi certissime probavit, et curatores ejusdem loci et alii e ministris confirmaverunt. Sir Andrew Smith et Brehm notabant idem in Cynocephalo. Illustrissimus Cuvier etiam narrat multa de hâc re, quâ ut opinor, nihil turpius potest indicari inter omnia hominibus et Quadrumanis communia. Narrat enim Cynocephalum quendam in furorem incidere aspectu feminarum aliquarem, sed nequaquam accendi tanto furore ab omnibus. Semper eilgebat juniores, et dignoscebat in turbâ, et advocabat voce gestûque.

[14] This remark is made with respect to Cynocephalus and the anthropomorphous apes by Geoffroy Saint-Hilaire and F. Cuvier, 'Hist. Nat. des Mammifères,' tom. i. 1824.

[15] Huxley, 'Man's Place in Nature,' 1863, p. 34.

[16] 'Man's Place in Nature,' 1863, p. 67.

developments, as the man does. Startling as this last assertion may appear to be, it is demonstrably true."

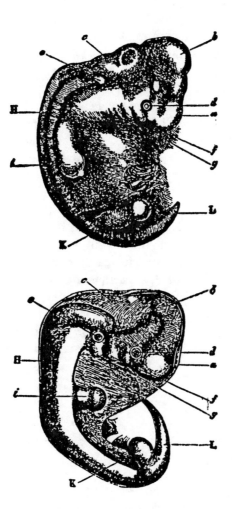

Fig. 1.—Upper figure human embryo, from Ecker. Lower figure that of a dog, from Bischoff.

    a. Forebrain, cerebral hemispheres, &c.

    b. Mid-brain, corpora, quadrigemina.

    c. Hind-brain, cerebellum, medulla oblongata.

    d. Eye.   e. Ear.   f. First visceral arch.   g. Second visceral arch.

    H. Vertebral columns and muscles in process of development.

    i. Anterior (extremities)

    K. Posterior (extremities)

    L. Tail or os coccyx.

As some of my readers may never have seen a drawing of an embryo, I have given one of man and another of a dog, at about the same early stage of development, carefully copied from two works of undoubted accuracy.[17]

After the foregoing statements made by such high authorities, it would be superfluous on my part to give a number of borrowed details, shewing that the embryo of man closely resembles that of other mammals. It may, however, be added, that the human embryo likewise resembles certain low forms when adult in various points of structure. For instance, the heart at first exists as a simple pulsating vessel; the excreta are voided through a cloacal passage; and the os coccyx projects like a true tail, "extending considerably beyond the rudimentary legs."[18] In the embryos of all air-breathing vertebrates, certain glands, called the corpora Wolffiana, correspond with, and act like the kidneys of mature fishes.[19] Even at a later embryonic period, some striking resemblances between man and the lower animals may be observed. Bischoff says "that the convolutions of the brain in a human fœtus at the end of the seventh month reach about the same stage of development as in a baboon when adult."[20] The great toe, as Professor Owen remarks,[21] "which forms the fulcrum when standing or walking, is perhaps the most characteristic peculiarity in the human structure;" but in an embryo, about an inch in length, Prof. Wyman[22] found "that the great toe was shorter than the others; and, instead of being parallel to them, projected at an angle from the side of the foot, thus corresponding with the permanent condition of this part in the quadrumana." I will conclude with a quotation from Huxley,[23] who after asking, does man originate in a different way from a dog, bird, frog or fish? says, "the reply is not doubtful for a moment; without question, the mode of origin, and the early stages of the development of man, are identical with those of the animals immediately below him in the scale: without a doubt in these respects, he is far nearer to apes than the apes are to the dog."

Rudiments

This subject, though not intrinsically more important than the two last, will for several reasons be treated here more fully.[24] Not one of the higher animals can be named

---

[17] The human embryo (upper fig.) is from Ecker, 'Icones Phys.,' 1851–1859, tab. xxx. fig. 2. This embryo was ten lines in length, so that the drawing is much magnified. The embryo of the dog is from Bischoff, 'Entwicklungsgeschichte des Hunde-Eies,' 1845, tab. xi. fig. 42 B. This drawing is five times magnified, the embryo being twenty-five days old. The internal viscera have been omitted, and the uterine appendages in both drawings removed. I was directed to these figures by Prof. Huxley, from whose work, 'Man's Place in Nature,' the idea of giving them was taken. Häckel has also given analogous drawings in his 'Schöpfungsgeschichte.'

[18] Prof. Wyman in 'Proc. of American Acad. of Sciences,' vol. iv. 1860, p. 17.

[19] Owen, 'Anatomy of Vertebrates,' vol. i. p. 533.

[20] 'Die Grosshirnwindungen des Menschen,' 1868, s. 95.

[21] 'Anatomy of Vertebrates,' vol. ii. p. 553.

[22] 'Proc. Soc. Nat. Hist.' Boston; 1863, vol. ix. p. 185.

[23] 'Man's Place in Nature,' p. 65.

[24] I had written a rough copy of this chapter before reading a valuable paper "Caratteri rudimentali in ordine all' origine dell' uomo" ('Annuario della Soc. d. Nat.,' Modena, 1867, p. 81), by G. Canestrini, to

which does not bear some part in a rudimentary condition; and man forms no exception to the rule. Rudimentary organs must be distinguished from those that are nascent; though in some cases the distinction is not easy. The former are either absolutely useless, such as the mammæ of male quadrupeds, or the incisor teeth of ruminants which never cut through the gums; or they are of such slight service to their present possessors, that we can hardly suppose that they were developed under the conditions which now exist. Organs in this latter state are not strictly rudimentary, but they are tending in this direction. Nascent organs, on the other hand, though not fully developed, are of high service to their possessors, and are capable of further development. Rudimentary organs are eminently variable; and this is partly intelligible, as they are useless, or nearly useless, and consequently are no longer subjected to natural selection. They often become wholly suppressed. When this occurs, they are nevertheless liable to occasional reappearance through reversion—a circumstance well worthy of attention.

The chief agents in causing organs to become rudimentary seem to have been disuse at that period of life when the organ is chiefly used (and this is generally during maturity), and also inheritance at a corresponding period of life. The term "disuse" does not relate merely to the lessened action of muscles, but includes a diminished flow of blood to a part or organ, from being subjected to fewer alterations of pressure, or from becoming in any way less habitually active. Rudiments, however, may occur in one sex of those parts which are normally present in the other sex; and such rudiments, as we shall hereafter see, have often originated in a way distinct from those here referred to. In some cases, organs have been reduced by means of natural selection, from having become injurious to the species under changed habits of life. The process of reduction is probably often aided through the two principles of compensation and economy of growth; but the later stages of reduction, after disuse has done all that can fairly be attributed to it, and when the saving to be effected by the economy of growth would be very small,[25] are difficult to understand. The final and complete suppression of a part, already useless and much reduced in size, in which case neither compensation nor economy can come into play, is perhaps intelligible by the aid of the hypothesis of pangenesis. But as the whole subject of rudimentary organs has been discussed and illustrated in my former works,[26] I need here say no more on this head.

Rudiments of various muscles have been observed in many parts of the human body;[27] and not a few muscles, which are regularly present in some of the lower animals

---

which paper I am considerably indebted. Häckel has given admirable discussions on this whole subject, under the title of Dysteleology, in his 'Generelle Morphologie' and 'Schöpfungsgeschichte.'

[25] Some good criticisms on this subject have been given by Messrs. Murie and Mivart, in 'Transact. Zoolog. Soc.' 1869, vol. vii p. 92.

[26] 'Variation of Animals and Plants under Domestication,' vol. ii. pp. 317 and 397. See also 'Origin of Species,' fifth edition, p. 535.

[27] For instance. M. Richard ('Annales des Sciences Nat.,' 3d series, Zoolog. 1852, tom. xviii. p. 13) describes and figures rudiments of what he calls the "muscle pédieux de la main," which he says is sometimes "infiniment petit." Another muscle, called "le tibial postérieur," is generally quite absent in the hand, but appears from time to time in a more or less rudimentary condition.

can occasionally be detected in man in a greatly reduced condition. Every one must have noticed the power which many animals, especially horses, possess of moving or twitching their skin; and this is effected by the *panniculus* with the comparative structure and development of man, and other mammals, should have believed that each was the work of a separate act of creation.

Chapter III
Comparison of the Mental Powers of Man and the Lower Animals

The difference in mental power between the highest ape and the lowest savage, immense — Certain instincts in common — The emotions — Curiosity — Imitation — Attention — Memory — Imagination — Reason — Progressive improvement — Tools and weapons used by animals — Abstraction, self-consciousness — Language — Sense of Beauty — Belief in God, spiritual agencies, superstitions.

We have seen in the last two chapters that man bears in his bodily structure clear traces of his descent from some lower form; but it may be urged that, as man differs so greatly in his mental power from all other animals, there must be some error in this conclusion. No doubt the difference in this respect is enormous, even if we compare the mind of one of the lowest savages, who has no words to express any number higher than four, and who uses hardly any abstract terms for common objects or for the affections,[28] with that of the most highly organised ape. The difference would, no doubt, still remain immense, even if one of the higher apes had been improved or civilised as much as a dog has been in comparison with its parent-form, the wolf or jackal. The Fuegians rank amongst the lowest barbarians; but I was continually struck with surprise how closely the three natives on board H. M. S. "Beagle," who had lived some years in England, and could talk a little English, resembled us in disposition and in most of our mental faculties. If no organic being excepting man had possessed any mental power, or if his powers had been of a wholly different nature from those of the lower animals, then we should never have been able to convince ourselves that our high faculties had been gradually developed. But it can be shewn that there is no fundamental difference of this kind. We must also admit that there is a much wider interval in mental power between one of the lowest fishes, as a lamprey or lancelet, and one of the higher apes, than between an ape and man; yet this interval is filled up by numberless gradations.

Nor is the difference slight in moral disposition between a barbarian, such as the man described by the old navigator Byron, who dashed his child on the rocks for dropping a basket of sea-urchins, and a Howard or Clarkson; and in intellect, between a savage who uses hardly any abstract terms, and a Newton or Shakespeare. Differences of this kind between the highest men of the highest races and the lowest savages, are connected by the finest gradations. Therefore it is possible that they might pass and be developed into each other.

---

[28] See the evidence on those points, as given by Lubbock, 'Prehistoric Times,' p. 354, &c.

My object in this chapter is to shew that there is no fundamental difference between man and the higher mammals in their mental faculties. Each division of the subject might have been extended into a separate essay, but must here be treated briefly. As no classification of the mental powers has been universally accepted, I shall arrange my remarks in the order most convenient for my purpose; and will select those facts which have struck me most, with the hope that they may produce some effect on the reader.

* * * The lower animals, like man, manifestly feel pleasure and pain, happiness and misery. Happiness is never better exhibited than by young animals, such as puppies, kittens, lambs, &c., when playing together, like our own children. Even insects play together, as has been described by that excellent observer, P. Huber,[29] who saw ants chasing and pretending to bite each other, like so many puppies.

The fact that the lower animals are excited by the same emotions as ourselves is so well established, that it will not be necessary to weary the reader by many details. Terror acts in the same manner on them as on us, causing the muscles to tremble, the heart to palpitate, the sphincters to be relaxed, and the hair to stand on end. Suspicion, the offspring of fear, is eminently characteristic of most wild animals. It is, I think, impossible to read the account given by Sir E. Tennent, of the behaviour of the female elephants, used as decoys, without admitting that they intentionally practise deceit, and well know what they are about. Courage and timidity are extremely variable qualities in the individuals of the same species, as is plainly seen in our dogs. Some dogs and horses are ill-tempered, and easily turn sulky; others are good-tempered; and these qualities are certainly inherited. Every one knows how liable animals are to furious rage, and how plainly they shew it. Many, and probably true, anecdotes have been published on the long-delayed and artful revenge of various animals. The accurate Rengger, and Brehm[30] state that the American and African monkeys which they kept tame, certainly revenged themselves. Sir Andrew Smith, a zoologist whose scrupulous accuracy was known to many persons, told me the following story of which he was himself an eye-witness; at the Cape of Good Hope an officer had often plagued a certain baboon, and the animal, seeing him approaching one Sunday for parade, poured water into a hole and hastily made some thick mud, which he skilfully dashed over the officer as he passed by, to the amusement of many bystanders. For long afterwards the baboon rejoiced and triumphed whenever he saw his victim.

The love of a dog for his master is notorious; as an old writer quaintly says,[31] "A dog is the only thing on this earth that luvs you more than he luvs himself."

In the agony of death a dog has been known to caress his master, and every one has heard of the dog suffering under vivisection, who licked the hand of the operator; this man, unless the operation was fully justified by an increase of our knowledge, or unless he had a heart of stone, must have felt remorse to the last hour of his life.

---

[29] 'Recherches sur les Mœurs des Fourmis,' 1810, p. 173.

[30] All the following statements, given on the authority of these two naturalists, are taken from Rengger's 'Naturgesch. der Säugethiere von Paraguay,' 1830's. 41–57, and from Brehm's 'Thierleben,' B. i. s. 10–87.

[31] Quoted by Dr. Lauder Lindsay, in his 'Physiology of Mind in the Lower Animals;' 'Journal of Mental Science,' April 1871, p. 38.

As Whewell[32] has well asked, "who that reads the touching instances of maternal affection, related so often of the women of all nations, and of the females of all animals, can doubt that the principle of action is the same in the two cases?" We see maternal affection exhibited in the most trifling details; thus Rengger observed an American monkey (a Cebus) carefully driving away the flies which plagued her infant; and Duvaucel saw a Hylobates washing the faces of her young ones in a stream. So intense is the grief of female monkeys for the loss of their young, that it invariably caused the death of certain kinds kept under confinement by Brehm in N. Africa. Orphan monkeys were always adopted and carefully guarded by the other monkeys, both males and females. One female baboon had so capacious a heart that she not only adopted young monkeys of other species, but stole young dogs and cats, which she continually carried about. Her kindness, however, did not go so far as to share her food with her adopted offspring, at which Brehm was surprised, as his monkeys always divided everything quite fairly with their own young ones. An adopted kitten scratched this affectionate baboon, who certainly had a fine intellect, for she was much astonished at being scratched, and immediately examined the kitten's feet, and without more ado bit off the claws.[33] In the Zoological Gardens, I heard from the keeper that an old baboon (C. chacma) had adopted a Rhesus monkey; but when a young drill and mandrill were placed in the cage, she seemed to perceive that these monkeys, though distinct species, were her nearer relatives, for she at once rejected the Rhesus and adopted both of them. The young Rhesus, as I saw, was greatly discontented at being thus rejected, and it would, like a naughty child, annoy and attack the young drill and mandrill whenever it could do so with safety; this conduct exciting great indignation in the old baboon. Monkeys will also, according to Brehm, defend their master when attacked by any one, as well as dogs to whom they are attached, from the attacks of other dogs. But we here trench on the subjects of sympathy and fidelity, to which I shall recur. Some of Brehm's monkeys took much delight in teasing a certain old dog whom they disliked, as well as other animals, in various ingenious ways.

Most of the more complex emotions are common to the higher animals and ourselves. Every one has seen how jealous a dog is of his master's affection, if lavished on any other creature; and I have observed the same fact with monkeys. This shews that animals not only love, but have desire to be loved. Animals manifestly feel emulation. They love approbation or praise; and a dog carrying a basket for his master exhibits in a high degree self-complacency or pride. There can, I think, be no doubt that a dog feels shame, as distinct from fear, and something very like modesty when begging too often for food. A great dog scorns the snarling of a little dog, and this may be called magnanimity. Several observers have stated that monkeys certainly dislike being laughed at; and they sometimes invent imaginary offences. In the Zoological Gardens I saw a baboon who always got into a furious rage when his keeper took out a letter or

---

[32] 'Bridgewater Treatise,' p. 263.

[33] A critic, without any grounds ('Quarterly Review,' July, 1871, p. 72), disputes the possibility of this act as described by Brehm, for the sake of discrediting my work. Therefore I tried, and found that I could readily seize with my own teeth the sharp little claw of a kitten nearly five weeks old.

book and read it aloud to him; and his rage was so violent that, as I witnessed on one occasion, he bit his own leg till the blood flowed. Dogs shew what may be fairly called a sense of humour, as distinct from mere play; if a bit of stick or other such object be thrown to one, he will often carry it away for a short distance; and then squatting down with it on the ground close before him, will wait until his master comes quite close to take it away. The dog will then seize it and rush away in triumph, repeating the same manœuvre, and evidently enjoying the practical joke.

We will now turn to the more intellectual emotions and faculties, which are very important, as forming the basis for the development of the higher mental powers. Animals manifestly enjoy excitement, and suffer from ennui, as may be seen with dogs, and, according to Rengger, with monkeys. All animals feel Wonder, and many exhibit Curiosity. They sometimes suffer from this latter quality, as when the hunter plays antics and thus attracts them; I have witnessed this with deer, and so it is with the wary chamois, and with some kinds of wild-ducks. Brehm gives a curious account of the instinctive dread, which his monkeys exhibited, for snakes; but their curiosity was so great that they could not desist from occasionally satiating their horror in a most human fashion, by lifting up the lid of the box in which the snakes were kept. I was so much surprised at this account, that I took a stuffed and coiled-up snake into the monkey-house at the Zoological Gardens, and the excitement thus caused was one of the most curious spectacles which I ever beheld. Three species of Cercopithecus were the most alarmed; they dashed about their cages, and uttered sharp signal cries of danger, which were understood by the other monkeys. A few young monkeys and one old Anubis baboon alone took no notice of the snake. I then placed the stuffed specimen on the ground in one of the larger compartments. After a time all the monkeys collected round it in a large circle, and staring intently, presented a most ludicrous appearance. They became extremely nervous; so that when a wooden ball, with which they were familiar as a plaything, was accidentally moved in the straw, under which it was partly hidden, they all instantly started away. These monkeys behaved very differently when a dead fish, a mouse,[34] a living turtle, and other new objects were placed in their cages; for though at first frightened, they soon approached, handled and examined them. I then placed a live snake in a paper bag, with the mouth loosely closed, in one of the larger compartments. One of the monkeys immediately approached, cautiously opened the bag a little, peeped in, and instantly dashed away. Then I witnessed what Brehm has described, for monkey after monkey, with head raised high and turned on one side, could not resist taking a momentary peep into the upright bag, at the dreadful object lying quietly at the bottom. It would almost appear as if monkeys had some notion of zoological affinities, for those kept by Brehm exhibited a strange, though mistaken, instinctive dread of innocent lizards and frogs. An orang, also, has been known to be much alarmed at the first sight of a turtle.[35]

---

[34] I have given a short account of their behaviour on this occasion in my "Expression of the Emotions,' p. 43.
[35] W. C. L. Martin, 'Nat. Hist. of Mammalia,' 1841, p. 405.

The principle of Imitation is strong in man, and especially, as I have myself observed, with savages. In certain morbid states of the brain this tendency is exaggerated to an extraordinary degree: some hemiplegic patients and others, at the commencement of inflammatory softening of the brain, unconsciously imitate every word which is uttered, whether in their own or in a foreign language, and every gesture or action which is performed near them.[36] Desor[37] has remarked that no animal voluntarily imitates an action performed by man, until in the ascending scale we come to monkeys, which are well known to be ridiculous mockers. Animals, however, sometimes imitate each other's actions: thus two species of wolves, which had been reared by dogs, learned to bark, as does sometimes the jackal,[38] but whether this can be called voluntary imitation is another question. Birds imitate the songs of their parents, and sometimes of other birds; and parrots are notorious imitators of any sound which they often hear. Dureau de la Malle gives an account[39] of a dog reared by a cat, who learnt to imitate the well-known action of a cat licking her paws, and thus washing her ears and face; this was also witnessed by the celebrated naturalist Audouin. I have received several confirmatory accounts; in one of these, a dog had not been suckled by a cat, but had been brought up with one, together with kittens, and had thus acquired the above habit, which he ever afterwards practised during his life of thirteen years. Dureau de la Malle's dog likewise learnt from the kittens to play with a ball by rolling it about with his fore paws, and springing on it. A correspondent assures me that a cat in his house used to put her paws into jugs of milk having too narrow a mouth for her head. A kitten of this cat soon learned the same trick, and practised it ever afterwards, whenever there was an opportunity.

The parents of many animals, trusting to the principle of imitation in their young, and more especially to their instinctive or inherited tendencies, may be said to educate them. We see this when a cat brings a live mouse to her kittens; and Dureau de la Malle has given a curious account (in the paper above quoted) of his observations on hawks which taught their young dexterity, as well as judgment of distances, by first dropping through the air dead mice and sparrows, which the young generally failed to catch, and then bringing them live birds and letting them loose.

Hardly any faculty is more important for the intellectual progress of man than Attention. Animals clearly manifest this power, as when a cat watches by a hole and prepares to spring on its prey. Wild animals sometimes become so absorbed when thus engaged, that they may be easily approached. Mr. Bartlett has given me a curious proof how variable this faculty is in monkeys. A man who trains monkeys to act in plays, used to purchase common kinds from the Zoological Society at the price of five pounds for each; but he offered to give double the price, if he might keep three or four of them for a few days, in order to select one. When asked how he could possibly learn so soon, whether a particular monkey would turn out a good actor, he answered that it all

[36] Dr. Bateman 'On Aphasia,' 1870, p. 110.
[37] Quoted by Vogt, 'Mémoire sur les Microcéphales,' 1867, p. 168.
[38] 'The Variation of Animals and Plants under Domestication,' vol. i. p. 27.
[39] 'Annales des Sc. Nat.' (1st Series), tom. xxii. p. 397.

depended on their power of attention. If when he was talking and explaining anything to a monkey, its attention was easily distracted, as by a fly on the wall or other trifling object, the case was hopeless. If he tried by punishment to make an inattentive monkey act, it turned sulky. On the other hand, a monkey which carefully attended to him could always be trained.

It is almost superfluous to state that animals have excellent Memories for persons and places. A baboon at the Cape of Good Hope, as I have been informed by Sir Andrew Smith, recognised him with joy after an absence of nine months. I had a dog who was savage and averse to all strangers, and I purposely tried his memory after an absence of five years and two days. I went near the stable where he lived, and shouted to him in my old manner; he shewed no joy, but instantly followed me out walking, and obeyed me, exactly as if I had parted with him only half an hour before. A train of old associations, dormant during five years, had thus been instantaneously awakened in his mind. Even ants, as P. Huber[40] has clearly shewn, recognised their fellow-ants belonging to the same community after a separation of four months. Animals can certainly by some means judge of the intervals of time between recurrent events.

The Imagination is one of the highest prerogatives of man. By this faculty he unites former images and ideas, independently of the will, and thus creates brilliant and novel results. A poet, as Jean Paul Richter remarks,[41] "who must reflect whether he shall make a character say yes or no—to the devil with him; he is only a stupid corpse." Dreaming gives us the best notion of this power; as Jean Paul again says, "The dream is an involuntary art of poetry." The value of the products of our imagination depends of course on the number, accuracy, and clearness of our impressions, on our judgment and taste in selecting or rejecting the involuntary combinations, and to a certain extent on our power of voluntarily combining them. As dogs, cats, horses, and probably all the higher animals, even birds[42] have vivid dreams, and this is shewn by their movements and the sounds uttered, we must admit that they possess some power of imagination. There must be something special, which causes dogs to howl in the night, and especially during moonlight, in that remarkable and melancholy manner called baying. All dogs do not do so; and, according to Houzeau,[43] they do not then look at the moon, but at some fixed point near the horizon. Houzeau thinks that their imaginations are disturbed by the vague outlines of the surrounding objects, and conjure up before them fantastic images: if this be so, their feelings may almost be called superstitious.

Of all the faculties of the human mind, it will, I presume, be admitted that Reason stands at the summit. Only a few persons now dispute that animals possess some power of reasoning. Animals may constantly be seen to pause, deliberate, and resolve. It is a significant fact, that the more the habits of any particular animal are studied by a

---

[40] 'Les Mœurs des Fourmis,' 1810, p. 150.
[41] Quoted in Dr. Maudsley's 'Physiology and Pathology of Mind,' 1868, pp. 19, 220.
[42] Dr. Jerdon, 'Birds of India,' vol. i. 1862, p. xxi. Honzeau says that his parokeets and canary-birds dreamt: 'Facultés Mentales,' tom. ii. p. 136.
[43] 'Facultés Mentales des Animaux,' 1872, tom. ii. p. 181.

naturalist, the more he attributes to reason and the less to unlearnt instincts.[44] In future chapters we shall see that some animals extremely low in the scale apparently display a certain amount of reason. No doubt it is often difficult to distinguish between the power of reason and that of instinct. For instance, Dr. Hayes, in his work on 'The Open Polar Sea,' repeatedly remarks that his dogs, instead of continuing to draw the sledges in a compact body, diverged and separated when they came to thin ice, so that their weight might be more evenly distributed. This was often the first warning which the travellers received that the ice was becoming thin and dangerous. Now, did the dogs act thus from the experience of each individual, or from the example of the older and wiser dogs, or from an inherited habit, that is from instinct? This instinct, may possibly have arisen since the time, long ago, when dogs were first employed by the natives in drawing their sledges; or the Arctic wolves, the parent-stock of the Esquimaux dog, may have acquired an instinct impelling them not to attack their prey in a close pack, when on thin ice.

We can only judge by the circumstances under which actions are performed, whether they are due to instinct, or to reason, or to the mere association of ideas: this latter principle, however, is intimately connected with reason. A curious case has been given by Prof. Möbius,[45] of a pike, separated by a plate of glass from an adjoining aquarium stocked with fish, and who often dashed himself with such violence against the glass in trying to catch the other fishes, that he was sometimes completely stunned. The pike went on thus for three months, but at last learnt caution, and ceased to do so. The plate of glass was then removed, but the pike would not attack these particular fishes, though he would devour others which were afterwards introduced; so strongly was the idea of a violent shock associated in his feeble mind with the attempt on his former neighbours. If a savage, who had never seen a large plateglass window, were to dash himself even once against it, he would for a long time afterwards associate a shock with a window-frame; but very differently from the pike, he would probably reflect on the nature of the impediment, and be cautious under analogous circumstances. Now with monkeys, as we shall presently see, a painful or merely a disagreeable impression, from an action once performed, is sometimes sufficient to prevent the animal from repeating it. If we attribute this difference between the monkey and the pike solely to the association of ideas being so much stronger and more persistent in the one than the other, though the pike often received much the more severe injury, can we maintain in the case of man that a similar difference implies the possession of a fundamentally different mind?

Houzeau relates[46] that, whilst crossing a wide and arid plain in Texas, his two dogs suffered greatly from thirst, and that between thirty and forty times they rushed down the hollows to search for water. These hollows were not valleys, and there were no trees in them, or any other difference in the vegetation, and as they were absolutely dry there

---

[44] Mr. L. H. Morgan's work on 'The American Beaver,' 1868, offers a good illustration of this remark. I cannot help thinking, however, that he goes too far in underrating the power of instinct.

[45] 'Die Bewegungen der Thiere,' &c., 1873, p. 11.

[46] 'Facultés Mentales des Animaux,' 1872, tom. ii. p. 265.

could have been no smell of damp earth. The dogs behaved as if they knew that a dip in the ground offered them the best chance of finding water, and Honzeau has often witnessed the same behaviour in other animals.

I have seen, as I daresay have others, that when a small object is thrown on the ground beyond the reach of one of the elephants in the Zoological Gardens, he blows through his trunk on the ground beyond the object, so that the current reflected on all sides may drive the object within his reach. Again a well-known ethnologist, Mr. Westropp, informs me that he observed in Vienna a bear deliberately making with his paw a current in some water, which was close to the bars of his cage, so as to draw a piece of floating bread within his reach. These actions of the elephant and bear can hardly be attributed to instinct or inherited habit, as they would be of little use to an animal in a state of nature. Now, what is the difference between such actions, when performed by an uncultivated man, and by one of the higher animals?

The savage and the dog have often found water at a low level, and the coincidence under such circumstances has become associated in their minds. A cultivated man would perhaps make some general proposition on the subject; but from all that we know of savages it is extremely doubtful whether they would do so, and a dog certainly would not. But a savage, as well as a dog, would search in the same way, though frequently disappointed; and in both it seems to be equally an act of reason, whether or not any general proposition on the subject is consciously placed before the mind.[47] The same would apply to the elephant and the bear making currents in the air or water. The savage would certainly neither know nor care by what law the desired movements were effected; yet his act would be guided by a rude process of reasoning, as surely as would a philosopher in his longest chain of deductions. There would no doubt be this difference between him and one of the higher animals, that he would take notice of much slighter circumstances and conditions, and would observe any connection between them after much less experience and this would be of paramount importance. I kept a daily record of the actions of one of my infants, and when he was about eleven-months old, and before he could speak a single word, I was continually struck with the greater quickness, with which all sorts of objects and sounds were associated together in his mind, compared with that of the most intelligent dogs I ever knew. But the higher animals differ in exactly the same way in this power of association from those low in the scale, such as the pike, as well as in that of drawing inferences and of observation.

The promptings of reason, after very short experience, are well shewn by the following actions of American monkeys, which stand low in their order. Rengger, a most careful observer, states that when he first gave eggs to his monkeys in Paraguay, they smashed them, and thus lost much of their contents; afterwards they gently hit one end against some hard body, and picked off the bits of shell with their fingers. After cutting themselves only *once* with any sharp tool, they would not touch it again, or would handle it with the greatest caution. Lumps of sugar were often given them

---

[47] Prof. Huxley has analysed with admirable clearness the mental steps by which a man, as well as a dog, arrives at a conclusion in a case analogous to that given in my text. See his article, 'Mr. Darwin's Critics,' in the 'Contemporary Review' Nov. 1871, p. 462, and in his 'Critiques and Essays,' 1873, p. 279.

wrapped up in paper; and Rengger sometimes put a live wasp in the paper, so that in hastily unfolding it they got stung; after this had *once* happened, they always first held the packet to their ears to detect any movement within.[48]

The following cases relate to dogs. Mr. Colquhoun[49] winged two wild-ducks, which fell on the further side of a stream; his retriever tried to bring over both at once, but could not succeed; she then, though never before known to ruffle a feather, deliberately killed one, brought over the other, and returned for the dead bird. Col. Hutchinson relates that two partridges were shot at once, one being killed, the other wounded; the latter ran away, and was caught by the retriever, who on her return came across the dead bird; "she stopped, evidently greatly puzzled, and after one or two trials, finding she could not take it up without permitting the escape of the winged bird, she considered a moment, then deliberately murdered it by giving it a severe crunch, and afterwards brought away both together. This was the only known instance of her ever having wilfully injured any game." Here we have reason though not quite perfect, for the retriever might have brought the wounded bird first and then returned for the dead one, as in the case of the two wild-ducks. I give the above cases, as resting on the evidence of two independent witnesses, and because in both instances the retrievers, after deliberation, broke through a habit which is inherited by them (that of not killing the game retrieved), and because they shew how strong their reasoning faculty must have been to overcome a fixed habit.

I will conclude by quoting a remark by the illustrious Humboldt.[50] "The muleteers in S. America say, 'I will not give you the mule whose step is easiest, but *la mas racional*, — the one that reasons best;'" and as he adds, "this popular expression, dictated by long experience, combats the system of animated machines, better perhaps than all the arguments of speculative philosophy." Nevertheless some writers even yet deny that the higher animals possess a trace of reason; and they endeavor to explain away, by what appears to be mere verbiage,[51] all such facts as those above given.

It has, I think, now been shewn that man and the higher animals, especially the Primates, have some few instincts in common. * * *

---

[48] Mr. Belt, in his most interesting work, 'The Naturalist in Nicaragua,' 1874 (p. 119), likewise describes various actions of a tamed Cebus, which, I think, clearly shew that this animal possessed some reasoning power.

[49] 'The Moor and the Loch,' p. 45. Col. Hutchinson on 'Dog Breaking,' 1850, p. 46.

[50] 'Personal Narrative,' Eng. translat., vol. iii. p. 106.

[51] I am glad to find that so acute a reasoner as Mr. Leslie Stephen ('Darwinism and Divinity, Essays on Freethinking,' 1873, p. 80), in speaking of the supposed impassable barrier between the minds of man and the lower animals, says, "The distinctions, indeed, which have been drawn, seem to us to rest upon no better foundation than a great many other metaphysical distinctions; that is, the assumption that because you can give two things different names, they must therefore have different natures. It is difficult to understand how anybody who has ever kept a dog, or seen an elephant, can have any doubt as to an animal's power of performing the essential processes of reasoning."

Chapter VI
On the Affinities and Genealogy of Man

Position of man in the animal series — The natural system genealogical — Adaptive characters of slight value — Various small points of resemblance between man and the Quadrumana — Rank of man in the natural system — Birthplace and antiquity of man — Absence of fossil connecting links — Lower stages in the genealogy of man, as inferred, firstly from his affinities and secondly from his structure — Early androgynous condition of the Vertebrata — Conclusion.

Even if it be granted that the difference between man and his nearest allies is as great in corporeal structure as some naturalists maintain, and although we must grant that the difference between them is immense in mental power, yet the facts given in the earlier chapters appear to declare, in the plainest manner, that man is descended from some lower form, notwithstanding that connecting-links have not hitherto been discovered.

Man is liable to numerous, slight, and diversified variations, which are induced by the same general causes, are governed and transmitted in accordance with the same general laws, as in the lower animals. Man has multiplied so rapidly, that he has necessarily been exposed to struggle for existence, and consequently to natural selection. He has given rise to many races, some of which differ so much from each other, that they have often been ranked by naturalists as distinct species. His body is constructed on the same homological plan as that of other mammals. He passes through the same phases of embryological development. He retains many rudimentary and useless structures, which no doubt were once serviceable. Characters occasionally make their re-appearance in him, which we have reason to believe were possessed by his early progenitors. If the origin of man had been wholly different from that of all other animals, these various appearances would be mere empty deceptions; but such an admission is incredible. These appearances, on the other hand, are intelligible, at least to a large extent, if man is the co-descendant with other mammals of some unknown and lower form.

Some naturalists, from being deeply impressed with the mental and spiritual powers of man, have divided the whole organic world into three kingdoms, the Human, the Animal, and the Vegetable, thus giving to man a separate kingdom.[52] Spiritual powers cannot be compared or classed by the naturalist: but he may endeavour to shew, as I have done, that the mental faculties of man and the lower animals do not differ in kind, although immensely in degree. A difference in degree, however great, does not justify us in placing man in a distinct kingdom, as will perhaps be best illustrated by comparing the mental powers of two insects, namely, a coccus or scale-insect and an ant, which undoubtedly belong to the same class. The difference is here greater than, though of a somewhat different kind from, that between man and the highest mammal. The female coccus, whilst young, attaches itself by its proboscis to a plant; sucks the sap, but never moves again; is fertilised and lays eggs; and this is its whole history. On the other

---

[52] Isidore Geoffroy St.-Hilaire gives a detailed account of the position assigned to man by various naturalists in their classifications: 'Hist. Nat. Gén.' tom. ii. 1859, pp. 170-189.

hand, to describe the habits and mental powers of worker-ants, would require, as Pierre Huber has shewn, a large volume; I may, however, briefly specify a few points. Ants certainly communicate information to each other, and several unite for the same work, or for games of play. They recognise their fellow-ants after months of absence, and feel sympathy for each other. They build great edifices, keep them clean, close the doors in the evening, and post sentries. They make roads as well as tunnels under rivers, and temporary bridges over them, by clinging together. They collect food for the community and when an object, too large for entrance, is brought to the nest, they enlarge the door, and afterwards build it up again. They store up seeds, of which they prevent the germination, and which, if damp, are brought up to the surface to dry. They keep aphides and other insects as milch-cows. They go out to battle in regular bands, and freely sacrifice their lives for the common weal. They emigrate according to a preconcerted plan. They capture slaves. They move the eggs of their aphides, as well as their own eggs and cocoons, into warm parts of the nest, in order that they may be quickly hatched; and endless similar facts could be given.[53] On the whole, the difference in mental power between an ant and a coccus is immense; yet no one has ever dreamed of placing these insects in distinct classes, much less in distinct kingdoms. No doubt the difference is bridged over by other insects; and this is not the case with man and the higher apes. But we have every reason to believe that the breaks in the series are simply the results of many forms having become extinct.

Professor Owen, relying chiefly on the structure of the brain, has divided the mammalian series into four sub-classes. One of these he devotes to man; in another he places both the Marsupials and the Monotremata; so that he makes man as distinct from all other mammals as are these two latter groups conjoined. This view has not been accepted, as far as I am aware, by any naturalist capable of forming an independent judgment and therefore need not here be further considered.

We can understand why a classification founded on any single character or organ—even an organ so wonderfully complex and important as the brain—or on the high development of the mental faculties, is almost sure to prove unsatisfactory. This principle has indeed been tried with hymenopterous insects; but when thus classed by their habits or instincts, the arrangement proved thoroughly artificial.[54] Classifications may, of course, be based on any character whatever, as on size, colour, or the element inhabited; but naturalists have long felt a profound conviction that there is a natural system. This system, it is now generally admitted, must be, as far as possible, genealogical in arrangement,—that is the co-descendants of the same form must be kept together in one group, apart from the co-descendants of any other form; but if the parent-forms are related, so will be their descendants, and the two groups together will form a larger group. The amount of difference between the several groups—that is the amount of modification which each has undergone—is expressed by such terms as

---

[53] Some of the most interesting facts ever published on the habits of ants are given by Mr. Belt, in his 'Naturalist in Nicaragua,' 1874. See also Mr. Moggridge's admirable work, 'Harvesting Ants,' &c., 1873, also L'Instinct chez les Insectes,' by M. George Pouchet, 'Revue des Deux Mondes,' Feb. 1870, p. 682.
[54] Westwood, 'Modern Class of Insects,' vol. ii. 1840, p. 87.

genera, families, orders, and classes. As we have no record of the lines of descent, the pedigree can be discovered only by observing the degrees of resemblance between the beings which are to be classed. For this object numerous points of resemblance are of much more importance than the amount of similarity or dissimilarity in a few points. If two languages were found to resemble each other in a multitude of words and points of construction, they would be universally recognised as having sprung from a common source, notwithstanding that they differed greatly in some few words or points of construction. But with organic beings the points of resemblance must not consist of adaptations to similar habits of life: two animals may, for instance, have had their whole frames modified for living in the water, and yet they will not be brought any nearer to each other in the natural system. Hence we can see how it is that resemblances in several unimportant structures, in useless and rudimentary organs, or not now functionally active, or in an embryological condition, are by far the most serviceable for classification; for they can hardly be due to adaptations within a late period; and thus they reveal the old lines of descent or of true affinity.

We can further see why a great amount of modification in some one character ought not to lead us to separate widely any two organisms. A part which already differs much from the same part in other allied forms has already, according to the theory of evolution, varied much; consequently it would (as long as the organism remained exposed to the same exciting conditions) be liable to further variations of the same kind; and these, if beneficial, would be preserved, and thus be continually augmented. In many cases the continued development of a part, for instance, of the beak of a bird or of the teeth of a mammal, would not aid the species in gaining its food, or for any other object; but with man we can see no definite limit to the continued development of the brain and mental faculties, as far as advantage is concerned. Therefore in determining the position of man in the natural or genealogical system, the extreme development of his brain ought not to outweigh a multitude of resemblances in other less important or quite unimportant points.

The greater number of naturalists who have taken into consideration the whole structure of man, including his mental faculties, have followed Blumenbach and Cuvier, and have placed man in a separate Order, under the title of the Bimana, and therefore on an equality with the orders of the Quadrumana, Carnivora, &c. Recently many of our best naturalists have recurred to the view first propounded by Linnæus, so remarkable for his sagacity, and have placed man in the same Order with the Quadrumana, under the title of the Primates. The justice of this conclusion will be admitted: for in the first place, we must bear in mind the comparative insignificance for classification of the great development of the brain in man, and that the strongly-marked differences between the skulls of man and the Quadrumana (lately insisted upon by Bischoff, Aeby, and others) apparently follow from their differently developed brains. In the second place, we must remember that nearly all the other and more important differences between man and the quadrumana are manifestly adaptive in their nature, and relate chiefly to the erect position of man; such as the structure of his hand, foot, and pelvis, the curvature of his spine, and the position of his head. The family of Seals offers a good illustration of the small importance of adaptive characters for classification. These animals differ from all other Carnivora in the form of their bodies and in the structure of their limbs, far more than does man from the higher apes; yet in most systems, from that of Cuvier to the most recent one by Mr. Flower,[55] seals are ranked as a mere family in the Order of the Carnivora. If man had not been his own classifier, he would never have thought of founding a separate order for his own reception.

It would be beyond my limits, and quite beyond my knowledge, even to name the innumerable points of structure in which man agrees with the other Primates. Our great anatomist and philosopher, Prof. Huxley, has fully discussed this subject,[56] and concludes that man in all parts of his organization differs less from the higher apes, than these do from the lower members of the same group. Consequently there "is no justification for placing man in a distinct order." * * *

Lower Stacks in the Genealogy of Man

* * * We have thus far endeavoured rudely to trace the genealogy of the Vertebrata by the aid of their mutual affinities. We will now look to man as he exists; and we shall, I think, be able partially to restore the structure of our early progenitors, during successive periods, but not in due order of time. This can be effected by means of the rudiments which man still retains, by the characters which occasionally make their appearance in him through reversion, and by the aid of the principles of morphology and embryology. The various facts, to which I shall here allude, have been given in the previous chapters.

The early progenitors of man must have been once covered with hair, both sexes having beards; their ears were probably pointed, and capable of movement; and their bodies were provided with a tail, having the proper muscles. Their limbs and bodies were also acted on by many muscles which now only occasionally reappear, but are normally present in the Quadrumana. At this or some earlier period, the great artery and nerve of the humerus ran through a supra-condyloid foramen. The intestine gave forth a much larger diverticulum or cæcum than that now existing. The foot was then prehensile, judging from the condition of the great toe in the fœtus; and our progenitors, no doubt, were arboreal in their habits, and frequented some warm, forest-clad land. The males had great canine teeth, which served them as formidable weapons. At a much earlier period the uterus was double; the excreta were voided through a cloaca; and the eye was protected by a third eyelid or nictitating membrane. At a still earlier period the progenitors of man must have been aquatic in their habits; for morphology plainly tells us that our lungs consist of a modified swim-bladder, which once served as a float. The clefts on the neck in the embryo of man show where the branchiæ once existed. In the lunar or weekly recurrent periods of some of our functions we apparently still retain traces of our primordial birthplace, a shore washed by the tides. At about this same early period the true kidneys were replaced by the corpora wolffiana. The heart existed as a simple pulsating vessel; and the chorda dorsalis took the place of a vertebral

---

[55] 'Proc. Zoolog. Soc.' 1863, p. 4.
[56] 'Evidence as to Man's Place in Nature,' 1863, p. 70. *et passim.*

column. These early ancestors of man, thus seen in the dim recesses of time, must have been as simply, or even still more simply organised than the lancelet or amphioxus.

There is one other point deserving a fuller notice. It has long been known that in the vertebrate kingdom one sex bears rudiments of various accessory parts, appertaining to the reproductive system, which properly belongs to the opposite sex; and it has now been ascertained that at a very early embryonic period both sexes possess true male and female glands. Hence some remote progenitor of the whole vertebrate kingdom appears to have been hermaphrodite or androgynous.[57] But here we encounter a singular difficulty. In the mammalian class the males possess rudiments of a uterus with the adjacent passage, in their vesiculæ prostaticæ; they bear also rudiments of mammæ, and some male Marsupials have traces of a marsupial sack.[58] Other analogous facts could be added. Are we, then, to suppose that some extremely ancient mammal continued androgynous, after it had acquired the chief distinctions of its class, and therefore after it had diverged from the lower classes of the vertebrate kingdom? This seems very improbable, for we have to look to fishes, the lowest of all the classes, to find any still existent androgynous forms.[59] That various accessory parts, proper to each sex, are found in a rudimentary condition in the opposite sex, may be explained by such organs having been gradually acquired by the one sex, and then transmitted in a more or less imperfect state to the other. When we treat of sexual selection, we shall meet with innumerable instances of this form of transmission,—as in the case of the spurs, plumes, and brilliant colours, acquired for battle or ornament by male birds, and inherited by the females in an imperfect or rudimentary condition.

The possession by male mammals of functionally imperfect mammary organs is, in some respects, especially curious. The Monotremata have the proper milk-secreting glands with orifices, but no nipples; and as these animals stand at the very base of the mammalian series, it is probable that the progenitors of the class also had milk-secreting glands, but no nipples. This conclusion is supported by what is known of their manner of development; for Professor Turner informs me, on the authority of Kölliker and Langer, that in the embryo the mammary glands can be distinctly traced before the nipples are in the least visible; and the development of successive parts in the individual generally represents and accords with the development of successive beings in the same

---

[57] This is the conclusion of Prof Gegenbaur, one of the highest authorities in comparative anatomy: see 'Grundzüge der vergleich. Anat.' 1870, s. 876. The result has been arrived at chiefly from the study of the Amphibia; but it appears from the researches of Waldeyer (as quoted in 'Journal of Anat. and Phys.' 1869, p. 161), that the sexual organs of even "the higher vertebrata are, in their early condition, hermaphrodite." Similar views have long been held by some authors, though until recently without a firm basis.

[58] The male Thylacinus offers the best instance. Owen, 'Anatomy of Vertebrates,' vol. iii. p. 771.

[59] Hermaphroditism has been observed in several species of Serranus, as well as in some other fishes, where it is either normal and symmetrical, or abnormal and unilateral. Dr. Zouteveen has given me references on this subject, more especially to a paper by Prof. Halbertsma, in the 'Transact. of the Dutch Acad. of Sciences,' vol. xvi. Dr. Günther doubts the fact, but it has now been recorded by too many good observers to be any longer disputed. Dr. M. Lessona writes to me, that he has verified the observations made by Cavolini on Serranus. Prof. Ercolani has recently shewn ('Acad. delle Scienze,' Bologna, Dec. 28, 1871 that eels are androgynyous.

line of descent. The Marsupials differ from the Monotremata by possessing nipples; so that probably these organs were first acquired by the Marsupials, after they had diverged from, and risen above, the Monotremata, and were then transmitted to the placental mammals.[60] No one will suppose that the Marsupials still remained androgynous, after they had approximately acquired their present structure. How then are we to account for male mammals possessing mammæ? It is possible that they were first developed in the females and then transferred to the males, but from what follows this is hardly probable.

It may be suggested, as another view, that long after the progenitors of the whole mammalian class had ceased to be androgynous, both sexes yielded milk, and thus nourished their young; and in the case of the Marsupials, that both sexes carried their young in marsupial sacks. This will not appear altogether improbable, if we reflect that the males of existing syngnathous fishes receive the eggs of the females in their abdominal pouches, hatch them, and afterwards, as some believe, nourish the young;[61] — that certain other male fishes hatch the eggs within their mouths or branchial cavities, — that certain male toads take the chaplets of eggs from the females, and wind them round their own thighs, keeping them there until the tadpoles are born; — that certain male birds undertake the whole duty of incubation, and that male pigeons, as well as the females, feed their nestlings with a secretion from their crops. But the above suggestion first occurred to me from mammary glands of male mammals being so much more perfectly developed than the rudiments of the other accessory reproductive parts, which are found in the one sex though proper to the other. The mammary glands and nipples, as they exist in male mammals, can indeed hardly be called rudimentary; they are merely not fully developed, and not functionally active. They are sympathetically affected under the influence of certain diseases, like the same organs in the female. They often secrete a few drops of milk at birth and at puberty: this latter fact occurred in the curious case before referred to, where a young man possessed two pairs of mammæ. In man and some other male mammals these organs have been known occasionally to become so well developed during maturity as to yield a fair supply of milk. Now if we suppose that during a former prolonged period male mammals aided the females in nursing their offspring,[62] and that afterwards from some cause (as from the production of a smaller number of young) the males ceased to give this aid, disuse of the organs during maturity would lead to their becoming inactive; and from two well-known principles of inheritance, this state of inactivity would probably be transmitted to the

---

[60] Prof. Gegenbaur has shewn ('Jenaische Zeitschrift,' Bd. vii. p. 212) that two distinct types of nipples prevail throughout the several mammalian orders, but that it is quite intelligible how both could have been derived from the nipples of the Marsupials, and the latter from those of the Monotremata. See, also, a memoir by Dr. Max Huss, on the mammary glands, ibid. B. viii. p. 176.

[61] Mr. Lockwood believes (as quoted in 'Quart. Journal of Science,' April, 1868 p. 269), from what he has observed of the development of Hippocampus, that the walls of the abdominal pouch of the male in some way afford nourishment. On male fishes hatching the ova in their mouths, see a very interesting paper by Prof. Wyman, in 'Proc. Boston Soc. of Nat. Hist.' Sept. 15, 1857; also Prof. Turner, in 'Journal of Anat. and Phys.' Nov. 1, 1866, p. 78. Dr. Günther has likewise described similar cases.

[62] Maddle. C. Royer has suggested a similar view in her 'Origine de l'Homme,' &c., 1870.

males at the corresponding age of maturity. But at an earlier age these organs would be left unaffected, so that they would be almost equally well developed in the young of both sexes.

Conclusion

Von Baer has defined advancement or progress in the organic scale better than any one else, as resting on the amount of differentiation and specialisation of the several parts of a being,—when arrived at maturity, as I should be inclined to add. Now as organisms have become slowly adapted to diversified lines of life by means of natural selection, their parts will have become more and more differentiated and specialised for various functions from the advantage gained by the division of physiological labour. The same part appears often to have been modified first for one purpose, and then long afterwards for some other and quite distinct purpose; and thus all the parts are rendered more and more complex. But each organism still retains the general type of structure of the progenitor from which it was aboriginally derived. In accordance with this view it seems, if we turn to geological evidence, that organisation on the whole has advanced throughout the world by slow and interrupted steps. In the great kingdom of the Vertebrata it has culminated in man. It must not, however, be supposed that groups of organic beings are always supplanted, and disappear as soon as they have given birth to other and more perfect groups. The latter, though victorious over their predecessors, may not have become better adapted for all places in the economy of nature. Some old forms appear to have survived from inhabiting protected sites, where they have not been exposed to very severe competition; and these often aid us in constructing our genealogies, by giving us a fair idea of former and lost populations. But we must not fall into the error of looking at the existing members of any lowly-organised group as perfect representatives of their ancient predecessors.

The most ancient progenitors in the kingdom of the Vetebrata, at which we are able to obtain an obscure glance, apparently consisted of a group of marine animals,[63] resembling the larvæ of existing Ascidians. These animals probably gave rise to a group of fishes, as lowly organised as the lancelet; and from these the Ganoids, and other fishes like the Lepidosiren, must have been developed. From such fish a very small advance would carry us on to the Amphibians. We have seen that birds and reptiles were once intimately connected together; and the Monotremata now connect mammals with reptiles in a slight degree. But no one can at present say by what line of descent the three higher and related classes, namely, mammals, birds, and reptiles, were derived from the two lower vertebrate classes, namely, amphibians and fishes. In the class of mammals the steps are not difficult to conceive which led from the ancient Monotremata to the ancient Marsupials; and from these to the early progenitors of the placental mammals. We may thus ascend to the Lemuridæ; and the interval is not very wide from these to the Simiadæ. The Simiadæ then branched off into two great stems, the New World and Old World monkeys; and from the latter, at a remote period, Man, the wonder and glory of the Universe, proceeded.

Thus we have given to man a pedigree of prodigious length, but not, it may be said, of noble quality. The world, it has often been remarked, appears as if it had long been preparing for the advent of man: and this, in one sense is strictly true, for he owes his birth to a long line of progenitors. If any single link in this chain had never existed, man would not have been exactly what he now is. Unless we wilfully close our eyes, we may, with our present knowledge, approximately recognise our parentage; nor need we feel ashamed of it. The most humble organism is something much higher than the inorganic dust under our feet; and no one with an unbiased mind can study any living creature, however humble, without being struck with enthusiasm at its marvellous structure and properties.

---

[63] The inhabitants of the seashore must be greatly affected by the tides; animals living either about the *mean* high-water mark, or about the *mean* low-water mark, pass through a complete cycle of tidal changes in a fortnight. Consequently, their food supply will undergo marked changes week by week. The vital functions of such animals, living under these conditions for many generations, can hardly fail to run their course in regular weekly periods. Now it is a mysterious fact that in the highest and now terrestrial Vertebrata, as well as in other classes, many normal and abnormal processes have one or more whole weeks as their periods; this would be rendered intelligible if the Vetebrata are descended from an animal allied to the existing tidal Ascidians. Many instances of such periodic processes might be given, as the gestation of mammals, the duration of fevers, &c. The hatching of eggs affords also a good example, for according to Mr. Bartlett ('Land and Water,' Jan. 7, 1871), the eggs of the pigeon are hatched in two weeks; those of the fowl in three; those of the duck in four; those of the goose in five; and those of the ostrich in seven weeks. As far as we can judge, a recurrent period, if approximately of the right duration for any process or function, would not, when once gained, be liable to change; consequently it might be thus transmitted through almost any number of generations. But if the function changed, the period would have to change, and would be apt to change almost abruptly by a whole week. This conclusion, if sound, is highly remarkable; for the period of gestation in each mammal, and the hatching of each bird's eggs, and many other vital processes, thus betray to us the primordial birthplace of these animals.

Chapter XXI
General Summary and Conclusion

Main conclusion that man is descended from some lower form — Manner of development — Genealogy of man — Intellectual and moral faculties — Sexual Selection — Concluding remarks.

A brief summary will be sufficient to recall to the reader's mind the more salient points in this work. Many of the views which have been advanced are highly speculative, and some no doubt will prove erroneous; but I have in every case given the reasons which have led me to one view rather than to another. It seemed worth while to try how far the principle of evolution would throw light on some of the more complex problems in the natural history of man. False facts are highly injurious to the progress of science, for they often endure long; but false views, if supported by some evidence, do little harm, for every one takes a salutary pleasure in proving their falseness and when this is done, one path towards error is closed and the road to truth is often at the same time opened.

The main conclusion here arrived at, and now held by many naturalists who are well competent to form a sound judgment, is that man is descended from some less highly organised form. The grounds upon which this conclusion rests will never be shaken, for the close similarity between man and the lower animals in embryonic development, as well as in innumerable points of structure and constitution, both of high and of the most trifling importance, — the rudiments which he retains, and the abnormal reversions to which he is occasionally liable, — are facts which cannot be disputed. They have long been known, but until recently they told us nothing with respect to the origin of man. Now when viewed by the light of our knowledge of the whole organic world, their meaning is unmistakable. The great principle of evolution stands up clear and firm, when these groups or facts are considered in connection with others, such as the mutual affinities of the members of the same group, their geographical distribution in past and present times, and their geological succession. It is incredible that all these facts should speak falsely. He who is not content to look, like a savage, at the phenomena of nature as disconnected, cannot any longer believe that man is the work of a separate act of creation. He will be forced to admit that the close resemblance of the embryo of man to that, for instance, of a dog — the construction of his skull, limbs and whole frame on the same plan with that of other mammals, independently of the uses to which the parts may be put — the occasional re-appearance of various structures, for instance of several muscles, which man does not normally possess, but which are common to the Quadrumana — and a crowd of analogous facts — all point in the plainest manner to the conclusion that man is the co-descendant with other mammals of a common progenitor.

We have seen that man incessantly presents individual differences in all parts of his body and in his mental faculties. These differences or variations seem to be induced by the same general causes, and to obey the same laws as with the lower animals. In both cases similar laws of inheritance prevail. Man tends to increase at a greater rate than his means of subsistence; consequently he is occasionally subjected to a severe struggle for existence, and natural selection will have effected whatever lies within its scope. A succession of strongly-marked variations of a similar nature is by no means requisite; slight fluctuating differences in the individual suffice for the work of natural selection; not that we have any reason to suppose that in the same species, all parts of the organisation tend to vary to the same degree. We may feel assured that the inherited effects of the long-continued use or disuse of parts will have done much in the same direction with natural selection. Modifications formerly of importance, though no longer of any special use, are long-inherited. When one part is modified, other parts change through the principle of correlation, of which we have instances in many curious cases of correlated monstrosities. Something may be attributed to the direct and definite action of the surrounding conditions of life, such as abundant food, heat or moisture; and lastly, many characters of slight physiological importance, some indeed of considerable importance, have been gained through sexual selection.

No doubt man, as well as every other animal, presents structures, which seem to our limited knowledge, not to be now of any service to him, nor to have been so formerly, either for the general conditions of life, or in the relations of one sex to the other. Such structures cannot be accounted for by any form of selection, or by the inherited effects of the use and disuse of parts. We know, however, that many strange and strongly-marked peculiarities of structure occasionally appear in our domesticated productions, and if their unknown causes were to act more uniformly, they would probably become common to all the individuals of the species. We may hope hereafter to understand something about the causes of such occasional modifications, especially through the study of monstrosities: hence the labours of experimentalists such as those of M. Camille Dareste, are full of promise for the future. In general we can only say that the cause of each slight variation and of each monstrosity lies much more in the constitution of the organism, than in the nature of the surrounding conditions; though new and changed conditions certainly play an important part in exciting organic changes of many kinds.

Through the means just specified, aided perhaps by others as yet undiscovered, man has been raised to his resent state. But since he attained to the rank of manhood, he has diverged into distinct races, or as they may be more fitly called, sub-species. Some of these, such as the Negro and European, are so distinct that, if specimens had been brought to a naturalist without any further information, they would undoubtedly have been considered by him as good and true species. Nevertheless all the races agree in so many unimportant details of structure and in so many mental peculiarities that these can be accounted for only by inheritance from a common progenitor; and a progenitor thus characterised would probably deserve to rank as man.

It must not be supposed that the divergence of each race from the other races, and of all from a common stock, can be traced back to any one pair of progenitors. On the contrary, at every stage in the process of modification, all the individuals which were in any way better fitted for their conditions of life, though in different degrees, would have survived in greater numbers than the less well-fitted. The process would have been like that followed by man, when he does not intentionally select particular individuals, but breeds from all the superior individuals, and neglects the inferior. He thus slowly but surely modifies his stock, and unconciously forms a new strain. So with respect to modifications acquired independently of selection, and due to variations arising from the nature of the organism and the action of the surrounding conditions, or from changed habits of life, no single pair will have been modified much more than the other pairs inhabiting the same country, for all will have been continually blended through free intercrossing.

By considering the embryological structure of man, — the homologies which he presents with the lower animals, — the rudiments which he retains, — and the reversions to which he is liable, we can partly recall in imagination the former condition of our early progenitors; and can approximately place them in their proper place in the zoological series. We thus learn that man is descended from a hairy, tailed quadruped, probably arboreal in its habits, and an inhabitant of the Old World. This creature, if its whole structure had been examined by a naturalist, would have been classed amongst the Quadrumana, as surely as the still more ancient progenitor of the Old and New World monkeys. The Quadrumana and all the higher mammals are probably derived from an ancient marsupial animal, and this through a long series of diversified forms, from some amphibian-like creature, and this again from some fish-like animal. In the dim obscurity of the past we can see that the early progenitor of all the Vertebrata must have been an aquatic animal provided with branchiæ, with the two sexes united in the same individual, and with the most important organs of the body (such as the brain and heart) imperfectly or not at all developed. This animal seems to have been more like the larvæ of the existing marine Ascidians than any other known form.

The high standard of our intellectual powers and moral disposition is the greatest difficulty which presents itself, after we have been driven to this conclusion on the origin of man. But every one who admits the principle of evolution, must see that the mental powers of the higher animals, which are the same in kind with those of man, though so different in degree, are capable of advancement. Thus the interval between the mental powers of one of the higher apes and of a fish, or between those of an ant and scale-insect, is immense; yet their development does not offer any special difficulty; for with our domesticated animals, the mental faculties are certainly variable, and the variations are inherited. No one doubts that they are of the utmost importance to animals in a state of nature. Therefore the conditions are favourable for their development through natural selection. The same conclusion may be extended to man; the intellect must have been all-important to him, even at a very remote period, as enabling him to invent and use language, to make weapons, tools, traps, &c., whereby with the aid of his social habits, he long ago became the most dominant of all living creatures.

A great stride in the development of the intellect will have followed, as soon as the half-art and half-instinct of language came into use; for the continued use of language will have reacted on the brain and produced an inherited effect; and this again will have reacted on the improvement of language. As Mr. Chauncey Wright[64] has well remarked, the largeness of the brain in man relatively to his body, compared with the lower

---

[64] 'On the Limits of Natural Selection,' in the 'North American Review,' Oct. 1870, p. 295.

animals, may be attributed in chief part to the early use of some simple form of language,—that wonderful engine which affixes signs to all sorts of objects and qualities, and excites trains of thought which would never arise from the mere impression of the senses, or if they did arise could not be followed out. The higher intellectual powers of man, such as those of ratiocination, abstraction, self-consciousness, &c., probably follow from the continued improvement and exercise of the other mental faculties.

The development of the moral qualities is a more interesting problem. The foundation lies in the social instincts, including under this term the family ties. These instincts are highly complex, and in the case of the lower animals give special tendencies towards certain definite actions; but the more important elements are love, and the distinct emotion of sympathy. Animals endowed with the social instincts take pleasure in one another's company, warn one another of danger, defend and aid one another in many ways. These instincts do not extend to all the individuals of the species, but only to those of the same community. As they are highly beneficial to the species, they have in all probability been acquired through natural selection.

A moral being is one who is capable of reflecting on his past actions and their motives—of approving of some and disapproving of others; and the fact that man is the one being who certainly deserves this designation, is the greatest of all distinctions between him and the lower animals. But in the fourth chapter I have endeavoured to shew that the moral sense follows, firstly, from the enduring and ever-present nature of the social instincts; secondly, from man's appreciation of the approbation and disapprobation of his fellows; and thirdly, from the high activity of his mental faculties, with past impressions extremely vivid; and in these latter respects he differs from the lower animals. Owing to this condition of mind, man cannot avoid looking both backwards and forwards, and comparing past impressions. Hence after some temporary desire or passion has mastered his social instincts, he reflects and compares the now weakened impression of such past impulses with the ever-present social instincts; and he then feels that sense of dissatisfaction which all unsatisfied instincts leave behind them, he therefore resolves to act differently for the future,—and this is conscience. Any instinct, permanently stronger or more enduring than another, gives rise to a feeling which we express by saying that it ought to be obeyed. A pointer dog, if able to reflect on his past conduct, would say to himself, I ought (as indeed we say of him) to have pointed at that hare and not have yielded to the passing temptation of hunting it.

Social animals are impelled partly by a wish to aid the members of their community in a general manner, but more commonly to perform certain definite actions. Man is impelled by the same general wish to aid his fellows; but has few or no special instincts. He differs also from the lower animals in the power of expressing his desires by words, which thus become a guide to the aid required and bestowed. The motive to give aid is likewise much modified in man: it no longer consists solely of a blind instinctive impulse, but is much influenced by the praise or blame of his fellows. The appreciation and the bestowal of praise and blame both rest on sympathy; and this emotion, as we have seen, is one of the most important elements of the social instincts. Sympathy, though gained as an instinct, is also much strengthened by exercise or habit. As all men desire their own happiness, praise or blame is bestowed on actions and motives, according as they lead to this end; and as happiness is an essential part of the general good, the greatest-happiness principle indirectly serves as a nearly safe standard of right and wrong. As the reasoning powers advance and experience is gained, the remoter effects of certain lines of conduct on the character of the individual, and on the general good, are perceived; and then the self-regarding virtues come within the scope of public opinion, and receive praise, and their opposites blame. But with the less civilised nations reason often errs, and many bad customs and base superstitions come within the same scope, and are then esteemed as high virtues, and their breach as heavy crimes.

The moral faculties are generally and justly esteemed as of higher value than the intellectual powers. But we should bear in mind that the activity of the mind in vividly recalling past impressions is one of the fundamental though secondary bases of conscience. This affords the strongest argument for educating and stimulating in all possible ways the intellectual faculties of every human being. No doubt a man with a torpid mind, if his social affections and sympathies are well developed, will be led to good actions, and may have a fairly sensitive conscience. But whatever renders the imagination more vivid and strengthens the habit of recalling and comparing past impressions, will make the conscience more sensitive, and may even somewhat compensate for weak social affections and sympathies.

The moral nature of man has reached its present standard, partly through the advancement of his reasoning powers and consequently of a just public opinion, but especially from his sympathies having been rendered more tender and widely diffused through the effects of habit, example, instruction, and reflection. It is not improbable that after long practice virtuous tendencies may be inherited. With the more civilised races, the conviction of the existence of an all-seeing Deity has had a potent influence on the advance of morality. Ultimately man does not accept the praise or blame of his fellows as his sole guide, though few escape this influence, but his habitual convictions, controlled by reason, afford him the safest rule. His conscience then becomes the supreme judge and monitor. Nevertheless the first foundation or origin of the moral sense lies in the social instincts, including sympathy; and these instincts no doubt were primarily gained, as in the case of the lower animals, through natural selection.

The belief in God has often been advanced as not only the greatest, but the most complete of all the distinctions between man and the lower animals. It is however impossible, as we have seen, to maintain that this belief is innate or instinctive in man. On the other hand a belief in all-pervading spiritual agencies seems to be universal; and apparently follows from a considerable advance in man's reason, and from a still greater advance in his faculties of imagination, curiosity and wonder. I am aware that the assumed instinctive belief in God has been used by many persons as an argument for His existence. But this is a rash argument, as we should thus be compelled to believe in the existence of many cruel and malignant spirits, only a little more powerful than man; for the belief in them is far more general than in a beneficent Deity. The idea of a universal and beneficent Creator does not seem to arise in the mind of man, until he has been elevated by long-continued culture.

He who believes in the advancement of man from some low organised form, will naturally ask how does this bear on the belief in the immortality of the soul. The barbarous races of man, as Sir J. Lubbock has shewn, possess no clear belief of this kind; but arguments derived from the primeval beliefs of savages are, as we have just seen, of little or no avail. Few persons feel any anxiety from the impossibility of determining at what precise period in the development of the individual, from the first trace of a minute germinal vesicle, man becomes an immortal being; and there is no greater cause for anxiety because the period cannot possibly be determined in the gradually ascending organic scale.[65]

I am aware that the conclusions arrived at in this work will be denounced by some as highly irreligious; but he who denounces them is bound to shew why it is more irreligious to explain the origin of man as a distinct species by descent from some lower form, through the laws of variation and natural selection, than to explain the birth of the individual through the laws of ordinary reproduction. The birth both of the species and of the individual are equally parts of that grand sequence of events, which our minds refuse to accept as the result of blind chance. The understanding revolts at such a conclusion, whether or not we are able to believe that every slight variation of structure,—the union of each pair in marriage,—the dissemination of each seed,—and other such events, have all been ordained for some special purpose.

Sexual selection has been treated at great length in this work; for, as I have attempted to shew, it has played an important part in the history of the organic world. I am aware that much remains doubtful, but I have endeavoured to give a fair view of the whole case. In the lower divisions of the animal kingdom, sexual selection seems to have done nothing: such animals are often affixed for life to the same spot, or have the sexes combined in the same individual, or what is still more important, their perceptive and intellectual faculties are not sufficiently advanced to allow of the feelings of love and jealousy, or of the exertion of choice. When, however, we come to the Arthropoda and Vertebrata, even to the lowest classes in these two great Sub-Kingdoms, sexual selection has effected much.

In the several great classes of the animal kingdom,—in mammals, birds, reptiles, fishes, insects, and even crustaceans,—the differences between the sexes follow nearly the same rules. The males are almost always the wooers; and they alone are armed with special weapons for fighting with their rivals. They are generally stronger and larger than the females, and are endowed with the requisite qualities of courage and pugnacity. They are provided, either exclusively or in a much higher degree than the females, with organs for vocal or instrumental music, and with odoriferous glands. They are ornamental with infinitely diversified appendages, and with the most brilliant or conspicuous colours, often arranged in elegant patterns, whilst the females are unadorned. When the sexes differ in more important structures, it is the male which is provided with special sense-organs for discovering the female, with locomotive organs for reaching her, and often with prehensile organs for holding her. These various structures for charming or securing the female are often developed in the male during

---

[65] The Rev. J. A. Picton gives a discussion to this effect in his 'New Theories and the Old Faith,' 1870.

only part of the year, namely the breeding-season. They have in many cases been more or less transferred to the females; and in the latter case they often appear in her as mere rudiments. They are lost or never gained by the males after emasculation. Generally they are not developed in the male during early youth, but appear a short time before the age for reproduction. Hence in most cases the young of both sexes resemble each other; and the female somewhat resembles her young offspring throughout life. In almost every great class a few anomalous cases occur, where there has been an almost complete transposition of the characters proper to the two sexes; the females assuming characters which properly belong to the males. This surprising uniformity in the laws regulating the differences between the sexes in so many and such widely separated classes, is intelligible if we admit the action of one common cause, namely sexual selection.

Sexual selection depends on the success of certain individuals over others of the same sex, in relation to the propagation of the species; whilst natural selection depends on the success of both sexes, at all ages, in relation to the general conditions of life. The sexual struggle is of two kinds; in the one it is between individuals of the same sex, generally the males, in order to drive away or kill their rivals, the females remaining passive; whilst in the other, the struggle is likewise between the individuals of the same sex, in order to excite or charm those of the opposite sex, generally the females, which no longer remain passive, but select the more agreeable partners. This latter kind of selection is closely analogous to that which man unintentionally, yet effectually, brings to bear on his domesticated productions, when he preserves during a long period the most pleasing or useful individuals, without any wish to modify the breed.

The laws of inheritance determine whether characters gained through sexual selection by either sex shall be transmitted to the same sex, or to both; as well as the age at which they shall be developed. It appears that variations arising late in life are commonly transmitted to one and the same sex. Variability is the necessary basis for the action of selection, and is wholly independent of it. It follows from this, that variations of the same general nature have often been taken advantage of and accumulated through sexual selection in relation to the propagation of the species, as well as through natural selection in relation to the general purposes of life. Hence secondary sexual characters, when equally transmitted to both sexes can be distinguished from ordinary specific characters only by the light of analogy. The modifications acquired through sexual selection are often so strongly pronounced that the two sexes have frequently been ranked as distinct species, or even as distinct genera. Such strongly-marked differences must be in some manner highly important; and we know that they have been acquired in some instances at the cost not only of inconvenience, but of exposure to actual danger.

The belief in the power of sexual selection rests chiefly on the following considerations. Certain characters are confined to one sex; and this alone renders it probable that in most cases they are connected with the act of reproduction. In innumerable instances these characters are fully developed only at maturity, and often during only a part of the year, which is always the breeding-season. The males (passing over a few exceptional cases) are the more active in courtship; they are the better armed, and are rendered the more attractive in various ways. It is to be especially observed that the males display their attractions with elaborate care in the presence of the females; and that they rarely or never display them excepting during the season of love. It is incredible that all this should be purposeless. Lastly we have distinct evidence with some quadrupeds and birds, that the individuals of one sex are capable of feeling a strong antipathy or preference for certain individuals of the other sex.

Bearing in mind these facts, and the marked results of man's unconscious selection, when applied to domesticated animals and cultivated plants, it seems to me almost certain that if the individuals of one sex were during a long series of generations to prefer pairing with certain individuals of the other sex, characterised in some peculiar manner, the offspring would slowly but surely become modified in this same manner. I have not attempted to conceal that, excepting when the males are more numerous than the females, or when polygamy prevails, it is doubtful how the more attractive males succeed in leaving a large number of offspring to inherit their superiority in ornaments or other charms than the less attractive males; but I have shewn that this would probably follow from the females, — especially the more vigorous ones, which would be the first to breed, — preferring not only the more attractive but at the same time the more vigorous and victorious males.

Although we have some positive evidence that birds appreciate bright and beautiful objects, as with the bower-birds of Australia, and although they certainly appreciate the power of song, yet I fully admit that it is astonishing that the females of many birds and some mammals should be endowed with sufficient taste to appreciate ornaments, which we have reason to attribute to sexual selection; and this is even more astonishing in the case of reptiles, fish, and insects. But we really know little about the minds of the lower animals. It cannot be supposed, for instance, that male birds of paradise or peacocks should take such pains in erecting, spreading, and vibrating their beautiful plumes before the females for no purpose. We should remember the fact given on excellent authority in a former chapter, that several peahens, when debarred from an admired male, remained widows during a whole season rather than pair with another bird.

Nevertheless I know of no fact in natural history more wonderful than that of the female Argus pheasant should appreciate the exquisite shading of the ball-and-socket ornaments and the elegant patterns on the wing-feathers of the male. He who thinks that the male was created as he now exists must admit that the great plumes, which prevent the wings from being used for flight, and which are displayed during courtship and at no other time in a manner quite peculiar to this one species, were given to him as an ornament. If so, he must likewise admit that the female was created and endowed with the capacity of appreciating such ornaments. I differ only in the conviction that the male Argus pheasant acquired his beauty gradually, through the preference of the females during many generations for the more highly ornamented males; the æsthetic capacity of the females having been advanced through exercise or habit, just as our own taste is gradually improved. In the male through the fortunate chance of a few feathers being left unchanged, we can distinctly trace how simple spots with a little fulvous shading on one side may have been developed by small steps into the wonderful ball-and-socket ornaments; and it is probable that they were actually thus developed.

Everyone who admits the principle of evolution, and yet feels great difficulty in admitting that female mammals, birds, reptiles, and fish, could have acquired the high taste implied by the beauty of the males, and which generally coincides with our own standard, should reflect that the nerve-cells of the brain in the highest as well as in the lowest members of the Vertebrate series, are derived from those of the common progenitor of this great Kingdom. For we can thus see how it has come to pass that certain mental faculties, in various and widely distinct groups of animals, have been developed in nearly the same manner and to nearly the same degree.

The reader who has taken the trouble to go through the several chapters devoted to sexual selection, will be able to judge how far the conclusions at which I have arrived are supported by sufficient evidence. If he accepts these conclusions he may, I think, safely extend them to mankind; but it would be superfluous here to repeat what I have so lately said on the manner in which sexual selection apparently has acted on man, both on the male and female side, causing the two sexes to differ in body and mind, and the several races to differ from each other in various characters, as well as from their ancient and lowly-organised progenitors.

He who admits the principle of sexual selection will be led to the remarkable conclusion that the nervous system not only regulates most of the existing functions of the body, but has indirectly influenced the progressive development of various bodily structures and of certain mental qualities. Courage, pugnacity, perseverance, strength and size of body, weapons of all kinds, musical organs, both vocal and instrumental, bright colours and ornamental appendages, have all been indirectly gained by the one sex or the other, through the exertion of choice, the influence of love and jealousy, and the appreciation of the beautiful in sound, colour or form; and these powers of the mind manifestly depend on the development of the brain.

Man scans with scrupulous care the character and pedigree of his horses, cattle, and dogs before he matches them; but when he comes to his own marriage he rarely, or never, takes any such care. He is impelled by nearly the same motives as the lower animals, when they are left to their own free choice, though he is in so far superior to them that he highly values mental charms and virtues. On the other hand he is strongly attracted by mere wealth or rank. Yet he might by selection do something not only for the bodily constitution and frame of his offspring, but for their intellectual and moral qualities. Both sexes ought to refrain from marriage if they are in any marked degree inferior in body or mind; but such hopes are Utopian and will never be even partially realised until the laws of inheritance are thoroughly known. Everyone does good service, who aids toward this end. When the principles of breeding and inheritance are better understood, we shall not hear ignorant members of our legislature rejecting with scorn a plan for ascertaining whether or not consanguineous marriages are injurious to man.

The advancement of the welfare of mankind is a most intricate problem: all ought to refrain from marriage who cannot avoid abject poverty for their children; for poverty is not only a great evil, but tends to its own increase by leading to recklessness in marriage. On the other hand, as Mr. Galton has remarked, if the prudent avoid marriage, whilst the reckless marry, the inferior members tend to supplant the better members of society. Man, like every other animal, has no doubt advanced to his present high condition through a struggle for existence consequent on his rapid multiplication; and if he is to advance still higher, it is to be feared that he must remain subject to a severe struggle. Otherwise he would sink into indolence, and the more gifted men would not be more successful in the battle of life than the less gifted. Hence our natural rate of increase, though leading to many and obvious evils, must not be greatly diminished by any means. There should be open competition for all men; and the most able should not be prevented by laws or customs from succeeding best and rearing the largest number of offspring. Important as the struggle for existence has been and even still is, yet as far as the highest part of man's nature is concerned there are other agencies more important. For the moral qualities are advanced, either directly or indirectly, much more through the effects of habit, the reasoning powers, instruction, religion, &c., than through natural selection; though to this latter agency may be safely attributed the social instincts, which afforded the basis for the development of the moral sense.

The main conclusion arrived at in this work, namely, that man is descended from some lowly organised form, will, I regret to think, be highly distasteful to many. But there can hardly be a doubt that we are descended from barbarians. The astonishment which I felt on first seeing a party of Fuegians on a wild and broken shore will never be forgotten by me, for the reflection at once rushed into my mind—such were our ancestors. These men were absolutely naked and bedaubed with paint, their long hair was tangled, their mouths, frothed with excitement, and their expression was wild, startled, and distrustful. They possessed hardly any arts, and like wild animals lived on what they could catch; they had no government, and were merciless to every one not of their own small tribe. He who has seen a savage in his native land will not feel much shame, if forced to acknowledge that the blood of some more humble creature flows in his veins. For my own part I would as soon be descended from that heroic little monkey, who braved his dreaded enemy in order to save the life of his keeper, or from that old baboon, who descending from the mountains, carried away in triumph his young comrade from a crowd of astonished dogs—as from a savage who delights to torture his enemies, offers up bloody sacrifices, practises infanticide without remorse, treats his wives like slaves, knows no decency, and is haunted by the grossest superstitutions.

Man may be excused for feeling some pride at having risen, though not through his own exertions, to the very summit of the organic scale; and the fact of his having thus risen, instead of having been aboriginally placed there, may give him hope for a still higher destiny in the distant future. But we are not here concerned with hopes or fears, only with the truth as far as our reason permits us to discover it; and I have given the evidence to the best of my ability. We must, however, acknowledge, as it seems to me, that man with all his noble qualities, with sympathy which feels for the most debased, with benevolence which extends not only to other men but to the humblest living creature, with his god-like intellect which has penetrated into the movements and constitution of the solar system—with all these exalted powers—Man still bears in his bodily frame the indelible stamp of his lowly origin.

10

Louis L. Snyder, editor

THE IMPERIALISM READER: DOCUMENTS AND READINGS ON MODERN EXPANSIONISM

Thomas Carlyle Expounds on the Mission of the Great Anglo-Saxon "Race," 1849[1,2]

Thomas Carlyle (1795–1881), sometimes styled the father of British imperialism, believed it to be the mission of the great Anglo-Saxon "race" to take over control of the backward regions of the world. It was England's moral duty, he said, as well as a matter of great importance for civilization in general, to bring the blessings of Anglo-Saxon culture to backward peoples. He was convinced that it was mighty England's destiny to rule the world.

Carlyle, lonely genius, expressed these ideas in his socio-political writings from Chartism *(1839) on. In the first excerpt reprinted below, from* Horoscope, *Carlyle spoke of England's future, "wide as the world, if we have heart and heroism for it." In the second excerpt, from* Occasional Discourse on the Nigger Question, *he sought to demonstrate that mastership and servantship was a natural way of life and that it was the duty of the white man to control the Negro. It was plainly a bad-tempered defense of slavery, to which John Stuart Mill, until then Carlyle's close friend, wrote a stinging reply. The arrogant Carlyle and the liberal-minded Mill broke their friendship on this issue.*

1

...Why should there not be an "Emigration Service," and Secretary, with adjuncts, with funds, forces, idle Navy-ships, and ever-increasing apparatus; in fine an *effective system* of Emigration; so that, at length, before our twenty years of respite ended, every

---

[1] From *Horoscope*, in Carlyle's *Complete Works*, Sterling Edition (Boston, n.d.), XII, 256–257.
[2] From *Occasional Discourse on the Nigger Question*, in *ibid.*, XVI, 296–297, 316 lf.

Louis I. Snyder, ed., *The Imperialism Reader: Documents and Readings on Modern Expansionism* (Kennitat Press, Port Washington, NY, 1973), Part Three, 107–142, Part Four, 147–165, 393–395.

honest willing workman who found England too strait, and the "Organization of Labour" not yet sufficiently advanced, might find likewise a bridge built to carry him into new Western Lands, there to "organize" with more elbow-room, some labor for himself? There to be a real blessing, raising new corn for us; leaving us at least in peace;—instead of staying here to be a Physical-Force Chartist, unblessed and no blessing! Is it not scandalous to consider that a Prime Minister could raise within the year, as I have seen it done, a Hundred and Twenty Millions Sterling to shoot the French; and we are stopt short for want of a hundredth part of that to keep the English living? The bodies of the English living, and the souls of the English living:—these two "Services," an Education Service and an Emigration Service, these with others will actually have to be organized!

A free bridge for Emigrants: why, we should then be on a par with America itself, the most favored of all lands that have no government; and we should have, besides, so many traditions and mementos of priceless things which America has cast away. We could proceed deliberately to "organize Labour," not doomed to perish unless we effected it within year and day;—every willing Worker that proved superfluous, finding a bridge ready for him. This verily will have to be done; the Time is big with this. Our little Isle is grown too narrow for us; but the world is wide enough yet for another Six Thousand Years. England's sure markets will be among new Colonies of Englishmen in all quarters of the Globe. All men trade with all men, when mutually convenient; and are even bound to do it by the Maker of men. Our friends of China, who guiltily refused to trade, in these circumstances,—had we not to argue with them, in cannon-shot at last, and convince them that they ought to trader "Hostile Tariffs" will arise, to shut us out; and then again will fall, to let us in: but the Sons of England, speakers of the English language were it nothing more, will in all times have the ineradicable predisposition to trade with England. Mycale was the *Pan-Ionian*, rendezvous of all the Tribes of Ion, for old Greece: why should not London long continue the *All-Saxon-home*, rendezvous of all the "Children of the Harz-Rock," arriving, in select samples, from the Antipodes and elsewhere, by steam and otherwise, to the "season" here!—What a future; wide as the world, if we have the heart and heroism for it,—which, by Heaven's blessing, we shall:—

> "Keep not standing fixed and rooted,
> Briskly venture, briskly roam;
> Head and hand, where'er thou foot it,
> And stout heart are still at home.
>
> "In what land the sun does visit,
> Brisk are we, whate'er betide:
> To give space for wandering is it
> That the world was made so wide."[3]

---

[3] Goethe, *Wilhelm Meister.*

Fourteen hundred years ago, it was by a considerable "Emigration Service," never doubt it, by much enlistment, discussion and apparatus, that we ourselves arrived in this remarkable Island,—and got into our present difficulties among others!...

2

The West Indies, it appears, are short of labour; as indeed is very conceivable in those circumstances. Where a Black man, by working about half an hour a day (such is the calculation), can supply himself, by aid of sun and soil, with as much pumpkin as will suffice, he is likely to be a little stiff to raise into hard work! Supply and demand, which, science says should be brought to bear on him, have an uphill task of it with such a man. Strong sun supplies itself gratis; rich soil in those unpeopled or half-peopled regions almost gratis; these are *his* "supply;" and half an hour a day, directed upon these, will produce pumpkin, which is his "demand." The fortunate Black man, very swiftly does he settle *his* account with supply and demand:—not so swiftly the less fortunate White man of those tropical localities. A bad case, his, just now. He himself cannot work; and his black neighbour, rich in pumpkin, is in no haste to help him. Sunk to the ears in pumpkin, inbibing saccharine juices, and much at his ease in the Creation, he can listen to the less fortunate white man's "demand," and take his own time in supplying it. Higher wages, massa; higher, for your cane-crop cannot wait; still higher,—till no conceivable opulence of cane-crop will cover such wages....

I never thought the "rights of Negroes" worth much discussing, nor the rights of men in any form; the grand point, as I once said, is the *mights* of men,—what portion of their "rights" they have a chance of getting sorted out, and realizes, in this confused world....

West-Indian Islands, still full of waste fertility, produce abundant pumpkins: pumpkins, however, you will observe, are not the sole requisite for human well-being. No; for a pig they are the one thing needful; but for a man they are only the first of several things needful.... Well, all this fruit too, fruit spicy and commercial, fruit spiritual and celestial, so far beyond the merely pumpkinish and grossly terrene, lies in the West-India lands: and the ultimate "proprietorship" of them,—why, I suppose, it will vest in him who can the *best* educe from them whatever of noble produce they were created fit for yielding. He, I compute, is the real "Viceregent of the Maker" there; in him, better and better chosen, and not in another, is the "property" vested by decree of Heaven's chancery itself!

Up to this time it is the Saxon British mainly; they hitherto have cultivated with some manfulness: and when a manfuler class of cultivators, stronger, worthier to have such land, able to bring fruit from it, shall make their appearance,—they, doubt it not, by fortune of war, and other confused negotiation and vicissitude, will be declared by Nature and Fact to *be* the worthier, and will become proprietors,—perhaps also only for a time. That is the law, I take it; ultimate, supreme, for all lands in all countries under this sky. The one perfect eternal proprietor is the Maker who created them: the temporary or worse proprietor is he whom the Maker has sent on that mission; he who the best hitherto can educe from said lands the beneficent gifts the Maker endowed them with; or, which is but another definition of the same person, he who leads hitherto the manfulest life on that bit of soil, doing, better than another yet found can do, the Eternal Purpose and Supreme Will there.

And now observe, my friends, it was not Black Quashee, or those he represents, that made those West-India Islands what they are, or can, by any hypothesis, be considered to have the right of growing pumpkins there. For countless ages, since they first mounted oozy, on the back of earthquakes, from their dark bed in the Ocean deeps, and reeking saluted the tropical Sun, and ever onwards till the European white man first saw them some three short centuries ago, those Islands had produced mere jungle, savagery, poison-reptiles and swamp-malaria: till the white European first saw them, they were as if not yet created,—their noble elements of cinnamon, sugar, coffee, pepper black and gray, lying all asleep, waiting the white enchanter who would say to them, Awake! Till the end of human history and the sounding of the Trump of Doom, they might have lain so, had Quashee and the like of him been the only artists in the game. Swamps, fever-jungles, maneating Caribs, rattlesnakes, and reeking waste and putrefaction, this had been the produce of them under the incompetent Caribal (which we call Cannibal) possessors, till that time; and Quashee knows, himself, whether ever he could have introduced an improvement. Him, had he by a miraculous chance been wafted thither, the Caribals would have eaten, rolling him as a fat morsel under their tongue; for him, till the sounding of the Trump of Doom, the rattlesnakes and savageries would have been held on their way. It was not he, then; it was another than he! Never by art of his could one pumpkin have grown there to solace any human throat; nothing but savagery and reeking putrefaction could have been grown there. These plentiful pumpkins, I say therefore, are not his: no, they are another's; they are his only under conditions....

Sir Charles Wentworth Dilke Sees the Anglo-Saxons as Destined to Conquer the World, 1868[4]

In 1866–1867, at the age of 23, Charles Wentworth Dilke (1843–1911) made a voyage around the world. First visiting the United States, then New Zealand, Australia, Ceylon, India, and Egypt, the clever young man recorded his travel impressions in two volumes titled Greater Britain *(1868). The book turned out to be an enthusiastic tribute to the Anglo-Saxon "race" which, according to Dilke, was destined to conquer the world. Here was the only "extirpating race" which must inevitably displace the backward colored peoples. Dilke actually anticipated the new imperialism by emphasizing the economic and military value of uncivilized tropical areas and by deprecating the value of such white colonies as Canada.*

The British public, fascinated by Dilke's book, demanded more and more editions. Dilke later became an influential career man in the British Foreign Office, in which capacity he urged that Egypt be controlled in order permanently to protect the Suez Canal, "one of our roads to our Colonial Empire in Australia and New Zealand."

Reprinted here are the preface and last chapter of Dilke's Greater Britain.

---

[4] Sir Charles Wentworth Dilke, *Greater Britain: A Record of Travel in English-Speaking Countries* (2 vols., London, 1868), vol. 1, pp. vi–viii; vol. 2, pp. 405–407.

from Dilke's Greater Britain
Preface

In 1866 and 1867 I followed England round the world: everywhere I was in English-speaking, or in English-governed lands. If I remarked that climate, soil, manners of life, that mixture with other peoples had modified the blood, I saw, too, that in essentials the race was always one.

The idea which in all the length of my travels has been at once my fellow and my guide—a key wherewith to unlock the hidden things of strange new lands—is a conception, however imperfect, of the grandeur of our race, already girdling the earth, which it is destined, perhaps, eventually to overspread.

In America, the peoples of the world are being fused together, but they are run into an English mould: Alfred's laws and Chaucer's tongue are theirs whether they would or no. There are men who say that Britain in her age will claim the glory of having planted greater Englands across the seas. They fail to perceive that she has done more than found plantations of her own—that she has imposed her institutions upon the offshoots of Germany, of Ireland, of Scandinavia, and of Spain. Through America, England is speaking to the world.

Sketches of Saxendom may be of interest even upon humbler grounds: the development of the England of Elizabeth is to be found, not in the Britain of Victoria, but in half of the habitable globe. If two small islands are by courtesy styled "Great," America, Australia, India, must form a Greater Britain.

C.W.D.

76, Sloane Street, S.W.
1st November, 1868

Chapter XXIII— The English

In America we have seen the struggle of the dead races against the cheap—the endeavours of the English to hold their own against the Irish and Chinese. In New Zealand, we found the stronger and more energetic race pushing from the earth the shrewd and laborious descendants of the Asian Malays; in Australia, the English triumphant, and the cheaper races excluded from the soil not by distance merely, but by arbitrary legislation; in India, we saw the solution of the problem of officering of the cheaper by the dearer race. Everywhere we have found that the difficulties which impede the progress to universal dominion of the English people lie in the conflict with the cheaper races. The result of our survey is such as to give us reason for the belief that race distinctions will long continue, that miscegenation will go but little way towards blending races; that the dearer are, on the whole, likely to destroy the cheaper peoples, and that Saxendom will rise triumphant from the doubtful struggle.

The countries ruled by a race whose very scum and outcasts have founded empires in every portion of the globe, even now consists of 9½ millions of square miles, and contain a population of 300 millions of people. Their surface is five times as great as that of the empire of Darius, and four and a half times as large as the Roman Empire at its greatest extent. It is no exaggeration to say that in power the English countries would be more than a match for the remaining nations of the world, whom in the intelligence of their people and the extent and wealth of their dominions they already considerably surpass. Russia gains ground steadily, we are told, but so do we. If we take maps of the English-governed countries and of the Russian countries of fifty years ago, and compare them with the English and Russian countries of today, we find that the Saxon has outstripped the Muscovite in conquest and colonization. The extensions of the United States alone are equal to those of Russia. Chili, La Plata, and Peru must eventually become English: the Red Indian race that now occupies those countries cannot stand against our colonists; and the future of the table lands of Africa and that of Japan and of China is as clear. Even in the tropical plains, the negroes alone seem able to withstand us. No possible series of events can prevent the English race itself in 1970 numbering 300 millions of beings—of one national character and one tongue. Italy, Spain, France, Russia become pigmies by the side of such a people.

Many who are well aware of the power of the English nations are nevertheless disposed to believe that our own is morally, as well as physically, the least powerful of the sections of the race or, in other words, that we are overshadowed by America and Australia. The rise to power of our southern colonies is, however distant, and an alliance between ourselves and America is still one to be made on equal terms. Although we are forced to contemplate the speedy loss of our manufacturing supremacy as coal becomes cheaper in America and dearer in Old England, we have nevertheless as much to bestow on America as she has to confer on us. The possession of India offers to ourselves that element of vastness of dominion which, in this age, is needed to secure width of thought and nobility of purpose; but to the English race our possession of India, of the coasts of Africa, and of the ports of China offers the possibility of planting free institutions among the black-skinned races of the world.

The ultimate future of any one section of our race, however, is of little moment by the side of its triumph as a whole, but the power of English laws and English principles of government is not merely an English question—its continuance is essential to the freedom of mankind.

Disraeli's Crystal Palace Speech, 1872[5]

On June 24, 1872, Benjamin Disraeli, leader of the British Conservative Party, made a striking speech in the Crystal Palace in London before a large audience. In this address, from which selections are given here, Disraeli fervently attacked his political rival, the Liberal leader William Ewart Gladstone, who had insisted that colonies were a costly luxury. To Disraeli the destiny of Britain was tied up inextricably with the new imperialism.

If you look to the history of this country since the advent of liberalism—forty years ago—you will find that there has been no effort so continuous, so subtle, supported by so much energy, and carried on with so much ability and acumen, as the attempts of

---

[5] Quoted in W. F. Monypenny and G. E. Buckle, *The Life of Benjamin Disraeli* (London, 1929), II, 534–536.

liberalism to effect the disintegration of the empire of England. And, gentlemen, of all its efforts, this is the one which has been the nearest to success. Statesmen of the highest character, writers of the most distinguished ability, the most organized and efficient means, have been employed in this endeavour. It has proved to all of us that we have lost money by our colonies. It has been shown with precise, with mathematical demonstration, that there never was a jewel in the crown of England that was so truly costly as the possession of India. How often has it been suggested that we should at once emancipate ourselves from this incubus! Well, that result was nearly accomplished. When those subtle views were adopted by the country under the plausible plea of granting self-government to the colonies, I confess that I myself thought that the tie was broken. Not that I for one object to self-government; I cannot conceive how our distant colonies can have their affairs administered except by self-government.

But self-government, in my opinion, when it was conceded, ought to have been conceded as part of a great policy of imperial consolidation. It ought to have been accompanied by an imperial tariff, by securities for the people of England for the enjoyment of the unappropriated lands which belonged to the sovereign as their trustee, and by a military code which should have precisely defined the means and the responsibilities by which the colonies should be defended and by which, if necessary, this country should call for the aid from the colonies themselves. It ought, further, to have been accompanied by the institution of some representative council in the metropolis, which would have brought the colonies into constant and continuous relations with the home government. All this, however, was omitted because those who advised that policy—and I believe their convictions were sincere—looked upon the colonies of England, looked even upon our connection with India, as a burden upon this country; viewing everything in a financial aspect, and totally passing by those moral and political considerations which make nations great, and by the influence of which alone men are distinguished from animals.

Well, what has been the result of this attempt during the reign of liberalism for the disintegration of the empire? It has entirely failed. But how has it failed? Through the sympathy of the colonies for the mother country. They have decided that the empire shall not be destroyed; and in my opinion no minister in this country will do his duty who neglects any opportunity of reconstructing as much as possible our colonial empire, and of responding to those distant sympathies which may become the source of incalculable strength and happiness to this land....

The issue is not a mean one. It is whether you will be content to be a comfortable England, modeled and molded upon Continental principles and meeting in due course an inevitable fate, or whether you will be a great country, an imperial country, a country where your sons, when they rise, rise to paramount positions, and obtain not merely the esteem of their countrymen, but command the respect of the world.

Friedrich Fabri Urges Imperialism on Germany "If She Would Live," 1879[6]

A representative German propagandist for imperialism in the 'seventies and 'eighties was Friedrich Fabri, who had seen long service as an inspector of the Barmen Rhine Mission in South West Africa. In a popularly written little book titled Does Germany Need Colonies? *("Bedarf Deutschland der Kolonien?") [1879], Fabri argued that Germany must have colonial markets, new areas for investment, and outlets for her surplus population. It was Germany's Kultur-mission, he said, to spread her civilization among the backward races. The concluding section of Fabri's book is translated here.*

Should not the German nation, so seaworthy, so industrially and commercially minded, more than other peoples geared to agricultural colonization, and possessing a rich and available supply of labor, all these to a greater extent than other modern culture-peoples, should not this nation successfully hew a new path on the road of imperialism? We are convinced beyond doubt that the colonial question has become a matter of life-or-death for the development of Germany. Colonies will have a salutary effect on our economic situation as well as on our entire national progress.

Here is a solution for many of the problems that face us. In this new Reich of ours there is so much bitterness, so much unfruitful, sour, and poisoned political wrangling, that the opening of a new, promising road of national effort will act as a kind of liberating influence. Our national spirit will be renewed, a gratifying thing, a great asset. A people that has been led to a high level of power can maintain its historical position only as long as it understands and proves itself to be *the bearer of a culture-mission*. At the same time, this is the only way to stability and to the growth of national welfare, the necessary foundation for a lasting expansion of power.

At one time Germany contributed only intellectual and literary activity to the tasks of our century. That era is now over. As a people we have become politically minded and powerful. But if political power becomes the primal goal of a nation, it will lead to harshness, even to barbarism. We must be ready to serve for the ideal, moral, and economic culture-tasks of our time. The French national-economist, Leroy Beaulieu, closed his work on colonization with these words: "That nation is the greatest in the world which colonizes most; if she does not achieve that rank today, she will make it tomorrow."

No one can deny that in this direction England has by far surpassed all other countries. Much has been said, even in Germany, during the last few decades about the "disintegrating power of England." Indeed, there seems to be something to it when we consider the Palmerston era and Gladstonian politics. It has been customary in our age of military power to evaluate the strength of a state in terms of its combat-ready troops. But anyone who looks at the globe and notes the steadily increasing colonial possessions of Great Britain, how she extracts strength from them, the skill with which she governs them, how the Anglo-Saxon strain occupies a dominant position in the overseas territories, he will begin to see the military argument as the reasoning of a philistine.

---

[6] Friedrich Fabri, *Bedarf Deutschland der Kolonien?* (Gotha, 1879), pp. 110–112. Translated by the editor.

The fact is that England tenaciously holds on to its world-wide possessions with scarcely one-fourth the manpower of our continental military state. That is not only a great economic advantage but also a striking proof of the solid power and cultural fiber of England. Great Britain, of course isolates herself far from the mass warfare of the continent, or only goes into action with dependable allies; hence, the insular state has suffered and will suffer no real damage. In any case, it would be wise for us Germans to learn about colonial skills from our Anglo-Saxon cousins and to begin a friendly competition with them. When the German Reich centuries ago stood at the pinnacle of the states of Europe, it was the Number One trade and sea power. If the New Germany wants to protect its newly won position of power for a long time, it must heed its *Kultur*-mission and, above all, delay no longer in the task of renewing the call for colonies.

Josiah Strong on the Anglo-Saxon Destiny, 1885[7]

Nationalists and racialists in all the major countries argued eloquently that it was the destiny of their own "master race" to dominate "backward" peoples. In the United States, Josiah Strong, a Congregationalist minister, contended that it was the historic mission of the "Anglo-Saxon race" to carry its ideals of civil liberty and spiritual Christianity to remote peoples of the earth. Later, Rudyard Kipling substituted the phrase "white man's burden" for the "backward peoples" concept.

Every race which has deeply impressed itself on the human family has been the representative of some great idea—one or more—which has given direction to the nation's life and form to its civilization. Among the Egyptians this seminal idea was life, among the Persians it was light, among the Hebrews it was purity, among the Greeks it was beauty, among the Romans it was law. The Anglo-Saxon is the representative of two great ideas, which are closely related. One of them is that of civil liberty. Nearly all of the civil liberty in the world is enjoyed by Anglo-Saxons: the English, the British colonists, and the people of the United States....

The other great idea...is that of a pure *spiritual* Christianity.... That means that most of the spiritual Christianity in the world is found among Anglo-Saxons and their converts; for this is the great missionary race....

It follows, then, that the Anglo-Saxon, as the great representative of these two ideas, the depository of these two greatest blessings, sustains peculiar relations to the world's future, is divinely commissioned to be, in a peculiar sense, his brother's keeper....

...Another marked characteristic of the Anglo-Saxon is what may be called an instinct or genius for colonizing. His unequaled energy, his indomitable perseverance, and his personal independence, made him a pioneer. He excels all others in pushing his way into new countries. It was those in whom this tendency was strongest that came to America, and this inherited tendency has been further developed by the westward sweep of successive generations across the continent. So noticeable has this characteristic become that English visitors remark it. Charles Dickens once said that the

---

[7] Josiah Strong, *Our Country* (New York, 1885), pp. 159–179, *passim*.

typical American would hesitate to enter heaven unless assured that he could go further west....

It seems to me that God, with infinite wisdom and skill, is training the Anglo-Saxon race for an hour sure to come in the world's future....

Is there room for reasonable doubt that this race, unless devitalized by alcohol and tobacco, is destined to dispossess many weaker races, assimilate others, and mold the remainder, until, in a very true and important sense, it has Anglo-Saxonized mankind? Already "the English language, saturated with Christian ideas, gathering up into itself the best thought of all the ages, is the great agent of Christian civilization throughout the world; at this moment affecting the destinies and molding the character of half the human race." Jacob Grimm, the German philologist, said of this language: "It seems chosen, like its people, to rule in future times in still greater degree in all the corners of the earth." He predicted, indeed, that the language of Shakespeare would eventually become the language of mankind. Is not Tennyson's noble prophecy to find its fulfillment in Anglo-Saxondom's extending its dominion and influence—

"Till the war-drum throbs no longer, and the battle-flags are furl'd
"In the Parliament of man, the Federation of the world."

Joseph Chamberlain Preaches the Doctrine of Commercial Imperialism, 1893[8]

Joseph Chamberlain (1836–1914), an aggressive and highly successful Birmingham manufacturer and an outspoken champion of British imperialism, was convinced that the "British Empire is commerce." British workingmen could have employment, he was sure, only if there were a market for the products they made. The British colonies would afford that market then and for posterity. In the following speech Chamberlain made his views known to a Birmingham audience composed mostly of manufacturers and workingmen. In 1895 Chamberlain took over the Colonial Office. In 1903 he shocked both friends and foes alike by his schemes for preferential treatment of colonial imports and protective legislation to assist native manufacturers and prevent dumping of foreign goods in British markets.

We must look this matter in the face, and must recognize that in order that we may have more employment to give we must create more demand [*hear, hear*]. Give me the demand for more goods and then I will undertake to give plenty of employment in making the goods; and the only thing, in my opinion, that the government can do in order to meet this great difficulty that we are considering, is so to arrange its policy that every inducement shall be given to the demand; that new markets shall be created, and that old markets shall be effectually developed [*cheers*].

You are aware that some of my opponents please themselves occasionally by finding names for me [*laughter*], and among other names lately they have been calling me a Jingo [*laughter*]. I am no more a Jingo than you are [*hear, hear*]. But for the reasons and arguments I have put before you tonight I am convinced that it is a necessity as well as a duty for us to uphold the dominion and empire which we now possess [*loud cheers*]. For

---

[8] *Speeches of Joseph Chamberlain* (London, 1897), pp. 131 ff.

these reasons, among others, I would never lose the hold which we now have over our great Indian dependency [*hear, hear*], by far the greatest and most valuable of all the customers we have or ever shall have in this country. For the same reasons I approve of the continued occupation of Egypt, and for the same reasons I have urged upon this government, and upon previous governments, the necessity for using every legitimate opportunity to extend our influence and control in that great African continent which is now being opened up to civilization and to commerce; and, lastly, it is for the same reasons that I hold that our navy should be strengthened [*loud cheers*] until its supremacy is so assured that we cannot be shaken in any of the possessions which we hold or may hold hereafter.

Believe me, if in any one of the places to which I have referred any change took place which deprived us of that control and influence of which I have been speaking, the first to suffer would be the workingmen of this country. Then, indeed, we should see a distress which would not be temporary, but which would be chronic, and we should find that England was entirely unable to support the enormous population which is now maintained by the aid of her foreign trade. If the workingmen of this country understand their own interests, they will never lend any countenance to the doctrines of those politicians who never lose an opportunity of pouring contempt and abuse upon the brave Englishmen, who, even at this moment, in all parts of the world are carving out new dominions for Britain, and are opening up fresh markets for British commerce and laying out fresh fields for British labor [*applause*]. If the "Little Englanders" had their way, not only would they refrain from taking the legitimate opportunities which offer for extending the empire and for securing for us new markets, but I doubt whether they would even take the pains which are necessary to preserve the great heritage which has come down to us from our ancestors [*applause*].

When you are told that the British pioneers of civilization in Africa are filibusters, and when you are asked to call them back, and to leave this great continent to the barbarism and superstition in which it has been steeped for centuries, or to hand over to foreign countries the duty which you are unwilling to undertake, I ask you to consider what would have happened if, one hundred and fifty years ago, your ancestors had taken similar views of their responsibility? Where would be the empire on which now your livelihood depends? We should have been the United Kingdom of Great Britain and Ireland, but those vast dependencies, those hundreds of millions with whom we keep up a mutually beneficial relationship and commerce would have been the subjects of other nations, who would not have been slow to profit by our neglect of opportunities and obligations [*applause*]....

Ferdinando Martini Presents the Italian Case for "Imperialism of the Have-Nots," 1897[9]

Ferdinando Martini (1841–1928), a liberal politician from Tuscany, was the Italian spokesman for the "imperialism of the Have-Nots." In this selection from his book, Cose Africane

---

[9] Ferdinando Martini, *Cose Africane (Concerning Africa)* (Treves, Milan, 1897), *passim.*

(Concerning Africa), Martini supported the policy of emigration to Italian colonies not to foster the expansion of industrial and financial interests, nor to gain raw materials, nor to acquire strategic bases, but as a solution to Italy's problem of overpopulation. Martini became the first Italian civil governor of Eritrea after the Italian defeat at Adowa (1896) in Ethiopia.

...Italy has 108 inhabitants per square kilometer; France has only 73. In proportion to the territory, only three states in Europe surpass Italy in density of population: Belgium, Holland, and Great Britain. If we go on like this, soon there will be no state that surpasses Italy: in the ten years 1871–1881 the births surpassed the deaths by seven per cent, and in the ten following years by eleven per cent. Every year 100,000 farmers and agricultural laborers emigrate from Italy. In spite of this immense exodus, the country witnesses the fact that, to the greatest danger of her political and economic future, her place in the family of civilized peoples is growing smaller and smaller. In fact, during the last eighty years the English-speaking peoples have risen from 22 to 90 millions; the Russian-speaking peoples from 50 to 70; and so forth, down to the Spanish-speaking peoples who were 18 millions and are now 39. On the other hand, the Italian-speaking peoples have increased only from 20 to 31, and most of the increase has taken place within Italy's own geographical borders. And this is not surprising. Even though our emigrants at first seem to be spreading in foreign land the name, the language, and the prestige of Italy, since all or nearly all of them go to areas very advanced in civilization, their sons or their grandsons, being attracted and encircled by the vigorous peoples giving them hospitality, end up by forgetting the language of their fathers and ancestors. They merely increase the number of other nations, like branches grafted on a different plant....

...Since our stubbornness and our mistakes have cost all that they cost and are costing, even if one wants to leave aside all other considerations and to take into account only the expenditure and the chances of success, I believe that it is less safe and more expensive to endeavor to bring under culture three million hectares in Italy, than to insure the prosperity of a large agricultural colony in Eritrea....

It is easy to make jokes about Abyssinian huts. But, once one has made jokes and laughed, one has good reason to cry when comparing those huts—where our colonial officers yet are living without discomfort—with the sandstone caves where the ploughmen and the reapers of the Roman Compagna are sleeping; or with the crumbling slums of Basilicata, where men, women and children are heaped together, and where, according to medical descriptions, it is possible to breathe only because air filters through the cracks of the rotten walls.

Gustav Schmoller Calls for German Expansion, c. 1900[10]

Professor Gustav Schmoller, a distinguished lecturer on political economy at Berlin University, a member of the Prussian Privy Council, and a member of the Prussian Upper Chamber,

---

[10] Quoted in J. Ellis Barker, *Modern Germany: Its Rise, Growth, Downfall and Future* (6 ed., New York, 1919), pp. 84–95.

denounced other imperialisms while praising German expansion in a lecture which was widely circulated c. 1900. Here are significant passages from that lecture.

In various States, arrogant, reckless, cold-blooded daring bullies (*Gewaltmenschen*), men who possess the morals of a captain of pirates, as Professor Brentano called them so justly the other day, push themselves more and more forward and into the Government.... We must not forget that it is in the freest States, England and North America, where the tendencies of conquest, Imperial schemes, and hatred against new economic competitors are growing up amongst the masses. The leaders of these agitations are great speculators, who have the morals of a pirate, and who are at the same time party leaders and Ministers of State.... The conquest of Cuba and the Philippines by the United States alters their political and economical basis. Their tendency to exclude Europe from the North and South American markets must needs lead to new great conflicts. It must also not be forgotten how England tried to wreck our *Zollverein*, how she tried to prevent us from conquering Schleswig-Holstein, and how anti-German she was in 1870.... These bullies (*Gewaltmenschen*), these pirates and speculators *à la* Cecil Rhodes, act like poison within their State. They buy the press, corrupt ministers and the aristocracy, and bring on wars for the benefit of a bankrupt company or for the gain of filthy lucre. Where they govern modesty and decency disappear, as do honesty and respect for justice. Legitimate business cannot maintain itself, and all classes of society are exploited and ill-used by a small circle of capitalistic magnates, stockjobbers, and speculators.... We mean to extend our trade and industries far enough to enable us to live and sustain a growing population. We mean to defend our colonies, and, if possible, to acquire somewhere agricultural colonies. We mean to prevent extravagant mercantilism everywhere, and to prevent the division of the earth among the three world powers, which would exclude all other countries and destroy their trade. In order to attain this modest aim we require to-day so badly a large fleet. The German Empire must become the centre of a coalition of States, chiefly in order to be able to hold the balance in the death-struggle between Russia and England, but that is only possible if we possess a stronger fleet than that of to-day.... We must wish that at any price a German country, peopled by twenty to thirty million Germans, should grow up in Southern-Brazil. Without the possibility of energetic proceedings on the part of Germany our future over there is threatened.... We do not mean to press for an economic alliance with Holland, but if the Dutch are wise, if they do not want to lose their colonies someday, as Spain did, they will hasten to seek our alliance.

J. A. Hobson's Classic Assault on Imperialism, 1902[11]

A most important study of imperialism was published by John A. Hobson, an English economist, more than a half century ago. Hobson traced the origins of imperialism, discussed its theory and practice, evaluated its effects upon "lower" or alien peoples, and traced its moral reactions upon the Western nations. He found a common "taproot" for imperialism in the aim of capitalists to

---

[11] John A. Hobson, *Imperialism, A Study* (London, 1902). The first section is from the preface of the 1938 edition. The second section reproduced here is condensed from pp. 76–86 of the 1902 edition.

secure profitable investments overseas. Hobson's attack was utilized to some extent by Lenin in his analysis of imperialism as the final stage of a collapsing capitalism.

The Economic Parasites of Imperialism

Aggressive Imperialism, which costs the taxpayer so dear, which is of so little value to the manufacturer and trader, which is fraught with such grave incalculable peril to the citizen, is a source of great gain to the investor who cannot find at home the profitable uses he seeks for his capital, and insists that his Government should help him to profitable and secure investments abroad.

If, contemplating the enormous expenditure on armaments, the ruinous wars, the diplomatic audacity or knavery by which modern Governments seek to extend their territorial power, we put the plain, practical question, *Cui bono?* the first and most obvious answer is, the investor.

The annual income Great Britain derives from commissions on her whole foreign and colonial trade, import and export, was estimated by Sir R. Giflen at £18,000,000 for 1899 taken at 2½ per cent., upon a turnover of £800,000,000. This is the whole that we are entitled to regard as profits on external trade. Considerable as this sum is, it cannot serve to yield an economic motive-power adequate to explain the dominance which business considerations exercise over our imperial policy. Only when we set beside it some £90,000,000 or £100,000,000, representing pure profit upon investments, do we understand whence the economic impulse to Imperialism is derived.

Investors who have put their money in foreign lands, upon terms which take full account of the risks connected with the political conditions of the country, desire to use the resources of their Government to minimise these risks, and so to enhance the capital value and the interest of their private investments. The investing and speculative classes in general have also desired that Great Britain should take other foreign areas under her flag in order to secure new areas for profitable investments and speculation.

If the special interest of the investor is liable to clash with the public interest and to induce a wrecking policy, still more dangerous is the special interest of the financier, the general dealer in investments. In large measure the rank and file of the investors are, both for business and for politics, the cat's paws of the great financial houses, who use stocks and shares not so much as investments to yield them interest, but as material for speculation in the money market. In handling large masses of stocks and shares, in floating companies, in manipulating fluctuations of values, the magnates of the Bourse find their gain. These great businesses—banking, broking, bill discounting, loan floating, company promoting—form the central ganglion of international capitalism. United by the strongest bonds of organisation, always in closest and quickest touch with one another, situated in the very heart of the business capital of every State, controlled, so far as Europe is concerned, chiefly by men of a single and peculiar race, who have behind them many centuries of financial experience, they are in a unique position to manipulate the policy of nations. No great quick direction of capital is possible save by their consent and through their agency. Does any one seriously suppose that a great war could be undertaken by any European State, or a great State loan subscribed, if the house of Rothschild and its connexions set their face against it?...

The wealth of these houses, the scale of their operations, and their cosmopolitan organisation make them the prime determinants of imperial policy. They have the largest definite stake in the business of Imperialism, and the amplest means of forcing their will upon the policy of nations.

In view of the part which the non-economic factors of patriotism, adventure, military enterprise, political ambition, and philanthropy play in imperial expansion, it may appear that to impute to financiers so much power is to take a too narrowly view of history. And it is true that the motor-power of Imperialism is not chiefly financial: finance is rather the governor of the imperial engine, directing the energy and determining its work: it does not constitute the fuel of the engine, nor does it directly generate the power. Finance manipulates the patriotic forces which politicians, soldiers, philanthropists, and traders generate; the enthusiasm for expansion which issues from these sources, though strong and genuine, is irregular and blind; the financial interest has those qualities of concentration and clear-sighted calculation which are needed to set Imperialism to work. An ambitious statesman, a frontier soldier, an overzealous missionary, a pushing trader, may suggest or even initiate a step of imperial expansion, may assist in educating public opinion to the urgent need of some fresh advance, but the final determination rests with the financial power. The direct influence exercised by great financial houses in "high politics" is supported by the control which they exercise over the body of public opinion through the Press, which, in every "civilised" country, is becoming more and more their obedient instrument.... Add to this the natural sympathy with a sensational policy which a cheap Press always manifests, and it becomes evident that the Press has been strongly biased towards Imperialism, and has lent itself with great facility to the suggestion of financial or political Imperialists who have desired to work up patriotism for some new piece of expansion.

Such is the array of distinctively economic forces making for Imperialism, a large loose group of trades and professions seeking profitable business and lucrative employment from the expansion of military and civil services, and from the expenditure on military operations, the opening up of new tracts of territory and trade with the same, and the provision of new capital which these operations require, all these finding their central guiding and directing force in the power of the general financier.

The play of these forces does not openly appear. They are essentially parasites upon patriotism, and they adapt themselves to its protecting colours. In the mouth of their representatives are noble phrases, expressive of their desire to extend the area of civilisation, to establish good government, promote Christianity, extirpate slavery, and elevate the lower races. Some of the business men who hold such language may entertain a genuine, though usually a vague, desire to accomplish these ends, but they are primarily engaged in business, and they are not unaware of the utility of the more unselfish forces in furthering their ends. Their true attitude of mind was expressed by Mr. Rhodes in his famous description of "Her Majesty's Flag" as "the greatest commercial asset in the world."...

2

No mere array of facts and figures adduced to illustrate the economic nature of the new Imperialism will suffice to dispel the popular delusion that the use of national force to secure new markets by annexing fresh tracts of territory is a sound and a necessary policy for an advanced industrial country like Great Britain. It has indeed been proved that recent annexations of tropical countries, procured at great expense, have furnished poor and precarious markets, that our aggregate trade with our colonial possessions is virtually stationary, and that our most profitable and progressive trade is with rival industrial nations, whose territories we have no desire to annex, whose markets we cannot force, and whose active antagonism we are provoking by our expansive policy.

But these arguments are not conclusive. It is open to Imperialists to argue thus: "We must have markets for our growing manufactures, we must have new outlets for the investment of our surplus capital and for the energies of the adventurous surplus of our population; such expansion is a necessity of life to a nation with our great and growing powers of production. An ever larger share of our population is devoted to the manufactures and commerce of towns, and is thus dependent for life and work upon food and raw materials from foreign lands. In order to buy and pay for these things we must sell our goods abroad. During the first three-quarters of the century we could do so without difficulty by a natural expansion of commerce with continental nations and our colonies, all of which were far behind us in the main arts of manufacture and the carrying trades. So long as England held a virtual monopoly of the world markets for certain important classes of manufactured goods, Imperialism was unnecessary. During the last thirty years this manufacturing and trading supremacy has been greatly impaired; other nations, especially Germany, the United States, and Belgium, have advanced with great rapidity, and while they have not crushed or even stayed the increase of our external trade, their competition is making it more and more difficult to dispose of the full surplus of our manufactures at a profit. The encroachments made by these nations upon our old markets, even in our own possessions, make it most urgent that we should take energetic means to secure new markets. These new markets must lie in hitherto undeveloped countries, chiefly in the tropics, where vast populations live capable of growing economic needs which our manufacturers and merchants can supply. Our rivals are seizing and annexing territories for similar purposes, and when they have annexed them close them to our trade. The diplomacy and the arms of Great Britain must be used in order to compel the owners of the new markets to deal with us: and experience shows that the safest means of securing and developing such markets is by establishing 'protectorates' or by annexation....

"Far larger and more important is the pressure of capital for external fields of investment. Moreover, while the manufacturer and trader are well content to trade with foreign nations, the tendency for investors to work towards the political annexation of countries which contain their more speculative investments is very powerful. Of the fact of this pressure of capital there can be no question. Large savings are made which cannot find any profitable investment in this country; they must find employment elsewhere, and it is to the advantage of the nation that they should be employed as largely as possible in lands where they can be utilised in opening up markets for British trade and employment for British enterprise.

"However costly, however perilous, this process of imperial expansion may be, it is necessary to the continued existence and progress of our nation; if we abandoned it we must be content to leave the development of the world to other nations, who will everywhere cut into our trade, and even impair our means of securing the food and raw materials we require to support our population. Imperialism is thus seen to me, not a choice, but a necessity."

The practical force of this economic argument in politics is strikingly illustrated by the recent history of the United States. Here is a country which suddenly breaks through a conservative policy, strongly held by both political parties, bound up with every popular instinct and tradition, and flings itself into a rapid imperial career for which it possesses neither the material nor the moral equipment, risking the principles and practices of liberty and equality by the establishment of militarism and the forcible subjugation of peoples which it cannot safely admit to the condition of American citizenship.

Is this a mere wild freak of spread-eagleism, a burst of political ambition on the part of a nation coming to a sudden realisation of its destiny? Not at all. The spirit of adventure, the American "mission of civilisation," are, as forces making for Imperialism, clearly subordinate to the driving force of the economic factor. The dramatic character of the change is due to the unprecedented rapidity of the industrial revolution in the United States during the last two decades. During that period the United States, with her unrivalled natural resources, her immense resources of skilled and unskilled labour, and her genius for invention and organisation, has developed the best equipped and most productive manufacturing economy the world has yet seen. Fostered by rigid protective tariffs, her metal, textile, tool, clothing, furniture, and other manufactures have shot up in a single generation from infancy to full maturity, and, having passed through a period of intense competition, are attaining, under the able control of great trustmakers, a power of production greater than has been attained in the most advanced industrial countries of Europe.

An era of cut-throat competition, followed by a rapid process of amalgamation, has thrown an enormous quantity of wealth into the hands of a small number of captains of industry. No luxury of living to which this class could attain kept pace with its rise of income, and a process of automatic saving set in upon an unprecedented scale. The investment of these savings in other industries helped to bring these under the same concentrative forces. Thus a great increase of savings seeking profitable investment is synchronous with a stricter economy of the use of existing capital. No doubt the rapid growth of a population, accustomed to a high and an always ascending standard of comfort, absorbs in the satisfaction of its wants a large quantity of new capital. But the actual rate of saving, conjoined with a more economical application of forms of existing capital, has exceeded considerably the rise of the national consumption of manufactures. The power of production has far outstripped the actual rate of consumption, and, contrary to the older economic theory, has been unable to force a corresponding increase of consumption by lowering prices....

For the present argument it matters not which course is taken; the point is that this concentration of industry in "trusts," "combines," &c., at once limits the quantity of capital which can be effectively employed and increases the share of profits out of which fresh savings and fresh capital will spring. It is quite evident that a trust which is motivated by cut-throat competition, due to an excess of capital, cannot normally find inside the "trusted" industry employment for that portion of the profits which the trust-makers desire to save and to invest. New inventions and other economies of production or distribution within the trade may absorb some of the new capital, but there are rigid limits to this absorption. The trust-maker in oil or sugar must find other investments for his savings: if he is early in the application of the combination principles to his trade, he will naturally apply his surplus capital to establish similar combinations in other industries, economising capital still further, and rendering it ever harder for ordinary saving men to find investments for their savings.

Indeed, the conditions alike of cut-throat competition and of combination attest the congestion of capital in the manufacturing industries which have entered the machine economy. We are not here concerned with any theoretic question as to the possibility of producing by modern machine methods more goods than can find a market. It is sufficient to point out that the manufacturing power of a country like the United States may grow so fast as to exceed the demands of the home market. No one acquainted with trade will deny a fact which all American economists assert, that this is the condition which the United States has reached within the last few years, so far as the more developed industries are concerned. Her manufactures are saturated with capital and can absorb no more. One after another they are seeking refuge from the waste of competition in "combines" which secure a measure of profitable peace by restricting the quantity of operative capital. Industrial and financial princes in oil, steel, sugar, railroads, banking, &c., are faced with the dilemma of either spending more than they know how to spend, or forcing markets outside the home area. Two economic courses are open to them, both leading towards an abandonment of the political isolation of the past and the adoption of the imperialist methods in the future. Instead of shutting down inferior mills and rigidly restricting output to correspond with profitable sales in the home markets, they may employ their full productive power, applying their savings to increase their business capital, and, while still regulating output and prices for the home market, may "hustle" for foreign markets, dumping down their surplus goods at prices which would not be possible save for the profitable nature of their home market....

It is this sudden demand for foreign markets for manufactures and for investments which is avowedly responsible for the adoption of Imperialism as a political policy and practice by the Republican party to which the great industrial and financial chiefs belong, and which belongs to them. The adventurous enthusiasm of President Roosevelt and his "manifest destiny" and "mission of civilisation" party must not deceive us. It is Messrs. Rockefeller, Pierpont Morgan, Hanna, Schwab, and their associates who need Imperialism and who are fastening it upon the shoulders of the great Republic of the West. They need Imperialism because they desire to use the public resources of their country to find profitable employment for the capital which otherwise would be superfluous....

The suddenness of this political revolution is due to the rapid manifestation of the need. During a period of ten years the United States has nearly trebled the value of its manufacturing export trade, and, if the rate of progress of the last few years continues, within this decade it will overtake our more slowly advancing export trade, and stand first in the list of manufacture-exporting nations.

This is the avowed ambition, and no idle one, of the keenest business men of America; and with the natural resources, the labor and the administrative talents at their disposal, it is quite likely that they will achieve their object. The stronger and more direct control over politics exercised in America by business men enables them to drive more quickly and more straightly along the line of their economic interests than in Great Britain. American Imperialism is the natural product of the economic pressure of a sudden advance of capitalism which cannot find occupation at home and needs foreign markets for goods and for investments.

The same needs exist in European countries, and, as is admitted, drive Governments along the same path. Over-production in the sense of an excessive manufacturing plant, and surplus capital which cannot find sound investments within the country, force Great Britain, Germany, Holland, France to place larger and larger portions of their economic resources outside the area of their present political domain, and then stimulate a policy of political expansion so as to take in the new areas. The economic sources of this movement are laid bare by periodic trade-depressions due to an inability of producers to find adequate and profitable markets for what they can produce. The Majority Report of the Commission upon the Depression of Trade in 1885 put the matter in a nut-shell. "That, owing to the nature of the times, the demand for our commodities does not increase at the same rate as formerly; that our capacity for production is consequently in excess of our requirements, and could be considerably increased at short notice; that this is due partly to the competition of the capital which is being steadily accumulated in the country." The Minority Report straightly imputes the condition of affairs to "over-production." Germany is at the present time suffering severely from what is called a glut of capital and of manufacturing power: she must have new markets; her Consuls all over the world are "hustling" for trade; trading settlements are forced upon Asia Minor; in East and West Africa, in China and elsewhere the German Empire is impelled to a policy of colonisation and protectorates as outlets for German commercial energy.

Every improvement of methods of production, every concentration of ownership and control, seems to accentuate the tendency. As one nation after another enters the machine economy and adopts advanced industrial methods, it becomes more difficult for its manufacturers, merchants, and financiers to dispose profitably of their economic resources, and they are tempted more and more to use their Governments in order to secure for their particular use some distant undeveloped country by annexation and protection.

The process we may be told is inevitable, and so it seems upon a superficial inspection. Everywhere appear excessive powers of production, excessive capital in search of investment. It is admitted by all business men that the growth of the powers of production in their country exceeds the growth in consumption, that more goods can be produced than can be sold at a profit, and that more capital exists than can find remunerative investment.

It is this economic condition of affairs that forms the taproot of Imperialism. If the consuming public in this country raised its standard of consumption to keep pace with every rise of productive powers, there could be no excess of goods or capital clamorous to use Imperialism in order to find markets....

Socialist Leader Jean Jaurès Attacks French Imperialism, 1912[12]

Jean Jaurès (1859–1914), French Socialist politician under the Third Republic, was a strong opponent of militarism and imperialism. At first he believed that French penetration of Morocco might possibly fulfill a genuine moral mission, but he became a bitter critic of expansionism. Following are extracts from his remarks before the Chamber of Deputies on July 17, 1912, when the Moroccan protectorate treaty was being debated. Jaurès's attacks on militarism led to his assassination in 1914 by a half-crazed fanatic.

Don't tell me, Gentlemen, that we are subjugating Morocco by these brutal means for the sake of civilization.

I have never painted an idyllic picture of Moslem civilization, and I am fully aware of its chaotic side—the exploitation by an oligarchy of chieftains that exists in some areas. Nonetheless, Gentlemen, you must admit that there has existed a Moroccan civilization capable of evolution and progress, a civilization at once ancient and modern. The Berber tribes, as you know, have been established there for centuries past. They have a fine history, and despise them though we may, they are proud of their tradition. The leading historians of the Moslem world have recounted their exploits and praised their high intelligence. These were the tribes that once conquered Spain; in the city of Fez they raised human thought to a high level of philosophical genius. Again, it was the Moroccans who penetrated to the heart of Africa, establishing in what are now Senegal, Dutch Sudan, and the Niger Colony the foundations of civilization, on which Europe has been able to build.

And when, on the morrow of signing the protectorate treaty, the Sultan wrote, "Take care, Gentlemen, I represent a people never colonized, never subjugated, never enslaved; I represent an empire which, for countless generations, has been independent," he was expressing not only his own indignation and forebodings as a proud chieftain but those of his country as well. And now these people, whom we are about to turn into subjects through force and cunning, have shown that they are not only a nation of workers but also (for we must salute the heroism of the enemy as well as that of our own soldiers) a nation of warriors!

What has always struck me is the complexity and adaptability of Moroccan society: its readiness to change; the ease with which it has integrated all types of property organization, from collective ownership by tribes to individual ownership by the peasants who plow the land and sow the crops; the vitality of its craftsmen, makers of

---

[12] *Journal Officiel. Chambre des Députés*, July 17, 1912. Translated by Harvey Goldberg, in *French Colonialism* (New York, 1959), pp. 11–12. Courtesy of Harvey Goldberg and Rinehart & Company.

leather and metal goods working in little shops or in the bazaars; the flexibility of a country so receptive to European influence, its farmers sending their goods to the port cities, its children beginning to frequent European schools along the Mediterranean and Atlantic coasts. All of this I welcomed, and it gave hope for a fine future. And let me tell you that I shall never forgive those who have crushed the seeds of peaceful progress by brutal conquest....

But we are already witnessing the birth of a great new force. All the people of divers races, the races which seemed from the European standpoint to be sunk in a perpetual apathy, are now awakening, claiming their rights and asserting their strength.... In North Africa, too, we are faced with an awakening, a stirring which it would be unwise, Mr. President and colleagues, to scorn or disregard.

I tell you that all these peoples, for centuries oppressed, dormant, or severed from Europe by oceans of indifference, possess untapped spiritual resources, a thirst for freedom and independence, a sense of justice which often finds expression in words borrowed from our own vocabulary. And I tell you that any nation with the courage, wisdom, and farsighted generosity to eschew conquest and forcible expropriation will win the sympathy of these races, which are now awakening and demanding their rights, and which represent a powerful force for the future.

Edmund D. Morel on "The Black Man's Burden," 1920[13]

The campaign against maladministration of the Congo was led by a British journalist, Edmund D. Morel, founder of the newspaper, West African Mail. On March 24, 1904, Morel formally established the Congo Reform Association in the Philharmonic Hall in Liverpool with the support of such reformers as the Bishops of Durham, Liverpool, Rochester, and St. Asaph; Fabian Ware, editor of the Morning Post; *and W. T. Stead and Earl Beauchamp. The struggle between the Congo Reform Association and Leopold II, King of the Belgians, was waged seven years before reforms were instituted. The U.S. Senate in 1907 voted approval of the Association's program. Morel never ceased his attacks on imperialism. Reprinted below are excerpts from his book,* The Black Man's Burden *(1920), which stated the case for opponents of Western imperialism.*

It is [the peoples of Africa] who carry the "Black man's burden." They have not withered away before the white man's *occupation.* Indeed...Africa has ultimately absorbed within itself every Caucasian and, for that matter, every Semitic invader, too. In hewing out for himself a fixed abode in Africa, the white man has massacred the African in heaps. The African has survived, and it is well for the white settlers that he has....

What the partial occupation of his soil by the white man has failed to do; what the mapping out of European political "spheres of influence" has failed to do; what the maxim and the rifle, the slave gang, labour in the bowels of the earth and the lash, have failed to do; what imported measles, smallpox and syphilis have failed to do; what ever the overseas slave trade failed to do, the power of modern capitalistic exploitation, assisted by modern engines of destruction, may yet succeed in accomplishing.

---

[13] E. D. Morel, *The Black Man's Burden* (London, 1920), pp. 7–11, 112.

For from the evils of the latter, scientifically applied and enforced, there is no escape for the African. Its destructive effects are not spasmodic: they are permanent. In its permanence resides its fatal consequences. It kills not the body merely, but the soul. It breaks the spirit. It attacks the African at every turn, from every point of vantage. It wrecks his polity, uproots him from the land, invades his family life, destroys his natural pursuits and occupations, claims his whole time, enslaves him in his own home.

Economic bondage and wage slavery, the grinding pressure of a life of toil, the incessant demands of an industrial capitalism—these things a landless European proletariat physically endures, though hardly.... The recuperative forces of a temperate climate are there to arrest the ravages, which alleviating influences in the shape of prophylactic and curative remedies will still further circumscribe. But in Africa, especially in tropical Africa, which a capitalistic imperialism threatens and has, in part, already devastated, man is incapable of reacting against unnatural conditions. In those regions man is engaged in a perpetual struggle against disease and an exhausting climate, which tells heavily upon child-bearing; and there is no scientific machinery for salving the weaker members of the community. The African of the tropics is capable of tremendous physical labours. But he cannot accommodate himself to the European system of monotonous, uninterrupted labour, with its long and regular hours, involving, moreover, as it frequently does, severance from natural surroundings and nostalgia, the condition of melancholy resulting from separation from home, a malady to which the African is specially prone. Climatic conditions forbid it. When the system is forced upon him, the tropical African droops and dies.

Nor is violent physical opposition to abuse and injustice henceforth possible for the African in any part of Africa. His chances of effective resistance have been steadily dwindling with the increasing perfectibility in the killing power of modern armament.... Against the latest inventions, physical bravery, though associated with a perfect knowledge of the country, can do nothing....

Thus the African is really helpless against the material gods of the white man, as embodied in the trinity of imperialism, capitalistic-exploitation, and militarism....

To reduce all the varied and picturesque, and stimulating episodes in savage life to a dull routine of endless toil for uncomprehended ends; to dislocate social ties and disrupt social institutions; to stifle nascent desires and crush mental development; to graft upon primitive passions the annihilating evils of scientific slavery, and the bestial imaginings of civilized man, unrestrained by convention or law; in fine, to kill the soul in a people—this is a crime which transcends physical murder.

Senator Albert J. Beveridge Demands Annexation of the Philippines, 1900[14]

Albert Jeremiah Beveridge (1826–1927), Senator from Indiana, presented the case for annexation of the Philippines in terms of dramatic oratory. Mincing no words, he made it plain that, in his estimation, the Filipinos would prefer the just, humane, and civilizing government of the United States "to the savage, bloody rule from which we have rescued them." He pointed out that if the

---

[14] *Congressional Record*, XXXIII, Part I, January 9, 1900, 704–705, 707.

United States did not take the Philippines, they would be absorbed by either Germany, Russia, France, or even Japan.

Mr. President, I address the Senate at this time because Senators and Members of the House on both sides have asked that I give to Congress and the country my observations in the Philippines and the Far East, and the conclusions which those observations compel; and because of hurtful resolutions introduced and utterances made in the Senate, every word of which will cost and is costing the lives of American soldiers.

Mr. President, the times call for candor. The Philippines are ours forever, "territory belonging to the United States," as the Constitution calls them. And just beyond the Philippines are China's illimitable markets. We will not repudiate our duty in the archipelago. We will not abandon our opportunity in the Orient. We will not renounce our part in the mission of our race, trustee, under God, of the civilization of the world. And we will move forward to our work, not howling out regrets like slaves whipped to their burdens, but with gratitude for a task worthy of our strength, and thanksgiving to Almighty God that He has marked us as His chosen people, henceforth to lead in the regeneration of the world.

This island empire [*the Philippines*] is the last land left in all the oceans. If it should prove a mistake to abandon it, the blunder once made would be irretrievable. If it proves a mistake to hold it, the error can be corrected when we will. Every other progressive nation stands ready to relieve us.

But to hold it will be no mistake. Our largest trade henceforth must be with Asia. The Pacific is our ocean. More and more Europe will manufacture the most it needs, secure from its colonies the most it consumes. Where shall we turn for consumers of our surplus? Geography answers the question. China is our natural customer.... The Philippines give us a base at the door of all the East....

Most future wars will be conflicts for commerce. The power that rules the Pacific, therefore, is the power that rules the world. And, with the Philippines, that power is and will forever be the American Republic....

The Philippines command the commercial situation of the entire East.... And yet American statesmen plan to surrender this commercial throne of the Orient where Providence and our soldiers' lives have placed us. When history comes to write the story of that suggested treason to American supremacy and therefore to the spread of American civilization, let her in mercy write that those who so proposed were merely blind and nothing more....

No land in America surpasses in fertility the plains and valleys of Luzon. Rice and coffee, sugar and coconuts, hemp and tobacco, and many products of the temperate as well as the tropic zone grow in various sections of the archipelago.... The mineral wealth of this empire of the ocean will one day surprise the world.... And the wood, hemp, copra, and other products of the Philippines supply what we need and cannot ourselves produce.... If we are willing to go to war rather than let England have a few feet of frozen Alaska, which affords no market and commands none, what should we not do rather than let England, Germany, Russia, or Japan have all the Philippines? And no man on the spot can fail to see that this would be their fate if we retired....

Here, then, Senators, is the situation. Two years ago there was no land in all the world which we could occupy for any purpose. Our commerce was daily turning toward the Orient, and geography and trade developments made necessary our commercial empire over the Pacific. And in that ocean we had no commercial, naval, or military base. Today we have one of the three great ocean possessions of the globe.... Shall we abandon it? That man little knows the common people of the Republic, little understands the instincts of our race, who thinks we will not hold it fast and hold it forever....

But, Senators, it would be better to abandon this combined garden and Gibraltar of the Pacific, and count our blood and treasure already spent a profitable loss, than to apply any academic arrangement of self-government to these children. They are not capable of self-government. How could they be? They are not of a self-governing race. They are Orientals, Malays, instructed by Spaniards in the latter's worst estate. They know nothing of practical government except as they have witnessed the weak, corrupt, cruel, and capricious rule of Spain....

No one need fear their competition with our labor. No reward could beguile, no force compel, these children of indolence to leave their trifling lives for the fierce and fervid industry of high-wrought America. The very reverse is the fact....

Mr. President, this question is deeper than any question of party politics; deeper than any question of the isolated policy of our country even; deeper even than any question of constitutional power. It is elemental. It is racial. God has not been preparing the English-speaking and Teutonic peoples for a thousand years for nothing but vain and idle self-contemplation and self-admiration. No! He has made us the master organizers of the world to establish system where chaos reigns. He has given us the spirit of progress to overwhelm the forces of reaction throughout the earth. He has made us adept in government that we may administer government among savage and senile peoples. Were it not for such a force as this the world would relapse into barbarism and night. And of all our race He has marked the American people as His chosen nation to finally lead in the regeneration of the world. This is the divine mission of America, and it holds for us all the profit, all the glory, all the happiness possible to man. We are trustees of the world's progress, guardians of its righteous peace....

[Our] flag has never paused in its onward march. Who dares halt it now—now, when history's largest events are carrying it forward; now, when we see at last one people, strong enough for any task, great enough for any glory destiny can bestow?...

And so, Senators, with reverent hearts, where dwells the fear of God, the American people move forward to the future of their hope and the doing of His work....

11

Olympe de Gouges

FROM DECLARATION OF THE RIGHTS OF WOMAN

The French revolution politicized millions of French men by transforming their status from subjects to citizens, but revolutionaries of all political stripes displayed extreme reluctance to incorporate women into the national political body. Heeding the new political discourse of equality, inalienable rights, and universal liberties, Olympe de Gouges, the self-educated daughter of a butcher, pointed up the revolutionaries' patent contradiction of applying tenets of natural law philosophy to one-half of the human race but not to the other. This pamphlet, published in September 1791, documents an important discussion during the revolution over the public roles and duties of women in civil society. Olympe de Gouges engaged her critical pen over a number of issues, which led to her arrest as a counterrevolutionary and her execution in 1793.

To be decreed by the National Assembly in its last sessions or by the next legislature.

Preamble

Mothers, daughters, sisters, female representatives of the nation ask to be constituted as a national assembly. Considering that ignorance, neglect, or contempt for the rights of woman are the sole causes of public misfortunes and governmental corruption, they have resolved to set forth in a solemn declaration the natural, inalienable, and sacred rights of woman: so that by being constantly present to all the members of the social body this declaration may always remind them of their rights and duties; so that by being liable at every moment to comparison with the aim of any and all political institutions the acts of women's and men's powers may be the more fully respected; and so that by being founded henceforward on simple and incontestable principles the demands of the citizenesses may always tend toward maintaining the constitution, good morals, and the general welfare.

Olympe de Gouges, "Declaration of the Rights of Woman" (1791) reproduced from Darline Levy, Harriet Applewhite, & Mary Johnson, eds., *Women in Revolutionary Paris, 1785–1795* (Champaign, IL, University of Illinois Press, 1979), 89–93.

In consequence, the sex that is superior in beauty as in courage, needed in maternal sufferings, recognizes and declares, in the presence and under the auspices of the Supreme Being, the following rights of woman and the citizeness.

1. Woman is born free and remains equal to man in rights. Social distinctions may be based only on common utility.

2. The purpose of all political association is the preservation of the natural and imprescriptible rights of woman and man. These rights are liberty, property, security, and especially resistance to oppression.

3. The principle of all sovereignty rests essentially in the nation, which is but the reuniting of woman and man. No body and no individual may exercise authority which does not emanate expressly from the nation.

4. Liberty and justice consist in restoring all that belongs to another; hence the exercise of the natural rights of woman has no other limits than those that the perpetual tyranny of man opposes to them; these limits must be reformed according to the laws of nature and reason.

5. The laws of nature and reason prohibit all actions which are injurious to society. No hindrance should be put in the way of anything not prohibited by these wise and divine laws, nor may anyone be forced to do what they do not require.

6. The law should be the expression of the general will. All citizenesses and citizens should take part, in person or by their representatives, in its formation. It must be the same for everyone. All citizenesses and citizens, being equal in its eyes, should be equally admissible to all public dignities, offices, and employments, according to their ability, and with no other distinction than that of their virtues and talents.

7. No woman is exempted; she is indicted, arrested, and detained in the cases determined by the law. Women like men obey this rigorous law.

8. Only strictly and obviously necessary punishments should be established by the law, and no one may be punished except by virtue of a law established and promulgated before the time of the offense, and legally applied to women.

9. Any woman being declared guilty, all rigor is exercised by the law.

10. No one should be disturbed for his fundamental opinions; woman has the right to mount the scaffold, so she should have the right equally to mount the tribune, provided that these manifestations do not trouble public order as established by law.

11. The free communication of thoughts and opinions is one of the most precious of the rights of woman, since this liberty assures the recognition of children by their fathers. Every citizeness may therefore say freely, I am the mother of your

child; a barbarous prejudice should not force her to hide the truth, so long as responsibility is accepted for any abuse of this liberty in cases determined by the law.

12. The safeguard of the rights of woman and citizeness requires public powers. These powers are instituted for the advantage of all and not for the private benefit of those to whom they are entrusted.

13. For maintenance of public authority and for expenses of administration, taxation of women and men is equal; she takes part in all forced labor service, in all painful tasks; she must therefore have the same proportion in the distribution of places, employments, offices, dignities, and in industry.

14. The citizenesses and citizens have the right, by themselves or through their representatives, to have demonstrated to them the necessity of public taxes. The citizenesses can only agree to them upon admission of an equal division, not only in wealth, but also in the public administration, and to determine the means of apportionment, assessment, and collection, and the duration of the taxes.

15. The mass of women, joining with men in paying taxes, have the right to hold accountable every public agent of the administration.

16. Any society in which the guarantee of rights is not assured or the separation of powers not settled has no constitution. The constitution is null and void if the majority of individuals composing the nation has not cooperated in its drafting.

17. Property belongs to both sexes whether united or separated; it is for each of them an inviolable and sacred right, and no one may be deprived of it as a true patrimony of nature, except when public necessity, certified by law, obviously requires it, and then on condition of a just compensation in advance.

Postscript

Women, wake up; the tocsin of reason sounds throughout the universe; recognize your rights. The powerful empire of nature is no longer surrounded by prejudice, fanaticism, superstition, and lies. The torch of truth has dispersed all the clouds of folly and usurpation. Enslaved man has multiplied his force and needs yours to break his chains. Having become free, he has become unjust toward his companion. Oh women! Women, when will you cease to be blind? What advantages have you gathered in the revolution? A scorn more marked, a disdain more conspicuous. During the centuries of corruption you only reigned over the weakness of men. Your empire is destroyed; what is left to you then? Firm belief in the injustices of men. The reclaiming of your patrimony founded on the wise decrees of nature; why should you fear such a beautiful enterprise?... Whatever the barriers set up against you, it is in your power to overcome them; you only have to want it. Let us pass now to the appalling account of what you have been in society; and since national education is an issue at this moment, let us see if our wise legislators will think sanely about the education of women.

* * *

If giving my sex an honorable and just consistency is considered to be at this time paradoxical on my part and an attempt at the impossible, I leave to future men the glory of dealing with this matter; but while waiting, we can prepare the way with national education, with the restoration of morals and with conjugal agreements.

Form for a Social Contract Between Man and Woman

We, _____ and _____, moved by our own will, unite for the length of our lives and for the duration of our mutual inclinations under the following conditions: We intend and wish to make our wealth communal property, while reserving the right to divide it in favor of our children and of those for whom we might have a special inclination, mutually recognizing that our goods belong directly to our children, from whatever bed they come, and that all of them without distinction have the right to bear the name of the fathers and mothers who have acknowledged them, and we impose on ourselves the obligation of subscribing to the law that punishes any rejection of one's own blood. We likewise obligate ourselves, in the case of a separation, to divide our fortune equally and to set aside the portion the law designates for our children. In the case of a perfect union, the one the one who dies first will give up half his property in favor of the children; and if there are no children, the survivor will inherit by right, unless the dying person has disposed of his half of the common property in favor of someone he judges appropriate.

12

Mary Wollstonecraft

FROM THE VINDICATION OF THE RIGHTS OF WOMAN

Mary Wollstonecraft (1759–1797), a teacher and writer, wrote this essay as a critical response to the French Revolution. An enthusiastic supporter of the Revolution, she was nonetheless angered that the National Assembly did not extend the same liberties to women as to men. Her essay, appealing to reason, utility, and natural law, exhorted both men and women to reform education for women and enable them to participate in civil society as useful members. Scorned as a radical francophile by contemporaries, her essay convincingly applies liberal reasoning to the cause of women at a critical juncture in European history.

After considering the historic page, and viewing the living world with anxious solicitude, the most melancholy emotions of sorrowful indignation have depressed my spirits, and I have sighed when obliged to confess that either Nature has made a great difference between man and man, or that the civilization which has hitherto taken place in the world has been very partial. I have turned over various books written on the subject of education, and patiently observed the conduct of parents and the management of schools; but what has been the result?—a profound conviction that the neglected education of my fellow-creatures is the grand source of the misery I deplore, and that women, in particular, are rendered weak and wretched by a variety of concurring causes, originating from one hasty conclusion. The conduct and manners of women, in fact, evidently prove that their minds are not in a healthy state; for, like the flowers which are planted in too rich a soil, strength and usefulness are sacrificed to beauty; and the flaunting leaves, after having pleased a fastidious eye, fade, disregarded on the stalk, long before the season when they ought to have arrived at maturity. One cause of this barren blooming I attribute to a false system of education, gathered from the books written on this subject by men who, considering females rather as women than human creatures, have been more anxious to make them alluring mistresses than affectionate wives and rational mothers; and the understanding of the sex has been so

Mary Wollstonecraft, *The Vindication of the Rights of Woman* (1792), selections reproduced from the edition by W. W. Norton (New York, 1970), 3–5.

bubbled by this specious homage, that the civilized women of the present century, with a few exceptions, are only anxious to inspire love, when they ought to cherish a nobler ambition, and by their abilities and virtues exact respect.

In a treatise, therefore, on female rights and manners, the works which have been particularly written for their improvement must not be overlooked, especially when it is asserted, in direct terms, that the minds of women are enfeebled by false refinement; that the books of instruction, written by men of genius, have had the same tendency as more frivolous productions; and that, in the true style of Mahometanism, they are treated as a kind of subordinate beings, and not as a part of the human species, when improvable reason is allowed to be the dignified distinction which raises men above the brute creation, and puts a natural sceptre in a feeble hand.

Yet, because I am a woman, I would not lead my readers to suppose that I mean violently to agitate the contested question respecting the quality or inferiority of the sex; but as the subject lies in my way, and I cannot pass it over without subjecting the main tendency of my reasoning to misconstruction, I shall stop a moment to deliver, in a few words, my opinion. In the government of the physical world it is observable that the female in point of strength is, in general, inferior to the male. This is the law of Nature; and it does not appear to be suspended or abrogated in favour of woman. A degree of physical superiority cannot, therefore, be denied, and it is a noble prerogative! But not content with this natural pre-eminence, men endeavour to sink us still lower, merely to render us alluring objects for a moment; and women, intoxicated by the adoration which men, under the influence of their senses, pay them, do not seek to obtain a durable interest in their hearts, or to become the friends of the fellow-creatures who find amusement in their society.

I am aware of an obvious inference. From every quarter have I heard exclamations against masculine women, but where are they to be found? If by this appellation men mean to inveigh against their ardour in hunting, shooting, and gaming, I shall most cordially join in the cry; but if it be against the imitation of manly virtues, or, more properly speaking, the attainment of those talents and virtues, the exercise of which ennobles the human character, and which raises females in the scale of animal being, when they are comprehensively termed mankind, all those who view them with a philosophic eye must, I should think, wish with me, that they may every day grow more and more masculine.

This discussion naturally divides the subject. I shall first consider women in the grand light of human creatures, who, in common with men, are placed on this earth to unfold their faculties; and afterwards I shall more particularly point out their peculiar designation.

I wish also to steer clear of an error which many respectable writers have fallen into; for the instruction which has hitherto been addressed to women, has rather been applicable to *ladies*, if the little indirect advice that is scattered through 'Sandford and Merton' be excepted; but, addressing my sex in a firmer tone, I pay particular attention to those in the middle class, because they appear to be in the most natural state. Perhaps the seeds of false refinement, immorality, and vanity, have ever been shed by the great. Weak, artificial beings, raised above the common wants and affections of their race, in a premature unnatural manner, undermine the very foundation of virtue, and spread corruption through the whole mass of society! As a class of mankind they have the strongest claim to pity; the education of the rich tends to render them vain and helpless, and the unfolding mind is not strengthened by the practice of those duties which dignify the human character. They only live to amuse themselves, and by the same law which in Nature invariably produces certain effects, they soon only afford barren amusement.

But as I purpose taking a separate view of the different ranks of society, and of the moral character of women in each, this hint is for the present sufficient; and I have only alluded to the subject because it appears to me to be the very essence of an introduction to give a cursory account of the contents of the work it introduces.

My own sex, I hope, will excuse me, if I treat them like rational creatures, instead of flattering their *fascinating* graces, and viewing them as if they were in a state of perpetual childhood, unable to stand alone. I earnestly wish to point out in what true dignity and human happiness consists. I wish to persuade women to endeavour to acquire strength, both of mind and body, and to convince them that the soft phrases, susceptibility of heart, delicacy of sentiment, and refinement of taste, are almost synonymous with epithets of weakness, and that those beings who are only the objects of pity, and that kind of love which has been termed its sister, will soon become objects of contempt.

Dismissing, then, those pretty feminine phrases, which the men condescendingly use to soften our slavish dependence, and despising that weak elegancy of mind, exquisite sensibility, and sweet docility of manners, supposed to be the sexual characteristics of the weaker vessel, I wish to show that elegance is inferior to virtue, that the first object of laudable ambition is to obtain a character as a human being, regardless of the distinction of sex, and that secondary views should be brought to this simple touchstone.

This is a rough sketch of my plan; and should I express my conviction with the energetic emotions that I feel whenever I think of the subject, the dictates of experience and reflection will be felt by some of my readers. Animated by this important object, I shall disdain to cull my phrases or polish my style. I aim at being useful, and sincerity will render me unaffected; for wishing rather to persuade by the force of my arguments than dazzle by the elegance of my language, I shall not waste my time in rounding periods, or in fabricating the turgid bombast of artificial feelings, which, coming from the head, never reach the heart. I shall be employed about things, not words! and, anxious to render my sex more respectable members of society, I shall try to avoid that flowery diction which has slided from essays into novels, and from novels into familiar letters and conversations.

These pretty superlatives, dropping glibly from the tongue, vitiate the taste, and create a kind of sickly delicacy that turns away from simple unadorned truth; and a deluge of false sentiments and overstretched feelings, stifling the natural emotions of the heart, render the domestic pleasures insipid, that ought to sweeten the exercise of those severe duties, which educate a rational and immortal being for a nobler field of action.

The education of women has of late been more attended to than formerly, yet they are still reckoned a frivolous sex, and ridiculed or pitied by the writers who endeavour by satire or instruction to improve them. It is acknowledged that they spend many of the first years of their lives in acquiring a smattering of accomplishments; meanwhile strength of body and mind are sacrificed to libertine notions of beauty, to the desire of establishing themselves—the only way women can rise in the world—by marriage. And this desire making mere animals of them, when they marry they act as such children may be expected to act—they dress, they paint, and nickname God's creatures. Surely these weak beings are only fit for a seraglio! Can they be expected to govern a family with judgement, or take care of the poor babes, whom they bring into the world?

If, then, it can be fairly deduced from the present conduct of the sex, from the prevalent fondness for pleasure which takes place of ambition and those nobler passions that open and enlarge the soul, that the instruction which women have hitherto received has only tended, with the constitution of civil society, to render them insignificant objects of desire—mere propagators of fools!—if it can be proved that in aiming to accomplish them, without cultivating their understandings, they are taken out of their sphere of duties, and made ridiculous and useless when the short-lived bloom of beauty is over, I presume that rational men will excuse me for endeavouring to persuade them to become more masculine and respectable.

Indeed the word masculine is only a bugbear; there is little reason to fear that women will acquire too much courage or fortitude, for their apparent inferiority with respect to bodily strength must render them in some degree dependent on men in the various relations of life; but why should it be increased by prejudices that give a sex to virtue, and confound simple truths with sensual reveries?

Women are, in fact, so much degraded by mistaken notions of female excellence, that I do not mean to add a paradox when I assert that this artificial weakness produces a propensity to tyrannize, and gives birth to cunning, the natural opponent of strength, which leads them to play off those contemptible infantine airs that undermine esteem even whilst they excite desire. Let men become more chaste and modest, and if women do not grow wiser in the same ratio it will be clear that they have weaker understandings. It seems scarcely necessary to say that I now speak of the sex in general. Many individuals have more sense than their male relatives; and, as nothing preponderates where there is a constant struggle for an equilibrium without it has naturally more gravity, some women govern their husbands without degrading themselves, because intellect will always govern.

13

John Stuart Mill

THE SUBJECTION OF WOMEN
THE ARGUMENT FOR EQUALITY

In his speech before Parliament while he argued for the franchise of women, John Stuart Mill (1806–1873) rejected the idea that women are innately inferior to men. For Mill the issue was one of education and legal rights, which women had been unfairly denied.

The social subordination of women thus stands out an isolated fact in modern social institutions; a solitary breach of what has become their fundamental law; a single relic of an old world of thought and practice exploded in everything else, but retained in the one thing of most universal interest....

The least that can be demanded is, that the question should not be considered as prejudged by existing fact and existing opinion, but open to discussion on its merits, as a question of justice and expediency; the decision on this, as on any of the other social arrangements of mankind, depending on what an enlightened estimate of tendencies and consequences may show to be most advantageous to humanity in general, without distinction of sex.

Neither does it avail anything to say that the *nature* of the two sexes adapts them to their present functions and position, and renders these appropriate to them. Standing on the ground of common sense and the constitution of the human mind, I deny that anyone knows, or can know, the nature of the two sexes, as long as they have only been seen in their present relation to one another. If men had ever been found in society without women, or women without men, or if there had been a society of men and women in which the women were not under the control of the men, something might have been positively known about the mental and moral differences which may be inherent in the nature of each. What is now called the nature of women is an eminently artificial thing — the result of forced repression in some directions, unnatural stimulation in others. It may be asserted without scruple, that no other class of dependents have had their character so entirely distorted from its natural proportions by their relation with

John Stuart Mill, *The Subjection of Women* (1869), selections reproduced from the edition by F. Stokes Co. of New York (1911), 42–51, 54.

their masters; for, if conquered and slave races have been, in some respects, more forcibly repressed, whatever in them has not been crushed down by an iron heel has generally been let alone, and if left with any liberty of development it has developed itself according to its own laws; but in the case of women, a hot-house and stove cultivation has always been carried on of some of the capabilities of their nature, for the benefit and pleasure of their masters. Then, because certain products of the general vital force sprout luxuriantly and reach a great development in this heated atmosphere and under this active nurture and watering, while other shoots from the same root, which are left outside in the wintry air, with ice purposely heaped all round them, have a stunted growth, and some are burnt off with fire and disappear; men, with that inability to recognize their own work which distinguishes the unanalytic mind, indolently believe that the tree grows of itself in the way they have made it grow, and that it would die if one-half of it were not kept in a vapor-bath and the other half in the snow.

Of all difficulties which impede the progress of thought, and the formation of well-grounded opinions on life and social arrangements, the greatest is now the unspeakable ignorance and inattention of mankind in respect to the influences which form human character. Whatever any portion of the human species now are, or seem to be, such, it is supposed, they have a natural tendency to be: even when the most elementary knowledge of the circumstances in which they have been placed, clearly points out the causes that made them what they are.

…Because women, as is often said, care nothing about politics except their personalities, it is supposed that the general good is naturally less interesting to women than to men. History, which is now so much better understood than formerly, teaches another lesson: if only by showing the extraordinary susceptibility of human nature to external influences, and the extreme variableness of those of its manifestations which are supposed to be most universal and uniform. But in history, as in traveling, men usually see only what they already had in their own minds; and few learn much from history, who do not bring much with them to its study.

Hence, in regard to that most difficult question, what are the natural differences between the two sexes—a subject on which it is impossible in the present state of society to obtain complete and correct knowledge—while almost everybody dogmatizes upon it, almost all neglect and make light of the only means by which any partial insight can be obtained into it. This is, an analytic study of the most important department of psychology, the laws of the influence of circumstances on character. For, however great and apparently ineradicable the moral and intellectual differences between men and women might be, the evidence of there being natural differences could only be negative. Those only could be inferred to be natural which could not possibly be artificial—the residuum, after deducting every characteristic of either sex which can admit of being explained from education or external circumstances. The profoundest knowledge of the laws of the formation of character is indispensable to entitle anyone to affirm even that there is any difference, much more what the difference is, between the two sexes considered as moral and rational beings; and since no one, as yet, has that knowledge (for there is hardly any subject which, in proportion to its importance, has been so little studied), no one is thus far entitled to any positive opinion on the subject.…

Even the preliminary knowledge, what the differences between the sexes now are, apart from all question as to how they are made what they are, is still in the crudest and most incomplete state. Medical practitioners and physiologists have ascertained, to some extent, the differences in bodily constitution; and this is an important element to the psychologist; but hardly any medical practitioner is a psychologist. Respecting the mental characteristics of women, their observations are of no more worth than those of common men. It is a subject on which nothing final can be known, so long as those who alone can really know it, women themselves, have given but little testimony, and that little, mostly suborned....

...We may safely assert that the knowledge which men can acquire of women, even as they have been and are, without reference to what they might be, is wretchedly imperfect and superficial, and always will be so, until women themselves have told all that they have to tell.

14

Clara Zetkin

WOMEN'S WORK AND THE
ORGANIZATION OF TRADE UNIONS

The German socialist Clara Zetkin (1857–1933) was well known throughout Europe for her ardent support of working women. Unlike the many left wing activists who rejected feminism in the belief that the workers' revolution would inevitably bring gender equality in its wake, Zetkin argued that an active commitment to women's rights must go hand in hand with the socialist struggle against capitalism. Although Zetkin was a strong supporter of women's right to vote, as a socialist she rejected the liberal feminism of middle-class suffragettes such as the Pankhursts (see chapter 24) and instead focused her efforts on seeking solutions to the specific forms of economic oppression suffered by women as workers.

The following article appeared in Gleichheit ("Equality"), the highly successful German Socialist women's newspaper that Zetkin edited between 1892 and 1917. Responding to male labor organizers who saw low-paid women workers as competitors and who wished to exclude women from the industrial work force, Zetkin argues here that the socialist movement would benefit more if male workers sought to bring working women into trade union organizations.

In all capitalist countries, women's work in industry plays an ever larger role. The number of industrial branches in which women nowadays toil and drudge from morning till night increases with every year. Factories which have traditionally employed women, employ more and more women workers. It is not only that the number of all industrially employed women is constantly growing, but their number in relation to the men who are working in industry and trade is also on the increase.

Some branches of industry (one has only to think of clothing) are virtually dominated by women's labor which constantly reduces and replaces men's labor.

For understandable reasons, particularly during periods of recession (like the one we are experiencing right now), the number of women workers has increased in both relative and absolute terms whereas the number of employed male laborers has decreased.

Clara Zetkin, "Women's Work and the Organization of Trade Unions" (1893) in *Clara Zetkin: Selected Writings*, edited by Philip S. Foner (New York, International Publishers, 1984), 51–58, ISBN: 0-7178-0620-0.

* * *

The reasons for the constantly growing use of female laborers have been repeatedly pointed out: their cheapness and the improvement of the mechanical means and methods of production. The automatic machine, which in many cases does not even stand in need of having to be regulated, works with the powers of a giant, possesses unbelievable skill, speed and exactness and renders muscle power and acquired skills superfluous. The capitalist entrepreneur can employ only female labor at those places where he previously had to use male employees. And he just loves to hire women because female labor is cheap, much cheaper than male labor.

Even though the productive capacity of female workers does not lag behind that of male workers, the difference between men's and women's wages is very significant. The latter is often only half of the former and often only a third.

* * *

...the living conditions of these female workers correspond to their miserable earnings. It is easily understandable that these customary starvation wages for female laborers push thousands of them from the proletariat into the lumpenproletariat.[1] Their dire straits force some of them to take up part-time or temporary prostitution so that by selling their bodies, they may earn the piece of bread that they cannot secure by the sale of their labor.

But it is not just the women workers who suffer because of the miserable payment of their labor. The male workers, too, suffer because of it. As a consequence of their low wages, the women are transformed from mere competitors into unfair competitors who push down the wages of men. Cheap women's labor eliminates the work of men and if the men want to continue to earn their daily bread, they must put up with low wages. Thus women's work is not only a cheap form of labor, it also cheapens the work of men and for that reason it is doubly appreciated by the capitalist, who craves profits.

* * *

The transfer of hundreds of thousands of female laborers to the modernized means of production that increase productivity ten or even a hundredfold should have resulted (and did result in some cases) in a higher standard of living for the proletariat, given a rationally organized society. But as far as the proletariat is concerned, capitalism has changed blessing into curse and wealth into bitter poverty. The economic advantages of the industrial activity of proletarian women only aid the tiny minority of the sacrosanct guild of coupon clippers and extortionists of profit.

Frightened by the economic consequences of women's work and the abuses connected with it, organized labor demanded for a while the prohibition of female

---

[1] In Marxist terminology, the *lumpenproletariat* consists of the lowest ranks of the working class. It verges on being a criminal underclass and is disinclined to join with honest workers in the struggle against capitalism.

labor. It was viewing this question merely from the narrow viewpoint of the wage question. Thanks to Socialist propaganda, the class-conscious proletariat has learned to view this question from another angle, from the angle of its historical importance for the liberation of women and the liberation of the proletariat. It understands now how impossible it is to abolish the industrial labor of women. Thus it has dropped its former demand and it attempts to lessen the bad economic consequences of women's work within capitalist society (and only within it!) by two other means; by the legal protection of female workers and by their inclusion in trade union organizations. We have already mentioned above the necessity and the advantageous effects of the legal protection of women workers. * * *

Given the fact that many thousands of female workers are active in industry, it is vital for the trade unions to incorporate them into their movement. In individual industries where female labor plays an important role, any movement advocating better wages, shorter working hours, etc., would be doomed from the start because of the attitude of those women workers who are not organized. Battles which began propitiously enough, ended up in failure because the employers were able to play off non-union female workers against those that are organized in unions. These non-union workers continued to work (or took up work) under any conditions, which transformed them from competitors in dirty work to scabs.

It is not only because of the successful economic battles of trade unions that women should be included in them. The improvement of the starvation wages of female workers and the limitation of competition among them requires their organization into unions.

The fact that the pay for female labor is so much lower than that of male labor has a variety of causes. Certainly one of the reasons for these poor wages for women is the circumstance that female workers are practically unorganized. They lack the strength which comes with unity. They lack the courage, the feeling of power, the spirit of resistance and the ability to resist which is produced by the strength of an organization in which the individual fights for everybody and everybody fights for the individual. Furthermore, they lack the enlightenment and the training which an organization provides. Without an understanding of modern economic life in whose machinery they are inextricably caught up, they will neither be able to take advantage of periods of boom through conscious, calculating and unified conduct nor will they be able to protect themselves against the disadvantages occurring during periods of economic recession. If, under the pressure of unbearable conditions they finally fight back, they usually do so at an inopportune moment and in a disorganized fashion.

This situation exercises a great influence upon the miserable state of women's work and is further reflected by the bitterness that male workers feel about women's competition. Thus in the interest of both men and women workers, it is urgently recommended that the latter be included in the trade unions. The larger the number of organized female workers who fight shoulder to shoulder with their comrades from the factory or workshop for better working conditions, the sooner and the greater will women's wages rise so that soon there may be the realization of the principle: Equal pay for equal work regardless of the difference in sex. The organized female worker who has become the equal of the male worker ceases to be his scab competitor.

The unionized male workers realize more and more just how important it is that the female workers are accepted into the ranks of their organization. During these past few years, there was no lack of effort on the part of the unions in regard to this endeavor. And yet how little has been accomplished and how incredibly much remains to be done in this respect.

*   *   *

Even in those industrial branches in which the trade union organization of women began, these organizations are still in their infancy.

*   *   *

As far as the percentage of female membership is concerned, the Tobacco Workers rank first, and yet these women workers do not even constitute a fourth of its entire membership. In 1882, 43.1% of all tobacco industry workers were women. In the other four trade unions which come next, as far as the percentage of women that work in the industries they represent are concerned, women workers do not even constitute 10% of the membership. The Organization of Gold and Silver Workers does not have a female membership of even 5% even though there are large numbers of women workers who are employed by the gold and silver industry. In 1882, 60% of all laborers in spinning mills and 30% of all laborers in weaving mills happened to be women, yet the percentage of them who were unionized amounted to only 9½%. These numbers, in conjunction with the slave wages which generally prevail in the textile industry, speak whole volumes about the necessity of unionizing women.

In recognition of this necessity, the trade unions should use all of their energies to work for the inclusion of women in their organizations.

We certainly do not fail to recognize the difficulties raised by women workers which are detrimental to the solution of this problem. Stupid resignation, lack of a feeling of solidarity, shyness, prejudices of all kinds and fear of the factory tyrant keep many women from joining unions. Even more than the just mentioned factors, the lack of time on the part of female workers represents a major obstacle against their mass organization because women are house as well as factory slaves and are forced to bear a double workload. The economic developments, however, as well as the increasing acuteness of the class struggle, educate both male and female laborers and force them to overcome the above-mentioned difficulties.

Theoretically, most male union members admit that the common unionization of both male and female workers of the same trade has become an unavoidable necessity. In practice, however, many of them do not make the effort that they could be making. Rather there are only a few unions and within them only certain individuals who pursue with energy and perseverance the organization of female workers. The majority of trade union members give them precious little support. They treat such endeavors as a hobby which should be tolerated but not supported "as long as there are still so many indifferent non-union male workers." This point of view is totally wrong.

The unionization of women workers will make significant progress only when it is no longer merely aided by the few, but by every single union member making every effort to enlist their female colleagues from factory and workshop. In order to fulfill this task, two things are necessary. The male workers must stop viewing the female worker primarily as a woman to be courted if she is young, beautiful, pleasant and cheerful (or not). They must stop (depending on their degree of culture or lack of it) molesting them with crude and fresh sexual advances. The workers must rather get accustomed to treat female laborers primarily as female proletarians, as working-class comrades fighting class slavery and as equal and indispensable co-fighters in the class struggle. The unions make such a big thing out of having all of the members and followers of the political party become members of the unions. It seems to us that it would be much more important to put the emphasis on enrolling the broad, amorphous masses in the labor movement. In our opinion, the main task of the unions is the enlightenment, disciplining and education of all workers for the class struggle. In view of the increasing use of female labor and the subsequent results, the labor movement will surely commit suicide if, in its effort to enroll the broad masses of the proletariat, it does not pay the same amount of attention to female workers as it does to male ones.

15

Emmeline Pankhurst
WHY WE ARE MILITANT

Agitation in Great Britain for woman suffrage reached a peak during the turbulent years of parliamentary reform, 1909–1911. Under the leadership of Emmeline Pankhurst (1858–1928) and her daughter Christabel, women engaged in demonstrations, disrupted political meetings, and when dragged off to jail, resorted to passive resistance and hunger strikes. Some hunger strikers were subjected to the cruelty of force feeding. In 1913 Emmeline Pankhurst carried her appeal to the United States, where she delivered the speech printed below.

I know that in your minds there are questions like these; you are saying, "Woman Suffrage is sure to come; the emancipation of humanity is an evolutionary process, and how is it that some women, instead of trusting to that evolution, instead of educating the masses of people of their country, instead of educating their own sex to prepare them for citizenship, how is it that these militant women are using violence and upsetting the business arrangements of the country in their undue impatience to attain their end?"

Lee me try to explain to you the situation....

The extensions of the franchise to the men of my country have been preceded by very great violence, by something like a revolution, by something like civil war. In 1832, you know we were on the edge of a civil war and on the edge of revolution, and it was at the point of the sword—no, not at the point of the sword—it was after the practice of arson on so large a scale that half the city of Bristol was burned down in a single night, it was because more and greater violence and arson were feared that the Reform Bill of 1832 [which gave the vote to the middle class] was allowed to pass into law. In 1867,...rioting went on all over the country, and as the result of that rioting, as the result of that unrest,...as a result of the fear of more rioting and violence the Reform Act of 1867 [which gave workers the vote] was put upon the statute books.

In 1884...rioting was threatened and feared, and so the agricultural labourers got the vote.

Emmeline Pankhurst, "Why We Are Militant" (1913), reproduced from Lynn Hunt, ed., *The French Revolution and Human Rights*, St. Martin's Press, (1996).

Meanwhile, during the '80's, women, like men, were asking for the franchise. Appeals, larger and more numerous than for any other reform, were presented in support of Woman's Suffrage. Meetings of the great corporations [group of principal officials in a town or city government], great town councils, and city councils, passed resolutions asking that women should have the vote. More meetings were held, and larger, for Woman Suffrage than were held for votes for men, and yet the women did not get it. Men got the vote because they were and would be violent. The women did not get it because they were constitutional and law-abiding....

I believed, as many women still in England believe, that women could get their way in some mysterious manner, by purely peaceful methods. We have been so accustomed, we women, to accept one standard for men and another standard for women, that we have even applied that variation of standard to the injury of our political welfare.

Having had better opportunities of education, and having had some training in politics, having in political life come so near to the "superior" being as to see that he was not altogether such a fount of wisdom as they had supposed, that he had his human weaknesses as we had, the twentieth century women began to say to themselves, "Is it not time, since our methods have failed and the men's have succeeded, that we should take a leaf out of their political book?"...

Well, we in Great Britain, on the eve of the General Election of 1905, a mere handful of us—why, you could almost count us on the fingers of both hands—set out on the wonderful adventure of forcing the strongest Government of modern times to give the women the vote....

The Suffrage movement was almost dead. The women had lost heart. You could not get a Suffrage meeting that was attended by members of the general public....

Two women changed that in a twinkling of an eye at a great Liberal demonstration in Manchester, where a Liberal leader, Sir Edward Grey, was explaining the programme to be carried out during the Liberals' next turn of office. The two women put the fateful question, "When are you going to give votes to women?" and refused to sit down until they had been answered. These two women were sent to gaol, and from that day to this the women's movement, both militant and constitutional, has never looked back. We had little more than one moribund society for Woman Suffrage in those days. Now we have nearly 50 societies for Woman Suffrage, and they are large in membership, they are rich in money, and their ranks are swelling every day that passes. That is how militancy has put back the clock of Woman Suffrage in Great Britain....

I want to say here and now that the only justification for violence, the only justification for damage to property, the only justification for risk to the comfort of other human beings is the fact that you have tried all other available means and have failed to secure justice, and as a law-abiding person—and I am by nature a law-abiding person, as one hating violence, hating disorder—I want to say that from the moment we began our militant agitation to this day I have felt absolutely guiltless in this matter.

I tell you that in Great Britain there is no other way....

Well, I say the time is long past when it became necessary for women to revolt in order to maintain their self respect in Great Britain. The women who are waging this war are women who would fight, if it were only for the idea of liberty—if it were only that they might be free citizens of a free country—I myself would fight for that idea alone. But we have, in addition to this love of freedom, intolerable grievances to redress....

Those grievances are so pressing that, so far from it being a duty to be patient and to wait for evolution, in thinking of those grievances the idea of patience is intolerable. We feel that patience is something akin to crime when our patience involves continued suffering on the part of the oppressed.

We are fighting to get the power to alter bad laws; but some people say to us, "Go to the representatives in the House of Commons, point out to them that these laws are bad, and you will find them quite ready to alter them."

Ladies and gentlemen, there are women in my country who have spent long and useful lives trying to get reforms, and because of their voteless condition, they are unable even to get the ear of Members of Parliament, much less are they able to secure those reforms.

Our marriage and divorce laws are a disgrace to civilisation. I sometimes wonder, looking back from the serenity of past middle age, at the courage of women. I wonder that women have the courage to take upon themselves the responsibilities of marriage and motherhood when I see how little protection the law of my country affords them. I wonder that a woman will face the ordeal of childbirth with the knowledge that after she has risked her life to bring a child into the world she has absolutely no parental rights over the future of that child. Think what trust women have in men when a woman will marry a man, knowing, if she has knowledge of the law, that if that man is not all she in her love for him thinks him, he may even bring a strange woman into the house, bring his mistress into the house to live with her, and she cannot get legal relief from such a marriage as that....

...[W]e realise how political power, how political influence, which would enable us to get better laws, would make it possible for thousands upon thousands of unhappy women to live happier lives....

Take the industrial side of the question: have men's wages for a hard day's work ever been so low and inadequate as are women's wages today? Have men ever had to suffer from the laws, more injustice than women suffer? Is there a single reason which men have had for demanding liberty that does not also apply to women?

Why, if you were talking to the *men* of any other nation you would not hesitate to reply in the affirmative. There is not a man in this meeting who has not felt sympathy with the uprising of the men of other lands when suffering from intolerable tyranny, when deprived of all representative rights. You are full of sympathy with men in Russia. You are full of sympathy with nations that rise against the domination of the Turk. You are full of sympathy with all struggling people striving for independence. How is it, then, that some of you have nothing but ridicule and contempt and [condemnation] for women who are fighting for exactly the same thing?

All my life I have tried to understand why it is that men who value their citizenship as their dearest possession seem to think citizenship ridiculous when it is to be applied to the women of their race. And I find an explanation, and it is the only one I can think of. It came to me when I was in a prison cell, remembering how I had seen men laugh at the idea of women going to prison. Why they would confess they could not bear a cell door to be shut upon themselves for a single hour without asking to be let out. A thought came to me in my prison cell, and it was this: that to men women are not human beings like themselves. Some men think we are superhuman; they put us on pedestals; they revere us; they think we are too fine and too delicate to come down into the hurly-burly of life. Other men think us sub-human; they think we are a strange species unfortunately having to exist for the perpetuation of the race. They think that we are fit for drudgery, but that in some strange way our minds are not like theirs, our love for great things is not like theirs, and so we are a sort of sub-human species.

We are neither superhuman nor are we sub-human. We are just human beings like yourselves.

Our hearts burn within us when we read the great mottoes which celebrate the liberty of your country; when we go to France and we read the words, liberty, fraternity and equality, don't you think that we appreciate the meaning of those words? And then when we wake to the knowledge that these things are not for us, they are only for our brothers, then there comes a sense of bitterness into the hearts of some women, and they say to themselves, "Will men never understand?" But so far as we in England are concerned, we have come to the conclusion that we are not going to leave men any illusions upon the question.

When we were patient, when we believed in argument and persuasion, they said, "You don't really want it because, if you did, you would do something unmistakable to show you were determined to have it." And then when we did something unmistakable they said, "You are behaving so badly that you show you are not fit for it."

Now, gentlemen, in your heart of hearts you do not believe that. You know perfectly well that there never was a thing worth having that was not worth fighting for. You know perfectly well that if the situation were reversed, if you had no constitutional rights and we had all of them, if you had the duty of paying and obeying and trying to look as pleasant, and we were the proud citizens who could decide our fate and yours, because we knew what was good for you better than you knew yourselves, you know perfectly well that you wouldn't stand it for a single day, and you would be perfectly justified in rebelling against such intolerable conditions.

16

Alexandra Kollontai

THE AUTOBIOGRAPHY OF A SEXUALLY EMANCIPATED COMMUNIST WOMAN

Alexandra Kollontai (1872–1952) grew up in an educated, affluent, and fairly liberal Russian family. She married young, but left her husband and son to study political economy in Switzerland, where she became actively involved in socialist organizing. Originally a Menshevik, Kollontai became a Bolshevik in 1915, largely because of the Bolshevik opposition to the war, and entered into a friendly correspondence with Lenin.

After the October Revolution, Kollontai was named People's Commissar of Social Welfare, becoming the only woman to hold a cabinet post in the new Bolshevik government. As director of the Women's Bureau (Zhenotdel) she agitated in favor of economic liberty for working women and state welfare benefits for mothers. Her advocacy of women's rights and free love was not universally popular, and in the years following the revolution she found herself increasingly at odds with the Communist Party leadership. In 1922, Kollontai was assigned a diplomatic post in Norway — a gentle form of exile — and she spent much of the rest of her life outside of Russia. In memoirs written in 1926, she recounted the heady early days of the revolution, when a total transformation of Russian society still seemed possible.

When one recalls the first months of the Workers' Government, months which were so rich in *magnificent illusions*,[1] plans, ardent initiatives to improve life, to organize the world anew, months of the real romanticism of the Revolution, one would in fact like to write about all else save about one's self. I occupied the post of Minister of Social Welfare from October of 1917 *to March of 1918*. It was not without opposition that I was received by the former officials of the Ministry. Most of them sabotaged us openly and simply did not show up for work. But precisely this office could not interrupt its work,

---

[1] By 1926, it was already necessary to be cautious about how one described one's involvement in the revolution, and Kollontai censored her own writing. Italics indicate passages in the original manuscript that were not included in the published version of her memoirs.

Alexandra Kollontai, *The Autobiography of a Sexually Emancipated Communist Woman* (1926), selections reproduced from the translated edition published by Herder and Herder in 1971, pp. 35-36, 37-39, 40, 41, 42-44.

included the whole welfare program for the war-disabled, hence for hundreds of thousands of crippled soldiers and officers, the pension system in general, foundling homes, homes for the aged, orphanages, hospitals for the needy, the work-shops making artificial limbs, the administration of playing-card factories (the manufacture of playing cards was a State monopoly), *the educational system*, clinical hospitals for women. In addition a whole series of educational institutes for young girls were also under the direction of this Ministry. One can easily imagine the enormous demands these tasks made upon a small group of people who, at the same time, were novices in State administration. In a clear awareness of these difficulties *I formed*, immediately, an auxiliary council in which experts such as physicians, jurists, pedagogues were represented alongside the workers and the minor officials of the Ministry. The sacrifice, the energy with which the minor employees bore the burden of this difficult task was truly exemplary. It was not only a matter of keeping the work of the Ministry going, but also of initiating reforms and improvements. New, fresh forces replaced the sabotaging officers of the old regime. A new life stirred in the offices of the formerly highly conservative Ministry. Days of grueling work! And at night the sessions of the councils of the People's Commissar (of the cabinet) under Lenin's chairmanship. A small, modest room and only one secretary who recorded the resolutions which changed Russia's life to its bottommost foundations.

*   *   *

My main work as People's Commissar consisted in the following: by decree to improve the situation of the war-disabled, to abolish religious instruction in the schools for young girls which were under the Ministry (this was still before the general separation of Church and State), and to transfer priests to the civil service, to introduce the right of self-administration for pupils in the schools for girls, to reorganize the former orphanages into government Children's Homes (*no distinction was to be made between orphaned children and those who still had fathers and mothers*), to set up the first hostels for the needy and street-urchins, to convene a committee, composed *only* of doctors, which was to be commissioned *to elaborate* the free public health system for the whole country. In my opinion the most important accomplishment of the People's Commissariat, however, was the legal foundation of a Central Office for Maternity and Infant Welfare. The draft of the bill relating to this Central Office was signed by me in January of 1918. A second decree followed in which *I* changed all maternity hospitals into free Homes for Maternity and Infant Care, in order thereby to set the groundwork for a comprehensive government system of pre-natal care. I was greatly assisted in coping with these tasks by Dr. Korolef. We also planned a "Pre-Natal Care Palace," a model home with an exhibition room in which courses for mothers would be held *and, among many other things*, model day nurseries were also to be established. We were just about completing preparations for such a facility in the building of a girls' boarding school at which formerly young girls of the nobility had been educated and which was still under the direction of a countess, when a fire destroyed our work, which had barely begun! Had the fire been set deliberately?... I was dragged out of bed in the middle of the night. I rushed to the scene of the fire; the beautiful exhibition room was totally ruined, as were all the other rooms. Only the huge nameplate "Pre-Natal Care Palace" still hung over the entrance door.

My efforts to nationalize maternity and infant care set off a new wave of insane attacks against me. All kinds of lies were related about the "nationalization of women," *about my legislative proposals which assertedly ordained that little girls of 12 were to become mothers.* A special fury gripped the religious followers of the old regime when, *on my own authority (the cabinet later criticized me for this action),* I transformed the famous Alexander Nevsky monastery into a home for war-invalids. The monks resisted and a shooting fray ensued. The press again raised a loud hue and cry against *me*. The Church organized street demonstrations *against my action* and also pronounced "anathema" against me...

I received countless threatening letters, but I never requested military protection. I always went out alone, unarmed and without any kind of a bodyguard. In fact I never gave a thought to any kind of danger, being all too engrossed in matters of an utterly different character. In February of 1918 a first State delegation of the Soviets was sent to Sweden *in order to clarify different economic and political questions.* As Peoples' Commissar I headed this delegation. But our vessel was shipwrecked; we were saved by landing on the Aland Islands which belonged to Finland. At this very time the struggle between the Whites and the Reds in the country had reached its most crucial moment and the German Army was also making ready to wage war against Finland.

*   *   *

Now began a *dark time* of my life which I cannot treat of here since the events are still too fresh in my mind. *But the day will also come when I will give an account of them.*

There were differences of opinion in the Party. I resigned from my post as People's Commissar *on the ground of total disagreement with the current policy. Little by little I was also relieved of all my other tasks. I again gave lectures and espoused my ideas on "the new woman" and "the new morality."* The Revolution was in full swing. The struggle was becoming increasingly irreconcilable and bloodier, *much of what was happening did not fit in with my outlook.* But after all there was still the unfinished task, women's liberation. Women, of course, had received all rights but in practice, of course, they still lived under the old yoke: without authority in family life, enslaved by a thousand menial household chores, bearing the whole burden of maternity, even the material cares, because many women now found life alone as a result of the war and other circumstances.

*   *   *

A flood of new work was waiting for me. The question now was one of drawing women into the people's kitchens and of educating them to devote their energies to children's homes and day-care centers, the school system, household reforms, and still many other pressing matters. The main thrust of all this activity was to implement, in fact, equal rights for women as a labor unit in the national economy and as a citizen in the political sphere and, of course, with the special proviso: maternity was to be appraised as a social function and therefore protected and provided for by the State.

* * *

A serious illness tore me away from the exciting work for months. Hardly having recovered—at that time I was in Moscow—I took over the direction of the Coordinating Office for Work among Women and again a new period of intensive, grueling work began. A communist women's *newspaper* was founded, conferences and congresses of women workers were convoked. The foundation was laid for work with the women of the East (Mohammedans). Two world conferences of communist women took place in Moscow. The law liberalizing abortion was put through and a number of regulations of benefit to women were introduced by our Coordinating Office and legally confirmed. *At this time I had to do more writing and speaking than ever before...*Our work received wholehearted support from Lenin. And Trotsky, although he was overburdened with military tasks, unfailingly and gladly appeared at our conferences. Energetic, gifted women, two of whom are no longer alive, sacrificially devoted all their energies to the work of the Coordinating Office.

At the eighth Soviet Congress, as a member of the Soviet executive *(now there were already several women on this body)*, I proposed a motion that the Soviets in all areas contribute to the creation of a consciousness of the struggle for equal rights for women and, accordingly, to involve them in State and communal work. I managed to push the motion through and to get it accepted but not without resistance. It was a great, an enduring victory.

A heated debate flared up when I published my thesis on the new morality. *For our Soviet marriage law, separated from the Church to be sure, is not essentially more progressive than the same laws that after all exist in other progressive democratic countries.* * * * [A]lthough the illegitimate child was placed on a legal par with the legitimate child, in practice a great deal of hypocrisy and injustice still exists in this area. When one speaks of the "immorality" which the Bolsheviks purportedly propagated, it suffices to submit our marriage laws to a close scrutiny to note that in the divorce question we are on a par with North America whereas in the question of the illegitimate child we have *not yet even* progressed as far as the Norwegians.

The most radical wing of the Party was formed around this question. My theses, my *sexual and moral* views, were bitterly fought *by many Party comrades of both sexes: as were still other differences of opinion in the Party regarding political guiding principles.* Personal and family cares were added thereto and thus months in 1922 went by without fruitful work. Then in the autumn of 1922 came my official appointment to the legation of the Russian Soviet representation in Norway. I really believed that this appointment would be purely formal and that therefore in Norway I would find time to devote to myself, to my literary activity. Things turned out quite differently. With the day of my entry into office in Norway I also entered upon a wholly new course of work in my life which drew upon all my energies to the highest degree.

17

Adolf Hitler

MEIN KAMPF

Adolf Hitler (1889–1945) was the son of an Austrian customs official in Braunau, Upper Austria. As a boy he held the ambition to become an artist, and in 1907 he went to Vienna with hopes of entering the Academy of Fine Arts. He was refused admission and for the next five years eked out a lonely, miserable existence in the capital of the Austro-Hungarian Empire, working as a casual laborer, living in a hostel for homeless men, sitting long hours in cafes, and producing cheap drawings and watercolors to earn a living. During these years, Hitler later claimed, he acquired his convictions on anti-Semitism, anti-Marxism, and racist nationalism.

In order to escape service in the Austrian army Hitler moved to Munich in 1913. At the outbreak of the First World War Hitler joined a Bavarian regiment as a volunteer. After the war he returned to Munich; in 1919 he became a member and (from 1921) the leader of the "German Workers' Party" (since 1920 the "National Socialist German Workers' Party"). After his abortive putsch in November 1923, Hitler was sentenced to five years in prison at the fortress of Landsberg (he served less than nine months). The enforced leisure allowed him to begin an account of his early life and thoughts, the first volume of which was published in 1925 under the title Mein Kampf. *This book articulated Hitler's fanatical ideas on anti-Semitism, racism, and anti-Marxist mass politics. Like early Nazi propaganda it also played upon German popular hatred of the postwar settlement, but it went beyond themes like the famous "Stab in the Back" legend of Germany's defeat to proffer a canon of expansive nationalism and social revolution in the aftermath of the Revolution of 1918/1919.* Mein Kampf *was thus, in rhetorical and thematic terms, as much a memoir of the anarchic rightism of the early 1920s as it was an anticipation of the horrors of the later 1930s.*

The National Socialist party was banned in 1923, but reconstituted by Hitler in 1925. The party grew quickly during the economic and political crises of the late Weimar Republic (810,000 votes in the 1928 national elections, 6.4 million in 1930, 13.7 million in 1932). In 1928 it had 12 representatives in the German Reichstag; 107 in 1930; 230 in July 1932 (reduced to 196 in November). On 30 January 1933 Hitler was nominated Chancellor of Germany by President von Hindenburg. He quickly eliminated all other parties and instituted a regime of institutional and racial barbarism unparalleled in modern history, which was responsible by 1945 for the deaths of

---

Adolf Hitler, *Mein Kampf* (1925), selections from John W. Boyer and Jan Goldstein, eds., *Twentieth-Century Europe: University of Chicago Readings in Western Civilization* (Chicago, University Press of Chicago, 1986), 191–218.

over 30 million people. After the collapse of the Third Reich, Hitler committed suicide in Berlin on 30 April 1945. The last words of his final Testament, written immediately before his death — urging "merciless struggle against the universal poisoner of all nations, international Jewry" — suggest both the fanaticism and the unspeakable cruelty of a man and a state poisoned by mass social hatred.

The following selections from Mein Kampf *consist of (1) Hitler's description of his life in Vienna before 1914; (2) his comments on the nature and purpose of the State; and (3) his description of propaganda in modern political movements.*

Vienna

What I knew about Social Democracy in my youth was precious little and highly erroneous.

Inwardly I was glad that the Social Democrats led in the struggle for universal and secret voting. Even then my understanding told me that this must lead to a weakening of the Hapsburg regime which I hated so much. In the conviction that the Danubian state could never be maintained without the sacrifice of its German character, but that even the price of a gradual Slavicization of the German elements would not in any way have guaranteed a really viable Empire because the ability of the Slavs to maintain a state had to be assessed as highly dubious, I welcomed every development that in my opinion would lead to the breakup of this impossible state which was condemning ten million people to the death of their Germanic character. The more the babble of different tongues ate into and decomposed the Parliament, the nearer the hour of the downfall of this Babylonian empire must come, and therewith also the hour of liberation for my Germanic-Austrian people. Only in this way, then, could union with the old Motherland come again.

Therefore I was not unsympathetic to this activity of Social Democracy. That they strove in the long run (as my simple soul was still stupid enough to believe) to raise the living conditions of the workers also seemed to me to speak for them rather than against them. What bothered me the most was their hostility toward the struggle for the preservation of German nationality, their deplorable illicit courtship of the favor of Slavic "comrades," who (for their part) readily accepted this wooing so long as it was tied to practical concessions, but who otherwise remained arrogantly and haughtily aloof, thus giving the importunate beggars their well-earned pay.

Thus, at the age of seventeen I scarcely knew the word "Marxism," while "Social Democracy" and socialism seemed to be identical terms. Here too the hand of Fate was required to open my eyes to this incredible national betrayal.

Until this time I had come to know the Social Democratic Party only as an onlooker at various mass demonstrations, without possessing so much as the slightest insight into the mentality of its followers or even into the essence of its teachings; now I came with a slap into sudden contact with the products of its education and world view. And what I might otherwise have realized only after decades, I now obtained in the course of a few months: an understanding of the pestilential whore, masking herself as social virtue and charitable love, from which, let us hope, mankind will free the earth as quickly as possible, since otherwise the earth could all too easily become rid of mankind instead.

My first encounter with Social Democrats took place when I was a construction worker.

From the beginning it was not very enjoyable. My clothing was still somewhat respectable, my speech was refined, and my manner was withdrawn. I was still so busy with my destiny that I was not able to concern myself much with my surroundings. I sought work so as not to starve, to obtain the possibility of a continuation, however gradual, of my education. Perhaps I would not have troubled myself at all about my new surroundings, if on the third or fourth day something had not happened that forced me at once to take a stand. I was called upon to join the union.

My knowledge of the trade union organization was then virtually nil. I would not have been able to prove either the expediency or the inexpediency of their existence. When it was explained to me that I had to join, I refused. I based my refusal on the ground that I did not understand the matter, but that under no circumstances would I permit myself to be forced into anything. Perhaps it was for the first of these reasons that they did not throw me out immediately. Possibly they hoped to convert me or to soften me up after a few days. At any rate they were basically fooling themselves. After a fortnight I could no longer have joined even if I had wanted to. In those fourteen days I came to know my surroundings so much better that no power on earth could have moved me to enlist in an organization whose supporters in the meantime had appeared to me in such an unfavorable light.

The first few days I was irritable.

At midday part of the workmen went to the nearby saloons while the others remained on the job site and consumed what was usually a very miserable lunch. These were the married men, whose wives brought them their midday soup in pitiable bowls. Toward the end of the week their number steadily increased; why, I understood only later. At this point they talked politics.

I drank my bottle of milk and ate my piece of bread somewhere off to the side and carefully studied my new surroundings or mulled over my wretched fate. Nevertheless, I heard more than enough; also, it often seemed to me that they inched closer to me intentionally, perhaps in order to lead me to take a stand. In any case, what I overheard was apt to infuriate me in the extreme. They rejected everything: the nation as an invention of the "capitalist"—how often I had to hear this word alone!—classes; the Fatherland as a device of the bourgeoisie for exploiting the workers; the authority of the law as a means for the suppression of the proletariat; the school as an institution for breeding slave material as well as slaveholders; religion as a means of stupefying people marked out for exploitation; morals as a sign of dumb sheeplike patience, etc. There was absolutely nothing that was not dragged through muck of a dreadful depth.

In the beginning I tried to keep silent. Finally it became impossible. I began to take a stand, began to contradict. But I had to realize that my efforts would be perfectly pointless so long as I did not have certain knowledge about the points in dispute, at the very least. Therefore I began to track down the sources from which they drew their alleged wisdom. Book after book, pamphlet after pamphlet now had its turn.

At work, however, the arguments often waxed hot. I quarreled, better informed day by day about their own theories than my opponents themselves, until one day those means were used which certainly win most easily over reason: terror and force. Some of the spokesmen for the opposition forced me to either leave the job site immediately or be thrown from the scaffolding. Since I was alone and resistance seemed pointless, I preferred to follow the first advice, one experience richer.

I left filled with disgust, but at the same time so affected that it would have been quite impossible for me to turn my back upon the whole thing. No: after the first rush of indignation, obstinacy regained the upper hand. I was firmly determined to get another construction job. I was strengthened in this decision by the privation which, several weeks later, after I had consumed what little I have saved from my wages, locked me in its heartless arms. I had to work whether I wanted to or not. And the game started over again, from the beginning, only to end as it had the first time.

I grappled then with my innermost soul: Are these still human beings, worthy of belonging to a great nation?

An agonizing question: because if it is answered with yes, then the struggle on behalf of a nationality is really no longer worth the trouble and sacrifice which the best of us have to bear for the sake of such dregs; but if the answer is no, then our nation is indeed poor in human beings. → worth of humans – boots are more worthy

With restless anxiety I saw, on such days of brooding and reflection, the masses of those who could be no longer counted as belonging to their own nation swell into a threatening army.

With what different feelings I now stared at the endless columns, four abreast, of a mass demonstration of Viennese workers that took place one day. For almost two hours I stood there and watched with bated breath the enormous human dragon's tail which slowly snaked past. In a state of anxious depression I finally left the square and wandered homeward. En route I caught sight of the "Workers Journal" [*Arbeiter-Zeitung*], the central organ of the old Austrian Social Democracy, in a tobacco shop. At a cheap popular café where I often went to read the papers it was also lying around. Until then I could not bring myself to look over that miserable rag for more than two minutes; its whole tone worked on me like spiritual vitriol. Under the depressing influence of the demonstration, an inner voice now drove me to buy the paper and read it thoroughly. That evening I did so, surmounting the sudden anger that rose up in me from time to time at this concentrated solution of lies.

More than from any theoretical literature, I was able from my daily reading of the Social Democratic press to study the inner character of this line of thinking.

What a contrast between the scintillating phrases about freedom, beauty, and dignity in the theoretical literature, the delusive light of a seemingly profound wisdom expressed in an irksome flock of lies, the repulsive humanitarian morality—all written down with the brazen effrontery of prophetic certainty—and the brutal daily press, which stops at no dirty trick, employs every means of libel and a truly girder-bending virtuosity for lying—all on behalf of this Gospel of the new humanity! The one is certainly for the simpletons from the middle class and, of course, also for the upper "intelligentsia," the other for the masses.

For me, plunging into the literature and press of this dogma and organization meant finding my own people again.

What at first appeared to me as an unbridgeable chasm now became the occasion for a greater love than ever before.

Only a fool could be aware of this monstrous work of poison and still damn the victim. The more independent I made myself in the next few years, increasing my distance from the matter, the more my insight into the inner reasons for the Social Democratic successes grew. Now I comprehended the significance of the brutal demands to subscribe only to Red newspapers, visit only Red meetings, read only Red books, etc. With plastic lucidity I saw before my eyes the unavoidable result of this dogma of intolerance.

The psyche of the masses is not receptive to half measures and weakness.

Just like the woman whose frame of mind is fixed less by the grounds of abstract reason than by an indefinable emotional yearning toward a strength that offers her completion, and who therefore prefers to bow to the strong man rather than dominate a weakling, the masses also love a sovereign more than a supplicant, and feel themselves inwardly more gratified by a dogma that suffers no other beside it, than by the grant of liberal freedom. For the most part, they hardly know what to do with the latter and, what is more, readily feel themselves abandoned. They are just as unconscious of the shamelessness of their spiritual terrorization as of the outrageous abuse of their human freedom, in no way suspecting the inner insanity of the entire doctrine. They see only the relentless strength and brutality of its purposeful expressions, to which they always bow in the end.

If Social Democracy is opposed by a doctrine of greater truthfulness but the same brutality of enforcement, the latter will conquer, if only after the heaviest fighting....

The more I obtained insight into the outward nature of Social Democracy the greater my longing became to grasp the inner core of this doctrine.

The official party literature was of little use here. It is, insofar as it deals with economic questions, incorrect in its assertions and its proofs; insofar as political goals are attended to, it lies. In addition, inwardly I felt myself especially repelled by their newfangled hair-splitting manner of expression and style of presentation. With an enormous outpouring of words of uncertain content or unintelligible meaning, sentences are stammered together which are supposed to be as clever as they are in fact senseless. Only the decadence of our cosmopolitan bohemians allows them to feel cosily at home in this labyrinth of reasoning, to cull an "inner experience" from the dung of this literary dadaism, endorsed by the proverbial modesty of one part of our people which always suspects the more profound wisdom is to be found in what is to them personally the most incomprehensible.

But by weighing out the theoretical falsehood and absurdity of this doctrine with the truth of the phenomenon, gradually I gained a clear idea of its inner will.

At such times I was seized by bleak presentiments and virulent fear. I saw before me a doctrine consisting of egoism and hate that could follow mathematical laws to victory, but which in doing so must also bring an end to the human race.

I had learned to understand by that time the connection between this doctrine of destruction and the nature of a people who until then had been as good as unknown to me.

A knowledge of Jewry alone offers the key to comprehending the inner and, with that, the real designs of Social Democracy.

Whoever knows this nation-race [Volk] has the veil of misconceptions concerning their aim and meaning fall from his eyes, and from the mist and fog of social catch-phrases there rises sneering the distorted face of Marxism.

It is difficult today, if not impossible, for me to say when the word "Jew" first gave me cause for particular thought. In the paternal household during the lifetime of my father I cannot remember ever having heard the word. I believe the old gentleman would have considered the particular emphasis on this term to be cultural backwardness. In the course of his life he had arrived at more or less cosmopolitan views which had not only maintained themselves despite his rugged sense of nationalism, but which had also colored my own views.

Nor did I find any inducement in school which could have led me to change this adopted point of view.

In high school, to be sure, I became well acquainted with a Jewish boy who was treated by all of us with circumspection, but only because we did not especially trust his discretion, having learned from various experiences; yet I gave the matter no particular thought any more than the others did.

Not until my fourteenth or fifteenth year did I come more frequently across the word "Jew," partly in connection with political discussions. I reacted with a mild aversion and could not resist an uncomfortable feeling that always overcame me whenever denominational bickering occurred in my presence.

But at that time I did not see the matter as a question of anything else.

Linz contained very few Jews. In the course of centuries their outward appearance had been Europeanized and had become humanized; yes, I even considered them to be Germans. The absurdity of this delusion was hardly clear to me because the only distinguishing feature I perceived was their alien religion. That they had, as I believed, been persecuted because of this, sometimes turned my antipathy against untoward remarks about them almost to disgust.

As yet I did not suspect at all the existence of an organized opposition to the Jews.

Then I came to Vienna.... [The transformation of my views on anti-Semitism] cost me the most inner spiritual struggles, and only after months of wrestling between understanding and sentiment did victory come down on the side of understanding. Two years later my sentiment had followed my understanding, from then on to be its most loyal guardian and monitor.

In the course of this bitter struggle between my spiritual upbringing and cold reason, the visual instruction of the Viennese streets had performed inestimable services. There came a time when I no longer ambled blindly through the vast city, as in the first days, but rather viewed not only the buildings but also the men with open eyes.

One time as I strolled in this way through the Inner City, I suddenly came upon an apparition in a long caftan and black hair locks.

Is this also a Jew? was my first thought.

Certainly they did not look this way in Linz. I studied the man secretly and charily, but the longer I stared into this strange face, searching it feature by feature, the more the first question transformed itself in my brain into another:

Is this also a German?

As always in such cases I now began to attempt to dispel my doubts through books. I bought for a few pennies the first anti-Semitic pamphlets of my life. Unfortunately they all started with the assumption that to a certain degree the reader was at least acquainted with or even comprehended the Jewish question. For the most part, the tone was such that doubt in the end always returned to me, in part due to the superficial and extraordinarily unscientific reasoning in support of the thesis.

I would then backslide again for weeks—indeed, once even for months.

The whole thing seemed to me so atrocious, the charge so excessive that, tormented by the fear of committing an injustice, I again became worried and uncertain.

To be sure, I could no longer very well doubt that the issue concerned itself not with Germans of a special denomination, but rather with a distinct nationality unto itself; for since I had begun to busy myself with this question, and first took notice of the Jews, Vienna appeared to me in a different light than previously. Wherever I went I now saw Jews, and the more of them I saw the more sharply my eyes segregated them from other men. The Inner City and the districts north of the Danube canal, in particular, swarmed with a people that no longer even superficially possessed any likeness to Germans.

But if I still might have doubted the matter, the vacillation was conclusively dispelled by the attitude of a portion of the Jews themselves.

A great movement among them, more than a little extensive in Vienna, advocated most sharply the acknowledgement of the national character of Jewry: Zionism.

To be sure, there was the appearance that only a portion of the Jews approved of this attitude, while the great majority condemned the arrangement, even inwardly disapproved. Upon closer inspection, however, this appearance dissipated into an evil mist of pretexts advanced for reasons of pure expediency, not to say lies. For the so-called Jews of liberal mentality did not reject the Zionists as non-Jews, but only as Jews with an unpractical, perhaps even dangerous manner of publicly declaring their Judaism.

Their inner solidarity didn't change itself a bit.

This apparent struggle between Zionistic and liberal Jews disgusted me in short order. It was false through and through, consequently mendacious and little suited to the ever maintained moral elevation and purity of this race of people.

On the whole, the moral and other cleanliness of this race of people was a point in itself. That the question here was of their lack of love for water one could see from outward appearances, unfortunately too often with your eyes shut. Later, the smell of these caftan-wearers often made me sick. Added to that, there was their unclean apparel and unheroic appearance.

All this could hardly produce a very charming impression; but it became repulsive when on top of their corporeal uncleanliness one suddenly discovered the blemished morality of this chosen people.

Nothing had made me so thoughtful in a brief time as my gradually increasing insight into the activity carried on by the Jews in certain areas.

Was there any form of shamelessness, then, any kind of filth, above all in cultural life, in which at least one Jew was not taking part?

As soon as one cut ever so carefully into such a tumor, one found, like the maggot in a rotting corpse, often totally blinded by the sudden light, a little Jew.

In my eyes, as I became acquainted with its activity in the press, in art, literature and theater, Judaism carried with it a heavy load. All the unctuous protestations were more or less useless then. It was enough to look at one of the advertising kiosks, to study the names of the intellectual producers of the ghastly concoctions for stage or screen which were hyped there, to harden yourself for a long time to come. This was pestilence, spiritual pestilence, worse than the Black Death of old, and with it they infected the nation. And what a multitude was engendered and propagated by this poisoning! Naturally, the lower the intellectual and moral level of one of these producers of art, the more boundless his fecundity, until such a fellow is like a centrifuge splashing his filth in the faces of other men. One should consider the infinitude of their numbers; one should bear in mind that for one Goethe, Nature easily dumps on the present generation ten thousand of these scribblers, who poison souls just like bacterial carriers of the worst kind.

It was dreadful, but not to be overlooked, that just the Jew seemed chosen by nature in superabundant numbers for this disgraceful calling.

Should their chosenness be sought for in this?

I began to check carefully the names of all the producers of these filthy products of public artistic life. The result was ever more unfavorable for my previous posture toward the Jews. Though feeling may resist a thousand times over, the understanding must draw its own conclusion.

The fact that nine-tenths of all the literary smut, artistic rubbish, and theatrical imbecility is to be ascribed to the account of one people, who amount to hardly one-hundredth of the inhabitants of the country, could not be easily denied; this was plainly the case.

I now began to check as well my beloved "world press" from this angle.

The more thoroughly I probed, the more the object of my former admiration shriveled. The style became ever more unbearable. I had to condemn the contents as inwardly shallow and superficial; the apparent objectivity of the presentation seemed to me now to be more lies than honest truth; the authors were again—Jews.

A thousand things that I had scarcely seen before impressed me now as noteworthy; still others which formerly gave me pause I learned to comprehend and understand.

I now saw the liberal convictions of these newspapers in a different light. Their refined tone when replying to some attacks, their deathly silence when replying to others, unmasked for me a trick as clever as it was underhanded; the press's radiantly written theater reviews were always directed toward a Jewish writer, and their hostile remarks were never aimed at anyone but a German. The faint taunting of Wilhelm II suggested their persistence, just like their praise for French culture and civilization. The trashy content of the short story bordered on indecency, and in the language I heard the sounds of an alien race; the disposition of the whole phenomenon was so obviously detrimental to German culture that it could only have been deliberate.

Yet who possessed such an interest?

Was this all mere chance?

So I gradually became uncertain.

My development was hastened, though, by insights which I gained in a succession of other proceedings. I refer to the general conception of customs and morals, which one could see flaunted and displayed quite openly by a great proportion of Jewry.

Here again the streets afforded at times a truly evil object lesson.

The relationship of Jewry to prostitution and even more to the white slave trade itself could be studied in Vienna as in no other west European city, perhaps excepting the seaports of southern France. If you went at night through the streets and alleys of Leopoldstadt, you witnessed at every step, whether you wanted to or not, proceedings which remained hidden from most of the German people until the war gave the soldiers on the eastern front the opportunity to see similar goings on—or, better put, forced them to see them.

When I thus for the first time recognized the Jew as the enterprising director of this scandalous trafficking in the scum of the city, as cold-hearted as he was shameless, a gentle shiver ran down my spine.

But then a flame flared up.

I no longer avoided consideration of the Jewish question; no, now I wanted to discuss it. But as I thus learned to seek out the Jew in all the branches of cultural and artistic life and in their various expressions, suddenly I came across him in a place where I would least have expected him.

As I recognized the Jew as leader of the Social Democracy, the scales began to fall from my eyes. Therewith a long spiritual struggle found its conclusion.

Already in my daily relations with my fellow workers I noticed the astonishing versatility with which they took different positions on the same question, at times within the space of a few days or even just a few hours. I could hardly understand how men who, when spoken to in private, always held reasonable views, suddenly lost them as soon as they came under the spell of the masses. Often it was enough to drive one mad. When I was convinced after long hours of argument that this time I had finally broken the ice or had thrown light upon some rigamarole and was heartily rejoicing at the success, to my dismay the next day I had to begin again from scratch; it had all been in vain. Like an eternal pendulum the insanity of their opinions seemed to swing back and forth again and again.

I could comprehend all this: that they were dissatisfied with their lot, that they condemned their Fate which often struck them so bitterly; that they hated their employers who seemed to them to be the hardhearted executors of that Fate; that they insulted the authorities who, in their eyes, had no feeling for their circumstances; that they demonstrated against food prices and marched on the street for their demands—all this could still at least be understood without regard for reason. But what had to remain inexplicable was the limitless hatred they exhibited toward their own nationality, defaming its greatness, dirtying its history, and dragging its great men into the gutter.

This fight against their own kind, their own nest, their own homeland was as absurd as it was incredible. It was unnatural.

One could cure them of this vice temporarily but only for a few days or at most a few weeks. If one met the supposed convert later, he had reverted to his old self.

The old unnatural state had him again in its possession.

I gradually came to know that the Social Democratic press was directed chiefly by Jews; in and of itself I ascribed no special significance to this fact since the situation at the other newspapers was exactly the same. One thing did perhaps strike me: not a single paper on whose staff there were Jews could truly be spoken of as national, along the lines of my education and interpretation.

I now overcame my scruples and tried to read the products of this kind of Marxist journalism, but my revulsion grew to unending proportions; I also tried now to get to know better the manufacturers of these collections of villainy.

Starting with the publisher, they were all Jews.

I took all the Social Democratic pamphlets I could get hold of and looked for the names of their authors: Jews. I noticed the names of almost all the leaders; far and away the largest part were also members of the "chosen people," whether they were Deputies in the Reichsrat or trade-union secretaries, the chairmen of the organizations or agitators in the streets. The same sinister picture always emerged. The names of the Austerlitzes, Davids, Adlers, Ellenbogens, etc., will forever remain in my memory.

One thing had become clear to me: the leadership of the party, with whose minor representatives I had for months waged the most vehement struggle, was almost exclusively in the hands of a foreign people; for I knew conclusively, to my inner joyful satisfaction, that the Jew was no German.

Only now did I first become thoroughly acquainted with the seducer of our nation.

One year of my stay in Vienna was already enough to bring me to the conviction that no worker could be so stubborn as not to succumb to better knowledge and better explanation. I slowly became an expert in their own dogma, and used this as a weapon in the battle for my inner belief.

Success almost always came down on my side.

The great masses could be saved, if only after the most difficult sacrifice of time and patience.

But a Jew could never be liberated from his views.

I was then still childish enough to want to make clear for them the insanity of their doctrine; in my small circle I talked until my tongue was sore and my throat was hoarse, thinking I must eventually succeed in persuading them of the perniciousness of their Marxian insanity; but all the more I only achieved the opposite. It seemed as though increasing insight into the devastating effect of Social-Democratic theories and their fulfillment only served to strengthen their resolution.

The more I quarreled with them, the better I became acquainted with their dialectic. First they counted upon the stupidity of their opponent, and then, when there was no other escape, they played dumb themselves. If all this was useless, then they didn't understand you correctly, or in the blink of an eye they jumped when challenged to another topic, advanced only truisms whose acceptance they immediately applied to fundamentally different matters, and then if again seized hold of, they side-stepped matters and pretended not to know anything in particular. Whenever one attacked one of these apostles, one's hand closed on a jelly-like slime; the slime oozed through one's fingers only to reassemble itself a moment later. If one struck a really annihilating blow so that he, having been observed by the audience, could do nothing else but agree, and if one believed that that was at least one step forward, then one's astonishment would be great the next day. The Jew knew not the least little bit from the day before, he vented his old nonsense again as though nothing at all had taken place, and, if angrily called to account, acted stunned, could remember absolutely nothing except the proven soundness of his assertions from the previous day.

At times I stood there dumbfounded.

You didn't know what to marvel at more: the dexterity of their tongues or the ingenuity of their lies.

Little by little I began to hate them.

All this had but one saving grace: that to the precise extent to which the identity of the real champions or at least the propagators of Social Democracy became clear to me, love for my own nation had to grow. Considering the devilish cleverness of these seducers, who could damn the unfortunate victims? How hard it was even for me to master the dialectical mendacity of this race! Yet how futile was this kind of success with people who twist the truth in their mouths, who flatly deny what was just said in order to claim it for themselves a moment later.

No. The more I became acquainted with the Jews, the more I had to forgive the worker.

In my eyes the heaviest guilt no longer belonged with him but with all those who found it not worth the trouble to have pity for him, to give the son of the nation his birthright with unrelenting justice, shoving the tempter and corrupter up against the wall.

Guided by the experience of daily life I now began to investigate the sources of Marxist doctrine itself. Its operation was clear to me in the particulars, its success presented itself daily to my attentive gaze, the consequences I was capable of drawing out with a little imagination. The only remaining question was whether the creators already had a notion of the consequences of their creation in its final form, or whether they were themselves the victims of an error.

Both were possible, I felt.

In one case, it was the duty of every thinking man to force himself to the front of this unfortunate movement, in order perhaps to prevent the worst from happening; in the other case, however, the erstwhile authors of this international disease must have been true devils, for only in the brain of a monster—not that of a man—could the plan of an organization take on sensible form whose activity must finally lead to the ruin of human culture and thus to the devastation of the world.

In this case only combat remains as the last means of salvation, combat with every weapon that the human spirit, understanding, and will can lay hold of, regardless to whom Fate tips the scale with her blessing.

Therefore I now began to familiarize myself with the founders of this dogma in order to study the basis of the movement. That I succeeded here more quickly than perhaps I originally considered possible was thanks to my newly won, though at that time hardly profound, awareness of the Jewish question. This knowledge alone permitted me the practical comparison of reality with the theoretical humbug of the founding apostles of Social Democracy, since it had taught me to understand the language of the Jewish race, who speak in order to hide or at least to mask their thoughts; their real objective therefore is not to be found in the lines themselves, but slumbers well hidden between them.

For me it was the time of the greatest inward upheaval that I had ever had to put myself through.

I went from weak cosmopolitan to fanatical anti-Semite.

Just once more—it was the last time—nerve-wrenching thoughts came to me in profound anxiety.

As I searchingly examined the activities of the Jewish race through long periods of human history, the disquieting question suddenly arose as to whether perhaps inexplicable Fate had not, for reasons that were unknown to us poor humans, with eternal and unalterable determination desired the final victory of this little people?

Should this race, who live eternally only for this world, be adjudged this world as a reward?

Do we have an objective right to fight for our own self-preservation, or is this right only subjectively grounded in us?

As I steeped myself in the teachings of Marxism, and so could subject the activities of the Jewish race to contemplation in peaceful lucidity, Fate itself gave me its answer.

The Jewish dogma of Marxism rejects the aristocratic principle of Nature and sets in the place of the everlasting prerogative of power and strength the mass of numbers and their dead weight. Therewith it denies the value of the individual in man, disputes the importance of nationality and race and with this deprives humanity of the prerequisite of its existence and its culture. As a basis for the universe, it would lead to the end of every order conceivable to man. And so, as in this greatest of all recognizable organisms the application of such a law could only result in chaos, on earth it could only bring about their own destruction for the inhabitants of this star.

If, with the aid of his Marxist faith, the Jew triumphs over the peoples of this world, then his crown will be the funeral wreath of the human race; then this planet will move through the ether empty of men as it did millions of years before.

Eternal Nature is relentless in taking vengeance for trespasses against her commandments.

So today I believe that I am acting in accordance with the almighty Creator: *by resisting the Jews, I am fighting for the work of the Lord.*

The State

For this glorious creative ability was given only to the Aryan, whether he bears it dormant within himself or gives it to awakening life, depending whether favorable circumstances permit this or an inhospitable Nature prevents it.

From this the following realization results:

The state is a means to an end. Its end lies in the preservation and advancement of a community of physically and psychically homogeneous creatures. This preservation itself comprises first of all existence as a race and thereby permits the free development of all the forces dormant in this race. Of them a part will always primarily serve the preservation of physical life, and only the remaining part the promotion of a further spiritual development. Actually the one always creates the precondition for the other.

States which do not serve this purpose are misbegotten, monstrosities in fact. The fact of their existence changes this no more than the success of a gang of bandits can justify robbery.

We National Socialists as champions of a new philosophy of life must never base ourselves on so-called "accepted facts"—and false ones at that. If we did, we would not be the champions of a new great idea, but the coolies of the present-day lie. We must distinguish in the sharpest way between the state as a vessel and the race as its content. This vessel has meaning only if it can preserve and protect the content; otherwise it is useless.

Thus, the highest purpose of a folkish state is concern for the preservation of those original racial elements which bestow culture and create the beauty and dignity of a higher mankind. We, as Aryans, can conceive of the state only as the living organism of a nationality which not only assures the preservation of this nationality, but by the development of its spiritual and ideal abilities leads it to the highest freedom.

But what they try to palm off on us as a state today is usually nothing but a monstrosity born of deepest human error, with untold misery as a consequence.

We National Socialists know that with this conception we stand as revolutionaries in the world of today and are also branded as such. But our thoughts and actions must in no way be determined by the approval or disapproval of our time, but by the binding obligation to a truth which we have recognized. Then we may be convinced that the higher insight of posterity will not only understand our actions of today, but will also confirm their correctness and exalt them.

From this, we National Socialists derive a standard for the evaluation of a state. This value will be relative from the standpoint of the individual nationality, absolute from that of humanity as such. This means, in other words:

The quality of a state cannot be evaluated according to the cultural level or the power of this state in the frame of the outside world, but solely and exclusively by the degree of this institution's virtue for the nationality involved in each special case.

A state can be designated as exemplary if it is not only compatible with the living conditions of the nationality it is intended to represent, but if in practice it keeps this nationality alive by its own very existence—quite regardless of the importance of this state formation within the framework of the outside world. For the function of the state is not to create abilities, but only to open the road for those forces which are present.

Thus, conversely, a state can be designated as bad if, despite a high cultural level, it dooms the bearer of this culture in his racial composition. For thus it destroys to all intents and purposes the premise for the survival of this culture which it did not create, but which is the fruit of a culture-creating nationality safeguarded by a living integration through the state. The state does not represent the content, but a form. *A people's cultural level at any time does not, therefore, provide a standard for measuring the quality of the state* in which it lives. It is easily understandable that a people highly endowed with culture offers a more valuable picture than a Negro tribe; nevertheless, the state organism of the former, viewed according to its fulfillment of purpose, can be inferior to that of the Negro. Though the best state and the best state form are not able to extract from a people abilities which are simply lacking and never did exist, a bad state is assuredly able to kill originally existing abilities by permitting or even promoting the destruction of the racial culture-bearer.

Hence our judgment concerning the quality of a state can primarily be determined only by the relative utility it possesses for a definite nationality, and in no event by the intrinsic importance attributable to it in the world.

This relative judgment can be passed quickly and easily, but the judgment concerning absolute value only with great difficulty, since this absolute judgment is no longer determined merely by the state, but by the quality and level of the nationality in question.

If, therefore, we speak of a higher mission of the state, we must not forget that the higher mission lies essentially in the nationality whose free development the state must merely make possible by the organic force of its being.

Hence, if we propound the question of how the state which we Germans need should be constituted, we must first clearly understand what kind of people it is to contain and what purpose it is to serve.

Our German nationality, unfortunately, is no longer based on a unified racial nucleus. The blending process of the various original components has advanced so far that we might speak of a new race. On the contrary, the poisonings of the blood which have befallen our people, especially since the Thirty Years' War, have led not only to a decomposition of our blood, but also of our soul. The open borders of our fatherland, the association with un-German foreign bodies along these frontier districts, but above all the strong and continuous influx of foreign blood into the interior of the Reich itself, due to its continuous renewal, leaves no time for an absolute blending. No new race is distilled out, the racial constituents remain side by side, with the result that, especially in critical moments in which otherwise a herd habitually gathers together, the German people scatters to all the four winds. Not only are the basic racial elements scattered territorially, but on a small scale within the same territory. Beside Nordic men Easterners, beside Easterners Dinarics, beside both of these Westerners, and mixtures in between. On the one hand, this is a great disadvantage: the German people lack that sure herd instinct which is based on unity of the blood and, especially in moments of threatening danger, preserves nations from destruction in so far as all petty inner differences in such peoples vanish at once on such occasions and the solid front of a unified herd confronts the common enemy. This co-existence of unblended basic racial elements of the most varying kind accounts for what is termed *hyper-individualism* in Germany. In peaceful periods it may sometimes do good services, but taking all things together, it has robbed us of world domination. If the German people in its historic development had possessed that herd unity which other peoples enjoyed, the German Reich today would doubtless be mistress of the globe. World history would have taken a different course, and no one can distinguish whether in this way we would not have obtained what so many blinded pacifists today hope to gain by begging, whining, and whimpering: *a peace, supported not by the palm branches of tearful, pacifist female mourners, but based on the victorious sword of a master people, putting the world into the service of a higher culture.*

The fact of the non-existence of a nationality of unified blood has brought us untold misery. It has given capital cities to many small German potentates, but deprived the German people of the master's right.

Today our people are still suffering from this inner division; but what brought us misfortune in the past and present can be our blessing for the future. For detrimental as it was on the one hand that a complete blending of our original racial components did not take place, and that the formation of a unified national body was thus prevented, it was equally fortunate on the other hand that in this way at least a part of our best blood was preserved pure and escaped racial degeneration.

Assuredly, if there had been a complete blending of our original racial elements, a unified national body would have arisen; however, as every racial cross-breeding proves, it would have been endowed with a smaller cultural capacity than the highest of the original components originally possessed. This is the blessing of the absence of complete blending: that today in our German national body we still possess great unmixed stocks of Nordic-Germanic people whom we may consider the most precious treasure for our future. In the confused period of ignorance of all racial laws, when a man appeared to be simply a man, with full equality—clarity may have been lacking with regard to the different value of the various original elements. Today we know that a complete intermixture of the components of our people might, in consequence of the unity thus produced, have given us outward power, but that the highest goal of mankind would have been unattainable, since the sole bearer, whom Fate had clearly chosen for this completion, would have perished in the general racial porridge of the unified people.

But what, through none of our doing, a kind Fate prevented, we must today examine and evaluate from the standpoint of the knowledge we have now acquired.

Anyone who speaks of a mission of the German people on earth must know that it can exist only in the formation of a state which sees its highest task in the preservation and promotion of the most noble elements of our nationality, indeed of all mankind, which still remain intact.

Thus, for the first time the state achieves a lofty inner goal. Compared to the absurd catchword about safeguarding law and order, thus laying a peaceable groundwork for mutual swindles, the task of preserving and advancing the highest humanity, given to this earth by the benevolence of the Almighty, seems a truly high mission.

From a dead mechanism which only lays claim to existence for its own sake, there must be formed a living organism with the exclusive aim of serving a higher idea.

The German Reich as a state must embrace all Germans and has the task, not only of assembling and preserving the most valuable stocks of basic racial elements in this people, but slowly and surely of raising them to a dominant position.

Thus, a condition which is fundamentally one of paralysis is replaced by a period of struggle, but as everywhere and always in this world, here, too, the saying remains valid that "he who rests—rusts," and, furthermore, that victory lies eternally and exclusively in attack. The greater the goal we have in mind in our struggle, and the smaller the understanding of the broad masses for it may be at the moment, all the more gigantic, as the experience of world history shows, will be the success—and the significance of this success if the goal is correctly comprehended and the struggle is carried through with unswerving perseverance.

Of course it may be more soothing for many of our present official helmsmen of the state to work for the preservation of an *existing* condition than having to fight for a new one. They will find it much easier to regard the state as a mechanism which exists simply in order to keep itself alive, since in turn their lives *"belong to the state"*—as they are accustomed to put it. As though something which sprang from the nationality could logically serve anything else than the nationality or man could work for anything else than man. *Of course, as I have said before, it is easier to see in state authority the mere formal mechanism of an organization than the sovereign embodiment of a nationality's instinct of self-preservation on earth.* For in the one case the state, as well as state authority, is for these weak minds a purpose in itself, while in the other, it is only a mighty weapon in the service of the great, eternal life struggle for existence, a weapon to which everyone must submit because it is not formal and mechanical, but the expression of a common will for preserving life.

Hence, in the struggle for our new conception, which is entirely in keeping with the primal meaning of things, we shall find few fellow warriors in a society which not only is physically senile but, sad to say, usually, mentally as well. Only exceptions, old men with young hearts and fresh minds, will come to us from those classes, never those who see the ultimate meaning of their life task in the preservation of an existing condition.

We are confronted by the endless army, not so much of the deliberately bad as of the mentally lazy and indifferent, including those with a stake in the preservation of the present condition. But precisely in this apparent hopelessness of our gigantic struggle lies the greatness of our task and also the possibility of our success. The battle-cry which either scares away the small spirits at the very start, or soon makes them despair, will be the signal for the assemblage of real fighting natures. And this we must see clearly: *If in a people a certain amount of the highest energy and active force seems concentrated upon one goal and hence is definitively removed from the inertia of the broad masses, this small percentage has risen to be master over the entire number. World history is made by minorities when this minority of number embodies the majority of will and determination.*

What, therefore, may appear as a difficulty today is in reality the premise for our victory. Precisely in the greatness and the difficulties of our task lies the probability that only the best fighters will step forward to struggle for it. And in this selection lies the guaranty of success....

If as the first task of the state in the service and for the welfare of its nationality we recognize the preservation, care, and development of the best racial elements, it is natural that this care must not only extend to the birth of every little national and racial comrade, but that it must educate the young offspring to become a valuable link in the chain of future reproduction.

And as in general the precondition for spiritual achievement lies in the racial quality of the human material at hand, education in particular must first of all consider and promote physical health; for taken in the mass, a healthy, forceful spirit will be found only in a healthy and forceful body. The fact that geniuses are sometimes physically not very fit, or actually sick, is no argument against this. Here we have to do with exceptions which—as everywhere—only confirm the rule. But if the mass of a people consists of physical degenerates, from this swamp a really great spirit will very seldom arise. In any case his activity will not meet with great success. The degenerate rabble will either not understand him at all, or it will be so weakened in will that it can no longer follow the lofty flight of such an eagle.

Realizing this, the folkish state must not adjust its entire educational work primarily to the inoculation of mere knowledge, but to the breeding of absolutely healthy bodies. The training of mental abilities is only secondary. And here again, first place must be taken by the development of character, especially the promotion of will-power and determination, combined with the training of joy in responsibility, and only in last place comes scientific schooling.

Here the folkish state must proceed from the assumption *that a man of little scientific education but physically healthy, with a good, firm character, imbued with the joy of determination and will-power, is more valuable for the national community than a clever weakling.* A people of scholars, if they are physically degenerate, weak-willed and cowardly pacifists, will not storm the heavens, indeed they will not even be able to safeguard their existence on this earth. In the hard struggle of destiny the man who knows least seldom succumbs, but always he who from his knowledge draws the weakest consequences and is most lamentable in transforming them into action. Here too, finally, a certain harmony must be present. *A decayed body is not made the least more aesthetic by a brilliant mind,* indeed the highest intellectual training could not be justified if its bearers were at the same time physically degenerate and crippled, weak-willed, wavering and cowardly individuals. What makes the Greek ideal of beauty a model is the wonderful combination of the most magnificent physical beauty with brilliant mind and noblest soul.

If Moltke's saying, "In the long run only the able man has luck," is anywhere applicable, it is surely to the relation between body and mind; the mind, too, if it is healthy, will as a rule and in the long run dwell only in the healthy body.

Physical training in the folkish state, therefore, is not an affair of the individual, and not even a matter which primarily regards the parents and only secondly or thirdly interests the community; it is a requirement for the self-preservation of the nationality, represented and protected by the state. Just as the state, as far as purely scientific education is concerned, even today interferes with the individual's right of self-determination and upholds the right of the totality toward him by subjecting the child to compulsory education without asking whether the parents want it or not—in far greater measure the folkish state must some day enforce its authority against the individual's ignorance or lack of understanding in questions regarding the preservation of the nationality. It must so organize its educational work that the young bodies are treated expediently in their earliest childhood and obtain the necessary steeling for later life. It must above all prevent the rearing of a generation of hothouse plants.

This work of care and education must begin with the young mother. Just as it became possible in the course of careful work over a period of decades to achieve antiseptic cleanliness in childbirth and reduce puerperal fever to a few cases, it must and will be possible, by a thorough training of nurses and mothers themselves, to achieve a treatment of the child in his first years that will serve as an excellent basis for future development.

The school as such in a folkish state must create infinitely more free time for physical training. It is not permissible to burden young brains with a ballast only a fraction of which they retain, as experience shows, not to mention the fact that as a rule it is unnecessary trifles that stick instead of essentials, since the young child cannot undertake a sensible sifting of the material that has been funneled into him. If today, even in the curriculum of the secondary schools, gymnastics gets barely two hours a week and participation in it is not even obligatory, but is left open to the individual, that is a gross incongruity compared to the purely mental training. Not a day should go by in which the young man does not receive one hour's physical training in the morning and one in the afternoon, covering every type of sport and gymnastics. And here one sport in particular must not be forgotten, which in the eyes of many "folkish" minded people is considered vulgar and undignified: boxing. It is incredible what false opinions are widespread in "educated" circles. It is regarded as natural and honorable that a young man should learn to fence and proceed to fight duels right and left, but if he boxes, it is supposed to be vulgar! Why? There is no sport that so much as this one promotes the spirit of attack, demands lightning decisions, and trains the body in steel dexterity. It is no more vulgar for two young men to fight out a difference of opinion with their fists than with a piece of whetted iron. It is not less noble if a man who has been attacked defends himself against his assailant with his fists, instead of running away and yelling for a policeman. But above all, the young, healthy body must also learn to suffer blows. Of course this may seem wild to the eyes of our present spiritual fighters. But it is not the function of the folkish state to breed a colony of peaceful aesthetes and physical degenerates. Not in the respectable shopkeeper or virtuous old maid does it see its ideal of humanity, but in the defiant embodiment of manly strength and in women who are able to bring men into the world.

And so sport does not exist only to make the individual strong, agile and bold; it should also toughen him and teach him to bear hardships.

If our entire intellectual upper crust had not been brought up so exclusively on upper-class etiquette; if instead they had learned boxing thoroughly, a German revolution of pimps, deserters, and such-like rabble would never have been possible; for what gave this revolution success was not the bold, courageous energy of the revolutionaries, but the cowardly, wretched indecision of those who led the state and were responsible for it.

The fact is that our whole intellectual leadership had received only "intellectual" education and hence could not help but be defenseless the moment not intellectual weapons but the crowbar went into action on the opposing side. All this was possible only because as a matter of principle especially our higher educational system did not train men, but officials, engineers, technicians, chemists, jurists, journalists, and to keep these intellectuals from dying out, professors.

Our intellectual leadership always performed brilliant feats, while our leadership in the matter of will-power usually remained beneath all criticism.

Certainly it will not be possible to turn a man of basically cowardly disposition into a courageous man by education, but just as certainly a man who in himself is not cowardly will be paralyzed in the development of his qualities if due to deficiencies in his education he is from the very start inferior to his neighbor in physical strength and dexterity. To what extent the conviction of physical ability promotes a man's sense of courage, even arouses his spirit of attack, can best be judged by the example of the army. Here, too, essentially, we have to deal not solely with heroes but with the broad average. But the superior training of the German soldier in peacetime inoculated the whole gigantic organism with that suggestive faith in its own superiority to an extent which even our foes had not considered possible. For the immortal offensive spirit and offensive courage achieved in the long months of midsummer and autumn 1914 by the forward-sweeping German armies was the result of that untiring training which in the long, long years of peace obtained the most incredible achievement often out of frail bodies, and thus cultivated that self-confidence which was not lost even in the terror of the greatest battles.

Particularly our German people which today lies broken and defenseless, exposed to the kicks of all the world, needs that suggestive force that lies in self-confidence. This self-confidence must be inculcated in the young national comrade from childhood on. His whole education and training must be so ordered as to give him the conviction that he is absolutely superior to others. Through his physical strength and dexterity, he must recover his faith in the invincibility of his whole people. For what formerly led the German army to victory was the sum of the confidence which each individual had in himself and all together in their leadership. What will raise the German people up again is confidence in the possibility of regaining its freedom. And this conviction can only be the final product of the same feeling in millions of individuals.

Here, too, we must not deceive ourselves:

Immense was the collapse of our people, and the exertion needed to end this misery some day will have to be just as immense. Anyone who thinks that our present bourgeois education for peace and order will give our people the strength some day to smash the present world order, which means our doom, and to hurl the links of our slavery into the face of our enemies, is bitterly mistaken. Only by super-abundance of national willpower, thirst for freedom, and highest passion, will we compensate for what we formerly lacked....

Propaganda and Organization

In several respects the year 1921 had assumed a special significance for me and the movement.

After my entrance into the German Workers' Party, I at once took over the management of propaganda. I regarded this department as by far the most important. For the present, it was less important to rack one's brains over organizational questions than to transmit the idea itself to a larger number of people. Propaganda had to run far in advance of organization and provide it with the human material to be worked on. Moreover, I am an enemy of too rapid and too pedantic organizing. It usually produces nothing but a dead mechanism, seldom a living organization. For organization is a thing that owes its existence to organic life, organic development. Ideas which have gripped a certain number of people will always strive for a greater order, and a great value must be attributed to this inner molding. Here, too, we must reckon with the weakness of men, which leads the individual, at first at least, instinctively to resist a superior mind. If an organization is mechanically ordered from above, there exists a great danger that a once appointed leader, not yet accurately evaluated and perhaps none too capable, will from jealousy strive to prevent the rise of abler elements within the movement. The harm that arises in such a case can, especially in a young movement, be of catastrophic significance.

For this reason it is more expedient for a time to disseminate an idea by propaganda from a central point and then carefully to search and examine the gradually gathering human material for leading minds. Sometimes it will turn out that men inconspicuous in themselves must nevertheless be regarded as born leaders.

But it would be absolutely mistaken to regard a wealth of theoretical knowledge as characteristic proof for the qualities and abilities of a leader.

The opposite is often the case.

The great *theoreticians* are only in the rarest cases great *organizers*, since the greatness of the *theoretician* and *program-maker* lies primarily in the *recognition* and *establishment of abstractly correct laws*, while the *organizer* must primarily be a *psychologist*. He must take people as they are and must therefore know them. He must not overestimate them, any more than he must underestimate them in the mass. On the contrary, he must endeavor to take weakness and bestiality equally into account, in order, considering all factors, to create a formation which will be a living organism, imbued with strong and stable power, and thus suited to upholding an idea and paving the way for its success.

Even more seldom, however, is a great theoretician a great leader. Much more readily will an *agitator* be one, something which many who only work scientifically on the question do not want to hear. And yet that is understandable. An agitator who demonstrates the ability to transmit an idea to the broad masses must always be a psychologist, even if he were only a demagogue. Then he will still be more suited for leadership than the unworldly theoretician, who is ignorant of people. *For leading means: being able to move masses.* The gift of shaping ideas has nothing to do with ability as a leader. And it is quite useless to argue which is of greater importance, to set up ideals and aims for mankind, or to realize them. Here, as so often in life: one would be utterly meaningless without the other. The finest theoretical insight remains without purpose and value if the leader does not set the masses in motion toward it. And conversely, of what avail would be all the genius and energy of a leader, if the brilliant theoretician did not set up aims for the human struggle? However, the combination of theoretician, organizer, and leader in one person is the rarest thing that can be found on this earth; this combination makes the great man.

As I have already remarked, I devoted myself to propaganda in the first period of my activity in the movement. What it had to do was gradually to fill a small nucleus of men with the new doctrine, and so prepare the material which could later furnish the first elements of an organization.

When a movement harbors the purpose of tearing down a world and building another in its place, complete clarity must reign in the ranks of its own leadership with regard to the following principles:

Every movement will first have to sift the human material it wins into two large groups: supporters and members.

The function of propaganda is to attract supporters, the function of organization is to win members.

A supporter of a movement is one who declares himself to be in agreement with its aims, a member is one who fights for them.

The supporter is made amenable to the movement by propaganda. The member is induced by the organization to participate personally in the recruiting of new supporters, from whom in turn members can be developed.

Since being a supporter requires only a passive recognition of an idea, while membership demands active advocacy and defense, to ten supporters there will at most be one or two members.

Being a supporter is rooted only in understanding, membership in the courage personally to advocate and disseminate what has been understood.

Understanding in its passive form corresponds to the majority of mankind which is lazy and cowardly. Membership requires an activistic frame of mind and thus corresponds only to the minority of men.

Propaganda will consequently have to see that an idea wins supporters, while the organization must take the greatest care only to make the most valuable elements among the supporters into members. Propaganda does not, therefore, need to rack its brains with regard to the importance of every individual instructed by it, with regard to his ability, capacity, and understanding, or character, while the organization must carefully gather from the mass of these elements those which really make possible the victory of the movement.

Propaganda tries to force a doctrine on the whole people; the organization embraces within its scope only those who do not threaten on psychological grounds to become a brake on the further dissemination of the idea.

Propaganda works on the general public from the standpoint of an idea and makes them ripe for the victory of this idea, while the organization achieves victory by the persistent, organic, and militant union of those supporters who seem willing and able to carry on the fight for victory.

The victory of an idea will be possible the sooner, the more comprehensively propaganda has prepared people as a whole and the more exclusive, rigid, and firm the organization which carries out the fight in practice.

From this it results that the number of supporters cannot be too large, but that the number of members can more readily be too large than too small.

If propaganda has imbued a whole people with an idea, the organization can draw the consequences with a handful of men. Propaganda and organization, in other words, supporters and members thus stand in a certain mutual relation. The better the propaganda has worked, the smaller the organization can be; and the larger the number of supporters, the more modest the number of members can be; and vice versa: the poorer the propaganda is, the larger the organization must be, and the smaller the host of followers of a movement remains, the more extensive the number of its members must be, if it still hopes to count on any success at all.

The first task of propaganda is to win people for subsequent organization; the first task of organization is to win men for the continuation of propaganda. The second task of propaganda is the disruption of the existing state of affairs and the permeation of this state of affairs with the new doctrine, while the second task of organization must be the struggle for power, thus to achieve the final success of the doctrine.

The most striking success of a revolution based on a philosophy of life will always have been achieved when the new philosophy of life as far as possible has been taught to all men, and, if necessary, later forced upon them, while the organization of the idea, in other words, the movement, should embrace only as many as are absolutely required for occupying the nerve centers of the state in question.

This, in other words, means the following:

In every really great world-shaking movement, propaganda will first have to spread the idea of this movement. Thus, it will indefatigably attempt to make the new thought processes clear to the others, and therefore to draw them over to their own ground, or to make them uncertain of their previous conviction. Now, since the dissemination of an idea, that is, propaganda, must have a firm backbone, the doctrine will have to give itself a solid organization. The organization obtains its members from the general body of supporters won by propaganda. The latter will grow the more rapidly, the more intensively the propaganda is carried on, and the latter in turn can work better, the stronger and more powerful the organization is that stands behind it.

Hence it is the highest task of the organization to make sure that no inner disunities within the membership of the movement lead to a split and hence a weakening of the movement's work; further, that the spirit of determined attack does not die out, but is continuously renewed and reinforced. The number of members need not grow infinitely; on the contrary: since only a small fraction of mankind is by nature energetic and bold, a movement which endlessly enlarges its organization would inevitably be weakened some day as a result. *Organizations, in other words, membership figures, which grow beyond a certain level gradually lose their fighting power and are no longer capable of supporting or utilizing the propaganda of an idea resolutely and aggressively.*

The greater and more essentially revolutionary an idea is, the more activistic its membership will become, since the revolutionary force of a doctrine involves a danger for its supporters, which seems calculated to keep cowardly little shopkeepers away from it. They will privately regard themselves as supporters, but decline to make a public avowal of this by membership. *By virtue of this fact, the organization of a really revolutionary idea obtains as members only the most active among the supporters won over by propaganda.* And precisely in this activity of a movement's membership, guaranteed by natural selection, lies the premise for equally active future propaganda as well as a successful struggle for the realization of the idea.

The greatest danger that can threaten a movement is a membership which has grown abnormally as a result of too rapid successes. For, just as a movement is shunned by all cowardly and egotistic individuals, as long as it has to fight bitterly, these same people rush with equal alacrity to acquire membership when a success of the party has been made probable or already realized by developments.

To this it must be ascribed why many victorious movements, on the point of success, or, rather, the ultimate completion of their will, suddenly from inexplicable inner weakness, flag, stop fighting, and finally die out. In consequence of their first victory, so many inferior, unworthy, and worst of all cowardly, elements have entered their organization that these inferior people finally achieve predominance over the militants and then force the movement into the service of their own interests, lower it to the level of their own scanty heroism, and do nothing to complete the victory of the original idea. The fanatical zeal has been blurred, the fighting force paralyzed, or, as the bourgeois world correctly puts it in such cases: "Water has been mixed with the wine." And when that happens, the trees can no longer grow skyward.

It is, therefore, most necessary that a movement, for pure reasons of self-preservation, should, once it has begun to achieve success, immediately block enrollments and henceforth increase its organization only with extreme caution and after the most thorough scrutiny. Only in this way will it be able to preserve the core of the movement in unvitiated freshness and health. *It must see to it that, from this point on, this core alone shall exclusively lead the movement, that is, determine the propaganda which should lead to its universal recognition, and, in full possession of the power, undertake the actions which are necessary for the practical realization of its ideas.*

It must not only occupy all the important positions of the conquered territory with the basic core of the old movement, but also constitute the entire leadership. And this until the principles and doctrines of the party have become the foundation and content of the new state. Only then can the reins gradually be handed over to the special government of this state, born of its spirit. This, however, in turn occurs for the most part only in mutual struggle, since it is less a question of human insight than of the play and workings of forces which can perhaps be recognized from the first, but cannot forever be guided.

All great movements, whether of a religious or a political nature, must attribute their mighty successes only to the recognition and application of these principles, and all lasting successes in particular are not even thinkable without consideration of these laws....

18

Benito Mussolini

THE DOCTRINE OF FASCISM

Benito Mussolini (1883–1945) was born in a small village in northern Italy, his father a blacksmith, his mother a schoolteacher. As a young man he worked briefly as a schoolteacher himself. He early became a socialist and lived for two years in Switzerland, where he attended lectures by Vilfredo Pareto at Lausanne and read the works of Sorel, Nietzsche, and Schopenhauer, all of whom influenced his later political visions. From 1912 to 1914 he was editor of Avanti! *the newspaper of the Italian Socialist party. A neutralist at the beginning of World War I, he soon moved to fervent interventionism, working for the entry of Italy into the war on the side of the Allies. In November 1914 he was expelled from the Socialist party and founded his own paper, the* Il Popolo d'Italia *in Milan. From 1915 to 1917 he served in the Italian army. In 1919 he founded the* Fasci di Combattimento, *a revolutionary network of political cells appealing to ex-socialists, disgruntled war veterans, syndicalists, intellectuals, and petty bourgeois voters which gained a reputation for terrorism and anti-Socialist propaganda. The maneuvering behind the Fascist "March on Rome" in October 1922 forced King Victor Emmanuel III to name Mussolini Prime Minister. In the following years Mussolini crushed all opposition and from 1925 ruled Italy as authoritarian leader (Duce). His dismissal from office in July 1943 brought the collapse of the Fascist regime. He was arrested and placed in custody at a ski resort on the Gran Sasso in the Apennines. Rescued by German commandos, he escaped to Germany and reentered Italy in September 1943, a broken man. In late April 1945 he was arrested by Italian partisans and executed with his mistress, Clara Petacci, near Lake Como on April 28.*

The essay printed below was first published in the Enciclopedia Italiana *in 1932.*

(i) Fundamental Ideas

1. Like every sound political conception, Fascism is both practice and thought; action in which a doctrine is immanent, and a doctrine which, arising out of a given system of historical forces, remains embedded in them and works there from within. Hence it has a form correlative to the contingencies of place and time, but it has also a

Benito Mussolini, "The Doctrine of Fascism" (1932), selections from John W. Boyer and Jan Goldstein, eds., *Twentieth-Century Europe: University of Chicago Readings in Western Civilization* (Chicago, University of Chicago Press, 1986), 219–233.

content of thought which raises it to a formula of truth in the higher level of the history of thought. In the world one does not act spiritually as a human will dominating other wills without a conception of the transient and particular reality under which it is necessary to act, and of the permanent and universal reality in which the first has its being and its life. In order to know men it is necessary to know man; and in order to know man it is necessary to know reality and its laws. There is no concept of the State which is not fundamentally a concept of life: philosophy or intuition, a system of ideas which develops logically or is gathered up into a vision or into a faith, but which is always, at least virtually, an organic conception of the world.

2. Thus Fascism could not be understood in many of its practical manifestations as a party organization, as a system of education, as a discipline, if it were not always looked at in the light of its whole way of conceiving life, a spiritualized way. The world seen through Fascism is not this material world which appears on the surface, in which man is an individual separated from all others and standing by himself, and in which he is governed by a natural law that makes him instinctively live a life of selfish and momentary pleasure. The man of Fascism is an individual who is nation and fatherland, which is a moral law, binding together individuals and the generations into a tradition and a mission, suppressing the instinct for a life enclosed within the brief round of pleasure in order to restore within duty a higher life free from the limits of time and space: a life in which the individual, through the denial of himself, through the sacrifice of his own private interests, through death itself, realizes that completely spiritual existence in which his value as a man lies.

3. Therefore it is a spiritualized conception, itself the result of the general reaction of modern times against the flabby materialistic positivism of the nineteenth century. Anti-positivistic, but positive: not sceptical, nor agnostic, nor pessimistic, nor passively optimistic, as are, in general, the doctrines (all negative) that put the centre of life outside man, who with his free will can and must create his own world. Fascism desires an active man, one engaged in activity with all his energies: it desires a man virilely conscious of the difficulties that exist in action and ready to face them. It conceives of life as a struggle, considering that it behoves man to conquer for himself that life truly worthy of him, creating first of all in himself the instrument (physical, moral, intellectual) in order to construct it. Thus for the single individual, thus for the nation, thus for humanity. Hence the high value of culture in all its forms (art, religion, science), and the enormous importance of education. Hence also the essential value of work, with which man conquers nature and creates the human world (economic, political, moral, intellectual).

4. This positive conception of life is clearly an ethical conception. It covers the whole of reality, not merely the human activity which controls it. No action can be divorced from moral judgement; there is nothing in the world which can be deprived of the value which belongs to everything in its relation to moral ends. Life, therefore, as conceived by the Fascist, is serious, austere, religious: the whole of it is poised in a world supported by the moral and responsible forces of the spirit. The Fascist disdains the "comfortable" life.

5. Fascism is a religious conception in which man is seen in his immanent relationship with a superior law and with an objective Will that transcends the particular individual and raises him to conscious membership of a spiritual society. Whoever has seen in the religious politics of the Fascist regime nothing but mere opportunism has not understood that Fascism besides being a system of government is also, and above all, a system of thought.

6. Fascism is an historical conception, in which man is what he is only in so far as he works with the spiritual process in which he finds himself, in the family or social group, in the nation and in the history in which all nations collaborate. From this follows the great value of tradition, in memories, in language, in customs, in the standards of social life. Outside history man is nothing. Consequently Fascism is opposed to all the individualistic abstractions of a materialistic nature like those of the eighteenth century; and it is opposed to all Jacobin utopias and innovations. It does not consider that "happiness" is possible upon earth, as it appeared to be in the desire of the economic literature of the eighteenth century, and hence it rejects all teleological theories according to which mankind would reach a definitive stabilized condition at a certain period in history. This implies putting oneself outside history and life, which is a continual change and coming to be. Politically, Fascism wishes to be a realistic doctrine; practically, it aspires to solve only the problems which arise historically of themselves and that of themselves find or suggest their own solution. To act among men, as to act in the natural world, it is necessary to enter into the process of reality and to master the already operating forces.

7. Against individualism, the Fascist conception is for the State; and it is for the individual in so far as he coincides with the State, which is the conscience and universal will of man in his historical existence. It is opposed to classical Liberalism, which arose from the necessity of reacting against absolutism, and which brought its historical purpose to an end when the State was transformed into the conscience and will of the people. Liberalism denied the State in the interests of the particular individual; Fascism reaffirms the State as the true reality of the individual. And if liberty is to be the attribute of the real man, and not of that abstract puppet envisaged by individualistic Liberalism, Fascism is for liberty. And for the only liberty which can be a real thing, the liberty of the State and of the individual within the State. Therefore, for the Fascist, everything is in the State, and nothing human or spiritual exists, much less has value, outside the State. In this sense Fascism is totalitarian, and the Fascist State, the synthesis and unity of all values, interprets, develops and gives strength to the whole life of the people.

8. Outside the State there can be neither individuals nor groups (political parties, associations, syndicates, classes). Therefore Fascism is opposed to Socialism, which confines the movement of history within the class struggle and ignores the unity of classes established in one economic and moral reality in the State; and analogously it is opposed to class syndicalism. Fascism recognizes the real exigencies for which the socialist and syndicalist movement arose, but while recognizing them wishes to bring them under the control of the State and give them a purpose within the corporative system of interests reconciled within the unity of the State.

9. Individuals form classes according to the similarity of their interests, they form syndicates according to differentiated economic activities within these interests; but they form first, and above all, the State, which is not to be thought of numerically as the sum-total of individuals forming the majority of a nation. And consequently Fascism is opposed to Democracy, which equates the nation to the majority, lowering it to the level of that majority; nevertheless it is the purest form of democracy if the nation is conceived, as it should be, qualitatively and not quantitatively, as the most powerful idea (most powerful because most moral, most coherent, most true) which acts within the nation as the conscience and the will of a few, even of One, which ideal tends to become active within the conscience and the will of all—that is to say, of all those who rightly constitute a nation by reason of nature, history or race, and have set out upon the same line of development and spiritual formation as one conscience and one sole will. Not a race, nor a geographically determined region, but as a community historically perpetuating itself, a multitude unified by a single idea, which is the will to existence and to power: consciousness of itself, personality.

10. This higher personality is truly the nation in so far as it is the State. It is not the nation that generates the State, as according to the old naturalistic concept which served as the basis of the political theories of the national States of the nineteenth century. Rather the nation is created by the State, which gives to the people, conscious of its own moral unity, a will and therefore an effective existence. The right of a nation to independence derives not from a literary and ideal consciousness of its own being, still less from a more or less unconscious and inert acceptance of a *de facto* situation, but from an active consciousness, from a political will in action and ready to demonstrate its own rights: that is to say, from a state already coming into being. The State, in fact, as the universal ethical will, is the creator of right.

11. The nation as the State is an ethical reality which exists and lives in so far as it develops. To arrest its development is to kill it. Therefore the State is not only the authority which governs and gives the form of laws and the value of spiritual life to the wills of individuals, but it is also a power that makes its will felt abroad, making it known and respected, in other words, demonstrating the fact of its universality in all the necessary directions of its development. It is consequently organization and expansion, at least virtually. Thus it can be likened to the human will which knows no limits to its development and realizes itself in testing its own limitlessness.

12. The Fascist State, the highest and most powerful form of personality, is a force, but a spiritual force, which takes over all the forms of the moral and intellectual life of man. It cannot therefore confine itself simply to the functions of order and supervision as Liberalism desired. It is not simply a mechanism which limits the sphere of the supposed liberties of the individual. It is the form, the inner standard and the discipline of the whole person; it saturates the will as well as the intelligence. Its principle, the central inspiration of the human personality living in the civil community, pierces into the depths and makes its home in the heart of the man of action as well as of the thinker, of the artist as well as of the scientist: it is the soul of the soul.

13. Fascism, in short, is not only the giver of laws and the founder of institutions, but the educator and promoter of spiritual life. It wants to remake, not the forms of human

life, but its content, man, character, faith. And to this end it requires discipline and authority that can enter into the spirits of men and there govern unopposed. Its sign, therefore, is the Lictors' rods, the symbol of unity, of strength and justice.

(ii) Political and Social Doctrine

1. When in the now distant March of 1919 I summoned to Milan, through the columns of the *Popolo d'Italia*, my surviving supporters who had followed me since the constitution of the Fasces of Revolutionary Action, founded in January 1915, there was no specific doctrinal plan in my mind. I had known and lived through only one doctrine, that of the Socialism of 1903–4 up to the winter of 1914, almost ten years. My experience in this had been that of a follower and of a leader, but not that of a theoretician. My doctrine, even in that period, had been a doctrine of action. An unequivocal Socialism, universally accepted, did not exist after 1905, when the Revisionist Movement began in Germany under Bernstein and there was formed in opposition to that, in the see-saw of tendencies, an extreme revolutionary movement, which in Italy never emerged from the condition of mere words, whilst in Russian Socialism it was the prelude to Bolshevism. Reform, Revolution, Centralization—even the echoes of the terminology are now spent; whilst in the great river of Fascism are to be found the streams which had their source in Sorel, Peguy, in the Lagardelle of the *Mouvement Socialiste* and the groups of Italian Syndicalists, who between 1904 and 1914 brought a note of novelty into Italian Socialism, which by that time had been devitalized and drugged by fornication with Giolitti, in *Pagine Libere* of Olivetti, *La Lupa* of Orano and *Divenire Sociale* of Enrico Leone.

In 1919, at the end of the War, Socialism as a doctrine was already dead: it existed only as hatred, it had still only one possibility, especially in Italy, that of revenge against those who had wished for the War and who should be made to expiate it. The *Popolo d'Italia* expressed it in its sub-title—"The Newspaper of Combatants and Producers." The word "producers" was already the expression of a tendency. Fascism was not given out to the wet nurse of a doctrine elaborated beforehand round a table: it was born of the need for action; it was not a party, but in its first two years it was a movement against all parties. The name which I gave to the organization defined its characteristics. Nevertheless, whoever rereads, in the now crumpled pages of the time, the account of the constituent assembly of the *Fasci italiani di Combattimento* will not find a doctrine, but a series of suggestions, of anticipations, of admonitions, which when freed from the inevitable vein of contingency, were destined later, after a few years, to develop into a series of doctrinal attitudes which made of Fascism a self-sufficient political doctrine able to face all others, both past and present. "If the bourgeoisie," I said at that time, "thinks to find in us a lightning-conductor, it is mistaken. We must go forward in opposition to Labour.... We want to accustom the working classes to being under a leader, to convince them also that it is not easy to direct an industry or a commercial undertaking successfully.... We shall fight against technical and spiritual retrogression.... The successors of the present regime still being undecided, we must not be unwilling to fight for it. We must hasten; when the present regime is superseded, we must be the ones to take its place. The right of succession belongs to us because we pushed the country into the War and we led it to victory. The present method of political representation cannot be sufficient for us, we wish for a direct representation of individual interests.... It might be said against this programme that it is a return to the corporations. It doesn't matter!... I should like, nevertheless, the Assembly to accept the claims of national syndicalism from the point of view of economics...."

Is it not surprising that from the first day in the Piazza San Sepolcro there should resound the word "Corporation" which was destined in the course of the revolution to signify one of the legislative and social creations at the base of the regime?

2. The years preceding the March on Rome were years during which the necessity of action did not tolerate enquiries or complete elaborations of doctrine. Battles were being fought in the cities and villages. There were discussions, but—and this is more sacred and important—there were deaths. People knew how to die. The doctrine—beautiful, well-formed, divided into chapters and paragraphs and surrounded by a commentary—might be missing; but there was present something more decisive to supplant it—Faith. Nevertheless, he who recalls the past with the aid of books, articles, votes in Parliament, the major and the minor speeches, he who knows how to investigate and weigh evidence, will find that the foundations of the doctrine were laid while the battle was raging. It was precisely in these years that Fascist thought armed itself, refined itself, moving towards one organization of its own. The problems of the individual and the State; the problems of authority and liberty; political and social problems and those more specifically national; the struggle against liberal, democratic, socialist, Masonic, demagogic doctrines was carried on at the same time as the "punitive expeditions." But since the "system" was lacking, adversaries ingenuously denied that Fascism had any power to make a doctrine of its own, while the doctrine rose up, even though tumultuously, at first under the aspect of a violent and dogmatic negation, as happens to all ideas that break new ground, then under the positive aspect of a constructive policy which, during the years 1926, 1927, 1928, was realized in the laws and institutions of the regime.

Fascism is to-day clearly defined not only as a regime but as a doctrine. And I mean by this that Fascism to-day, self-critical as well as critical of other movements, has an unequivocal point of view of its own, a criterion, and hence an aim, in face of all the material and intellectual problems which oppress the people of the world.

3. Above all, Fascism, in so far as it considers and observes the future and the development of humanity quite apart from the political considerations of the moment, believes neither in the possibility nor in the utility of perpetual peace. It thus repudiates the doctrine of Pacifism—born of a renunciation of the struggle and an act of cowardice in the face of sacrifice. War alone brings up to their highest tension all human energies and puts the stamp of nobility upon the peoples who have the courage to meet it. All other trials are substitutes, which never really put a man in front of himself in the alternative of life and death. A doctrine, therefore, which begins with a prejudice in favour of peace is foreign to Fascism; as are foreign to the spirit of Fascism, even though acceptable by reason of the utility which they might have in given political situations, all internationalistic and socialistic systems which, as history proves, can be blown to the

winds when emotional, idealistic and practical movements storm the hearts of peoples. Fascism carries over this anti-pacifist spirit even into the lives of individuals. The proud motto of the *Squadrista*, "Me ne frego," written on the bandages of a wound is an act of philosophy which is not only stoical, it is the epitome of a doctrine that is not only political: it is education for combat, the acceptance of the risks which it brings; it is a new way of life for Italy. Thus the Fascist accepts and loves life, he knows nothing of suicide and despises it; he looks on life as duty, ascent, conquest: life which must be noble and full: lived for oneself, but above all for those others near and far away, present and future.

4. The "demographic" policy of the regime follows from these premises. Even the Fascist does in fact love his neighbour, but this "neighbour" is not for him a vague and ill-defined concept; love for one's neighbour does not exclude necessary educational severities, and still less differentiations and distances. Fascism rejects universal concord, and, since it lives in the community of civilized peoples, it keeps them vigilantly and suspiciously before its eyes, it follows their states of mind and the changes in their interests and it does not let itself be deceived by temporary and fallacious appearances.

5. Such a conception of life makes Fascism the precise negation of that doctrine which formed the basis of the so-called Scientific or Marxian Socialism: the doctrine of historical Materialism, according to which the history of human civilizations can be explained only as the struggle of interest between the different social groups and as arising out of change in the means and instruments of production. That economic improvements—discoveries of raw materials, new methods of work, scientific inventions—should have an importance of their own, no one denies, but that they should suffice to explain human history to the exclusion of all other factors is absurd: Fascism believes, now and always, in holiness and in heroism, that is in acts in which no economic motive—remote or immediate—plays a part. With this negation of historical materialism, according to which men would be only by-products of history, who appear and disappear on the surface of the waves while in the depths the real directive forces are at work, there is also denied the immutable and irreparable "class struggle" which is the natural product of this economic conception of history, and above all it is denied that the class struggle can be the primary agent of social changes. Socialism, being thus wounded in these two primary tenets of its doctrine, nothing of it is left save the sentimental aspiration—old as humanity—towards a social order in which the sufferings and the pains of the humblest folk could be alleviated. But here Fascism rejects the concept of an economic "happiness" which would be realized socialistically and almost automatically at a given moment of economic evolution by assuring to all a maximum prosperity. Fascism denies the possibility of the materialistic conception of "happiness" and leaves it to the economists of the first half of the eighteenth century; it denies, that is, the equation of prosperity with happiness, which would transform men into animals with one sole preoccupation: that of being well-fed and fat, degraded in consequence to a merely physical existence.

6. After Socialism, Fascism attacks the whole complex of democratic ideologies and rejects them both in their theoretical premises and in their applications or practical manifestations. Fascism denies that the majority, through the mere fact of being a

majority, can rule human societies; it denies that this majority can govern by means of a periodical consultation; it affirms the irremediable, fruitful and beneficent inequality of men, who cannot be levelled by such a mechanical and extrinsic fact as universal suffrage. By democratic regimes we mean those in which from time to time the people is given the illusion of being sovereign, while true effective sovereignty lies in other, perhaps irresponsible and secret, forces. Democracy is a regime without a king, but with very many kings, perhaps more exclusive, tyrannical and violent than one king even though a tyrant. This explains why Fascism, although before 1922 for reasons of expediency it made a gesture of republicanism, renounced it before the March on Rome, convinced that the question of the political forms of a State is not preeminent to-day, and that studying past and present monarchies, past and present Republics, it becomes clear that monarchy and republic are not to be judged *sub specie aeternitatis*, but represent forms in which the political evolution, the history, the tradition, the psychology of a given country are manifested. Now Fascism overcomes the antithesis between monarchy and republic which retarded the movements of democracy, burdening the former with every defect and defending the latter as the regime of perfection. Now it has been seen that there are inherently reactionary and absolutistic republics, and monarchies that welcome the most daring political and social innovations.

7. "Reason, Science," said Renan (who was inspired before Fascism existed) in one of his philosophical Meditations, "are products of humanity, but to expect reason directly from the people and through the people is a chimera. It is not necessary for the existence of reason that everybody should know it. In any case, if such an initiation should be made, it would not be made by means of base democracy, which apparently must lead to the extinction of every difficult culture, and every higher discipline. The principle that society exists only for the prosperity and the liberty of the individuals who compose it does not seem to conform with the plans of nature, plans in which the species alone is taken into consideration and the individual seems to be sacrificed. It is strongly to be feared lest the last word of democracy thus understood (I hasten to say that it can also be understood in other ways) would be a social state in which a degenerate mass would have no other care than to enjoy the ignoble pleasures of vulgar men."

Thus far Renan. Fascism rejects in democracy the absurd conventional lie of political equalitarianism clothed in the dress of collective irresponsibility and the myth of happiness and indefinite progress. But if democracy can be understood in other ways, that is, if democracy means not to relegate the people to the periphery of the State, then Fascism could be defined as an "organized, centralized, authoritarian democracy."

8. In face of Liberal doctrines, Fascism takes up an attitude of absolute opposition both in the field of politics and in that of economics. It is not necessary to exaggerate—merely for the purpose of present controversies—the importance of Liberalism in the past century, and to make of that which was one of the numerous doctrines sketched in that century a religion of humanity for all times, present and future. Liberalism flourished for no more than some fifteen years. It was born in 1830, as a reaction against the Holy Alliance that wished to drag Europe back to what it had been before 1789, and it had its year of splendour in 1848 when even Pius IX was a Liberal. Immediately

afterwards the decay set in. If 1848 was a year of light and of poetry, 1849 was a year of darkness and of tragedy. The Republic of Rome was destroyed by another Republic, that of France. In the same year Marx launched the gospel of the religion of Socialism with the famous *Communist Manifesto*. In 1851 Napoleon III carried out his unliberal *coup d'état* and ruled over France until 1870, when he was dethroned by a popular revolt, but as a consequence of a military defeat which ranks among the most resounding that history can relate. The victor was Bismarck, who never knew the home of the religion of liberty or who were its prophets. It is symptomatic that a people of high culture like the Germans should have been completely ignorant of the religion of liberty during the whole of the nineteenth century. It was, there, no more than a parenthesis, represented by what has been called the "ridiculous Parliament of Frankfort" which lasted only a season. Germany has achieved her national unity outside the doctrines of Liberalism, against Liberalism, a doctrine which seems foreign to the German soul, a soul essentially monarchical, whilst Liberalism is the historical and logical beginning of anarchism. The stages of German unity are the three wars of 1864, 1866 and 1870, conducted by "Liberals" like Moltke and Bismarck. As for Italian unity, Liberalism has had in it a part absolutely inferior to the share of Mazzini and of Garibaldi, who were not Liberals. Without the intervention of the unliberal Napoleon we should not have gained Lombardy, and without the help of the unliberal Bismarck at Sadowa and Sedan, very probably we should not have gained Venice in 1866; and in 1870 we should not have entered Rome. From 1870–1915 there occurs the period in which the very priests of the new creed had to confess the twilight of their religion: defeated as it was by decadence in literature, by activism in practice. Activism: that is to say, Nationalism, Futurism, Fascism. The "Liberal" century, after having accumulated an infinity of Gordian knots, tried to untie them by the hecatomb of the World War. Never before has any religion imposed such a cruel sacrifice. Were the gods of Liberalism thirsty for blood? Now Liberalism is about to close the doors of its deserted temples because the peoples feel that its agnosticism in economics, its indifferentism in politics and in morals, would lead, as they have led, the States to certain ruin. In this way one can understand why all the political experiences of the contemporary world are anti-Liberal, and it is supremely ridiculous to wish on that account to class them outside of history; as if history were a hunting ground reserved to Liberalism and its professors, as if Liberalism were the definitive and no longer surpassable message of civilization.

9. But the Fascist repudiations of Socialism, Democracy, Liberalism must not make one think that Fascism wishes to make the world return to what it was before 1789, the year which has been indicated as the year of the beginning of the liberal-democratic age. One does not go backwards. The Fascist doctrine has not chosen De Maistre as its prophet. Monarchical absolutism is a thing of the past and so also is every theocracy. So also feudal privileges and division into impenetrable and isolated castes have had their day. The theory of Fascist authority has nothing to do with the police State. A party that governs a nation in a totalitarian way is a new fact in history. References and comparisons are not possible. Fascism takes over from the ruins of Liberal Socialistic democratic doctrines those elements which still have a living value. It preserves those that can be called the established facts of history, it rejects all the rest, that is to say the

idea of a doctrine which holds good for all times and all peoples. If it is admitted that the nineteenth century has been the century of Socialism, Liberalism and Democracy, it does not follow that the twentieth must also be the century of Liberalism, Socialism and Democracy. Political doctrines pass; peoples remain. It is to be expected that this century may be that of authority, a century of the "Right," a Fascist century. If the nineteenth was the century of the individual (Liberalism means individualism) it may be expected that this one may be the century of "collectivism" and therefore the century of the State. That a new doctrine should use the still vital elements of other doctrines is perfectly logical. No doctrine is born quite new, shining, never before seen. No doctrine can boast of an absolute "originality." It is bound, even if only historically, to other doctrines that have been, and to develop into other doctrines that will be. Thus the scientific socialism of Marx is bound to the Utopian Socialism of the Fouriers, the Owens and the Saint-Simons; thus the Liberalism of the nineteenth century is connected with the whole "Enlightenment" of the eighteenth century. Thus the doctrines of democracy are bound to the *Encyclopédie*. Every doctrine tends to direct the activity of men towards a determined objective; but the activity of man reacts upon the doctrine, transforms it, adapts it to new necessities or transcends it. The doctrine itself, therefore, must be, not words, but an act of life. Hence, the pragmatic veins in Fascism, its will to power, its will to be, its attitude in the face of the fact of "violence" and of its own courage.

10. The keystone of Fascist doctrine is the conception of the State, of its essence, of its tasks, of its ends. For Fascism the State is an absolute before which individuals and groups are relative. Individuals and groups are "thinkable" in so far as they are within the State. The Liberal State does not direct the interplay and the material and spiritual development of the groups, but limits itself to registering the results; the Fascist State has a consciousness of its own, a will of its own, on this account it is called an "ethical" State. In 1929, at the first quinquennial assembly of the regime, I said: "For Fascism, the State is not the night-watchman who is concerned only with the personal security of the citizens; nor is it an organization for purely material ends, such as that of guaranteeing a certain degree of prosperity and a relatively peaceful social order, to achieve which a council of administration would be sufficient, nor is it a creation of mere politics with no contact with the material and complex reality of the lives of individuals and the life of peoples. The State, as conceived by Fascism and as it acts, is a spiritual and moral fact because it makes concrete the political, juridical, economic organization of the nation and such an organization is, in its origin and in its development, a manifestation of the spirit. The State is the guarantor of internal and external security, but it is also the guardian and the transmitter of the spirit of the people as it has been elaborated through the centuries in language, custom, faith. The State is not only present, it is also past, and above all future. It is the State which, transcending the brief limit of individual lives, represents the immanent conscience of the nation. The forms in which States express themselves change, but the necessity of the State remains. It is the State which educates citizens for civic virtue, makes them conscious of their mission, calls them to unity; harmonizes their interests in justice; hands on the achievements of thought in the sciences, the arts, in law, in human solidarity; it carries men from the elementary life of the tribe to the highest human expression of power which is Empire; it entrusts to the

ages the names of those who died for its integrity or in obedience to its laws; it puts forward as an example and recommends to the generations that are to come the leaders who increased its territory and the men of genius who gave it glory. When the sense of the State declines and the disintegrating and centrifugal tendencies of individuals and groups prevail, national societies move to their decline."

11. From 1929 up to the present day these doctrinal positions have been strengthened by the whole economico-political evolution of the world. It is the State alone that grows in size, in power. It is the State alone that can solve the dramatic contradictions of capitalism. What is called the crisis cannot be overcome except by the State, within the State. Where are the shades of the Jules Simons who, at the dawn of liberalism, proclaimed that "the State must strive to render itself unnecessary and to prepare for its demise"; of the MacCullochs who, in the second half of the last century, affirmed that the State must abstain from too much governing? And faced with the continual, necessary and inevitable interventions of the State in economic affairs what would the Englishman Bentham now say, according to whom industry should have asked of the State only to be left in peace? Or the German Humboldt, according to whom the "idle" State must be considered the best? It is true that the second generation of liberal economists was less extremist than the first, and already Smith himself opened, even though cautiously, the door to State intervention in economics. But when one says liberalism, one says the individual; when one says Fascism, one says the State. But the Fascist State is unique; it is an original creation. It is not reactionary, but revolutionary in that it anticipates the solutions of certain universal problems. These problems are no longer seen in the same light: in the sphere of politics they are removed from party rivalries, from the supreme power of parliament, from the irresponsibility of assemblies; in the sphere of economics they are removed from the sphere of the syndicates' activities—activities that were ever widening their scope and increasing their power both on the workers' side and on the employers'—removed from their struggles and their designs; in the moral sphere they are divorced from ideas of the need for order, discipline and obedience, and lifted into the plane of the moral commandments of the fatherland. Fascism desires the State to be strong, organic and at the same time founded on a wide popular basis. The Fascist State has also claimed for itself the field of economics and, through the corporative, social and educational institutions which it has created, the meaning of the State reaches out to and includes the farthest off-shoots; and within the State, framed in their respective organizations, there revolve all the political, economic and spiritual forces of the nation. A State founded on millions of individuals who recognize it, feel it, are ready to serve it, is not the tyrannical State of the medieval lord. It has nothing in common with the absolutist States that existed either before or after 1789. In the Fascist State the individual is not suppressed, but rather multiplied, just as in a regiment a soldier is not weakened but multiplied by the number of his comrades. The Fascist State organizes the nation, but it leaves sufficient scope to individuals; it has limited useless or harmful liberties and has preserved those that are essential. It cannot be the individual who decides in this matter, but only the State.

12. The Fascist State does not remain indifferent to the fact of religion in general and to that particular positive religion which is Italian Catholicism. The State has no theology, but it has an ethic. In the Fascist State religion is looked upon as one of the deepest manifestations of the spirit; it is, therefore, not only respected, but defended and protected. The Fascist State does not create a "God" of its own, as Robespierre once, at the height of the Convention's foolishness, wished to do; nor does it vainly seek, like Bolshevism, to expel religion from the minds of men; Fascism respects the God of the ascetics, of the saints, of the heroes, and also God as seen and prayed to by the simple and primitive heart of the people.

13. The Fascist State is a will to power and to government. In it the tradition of Rome is an idea that has force. In the doctrine of Fascism Empire is not only a territorial, military or mercantile expression, but spiritual or moral. One can think of an empire, that is to say a nation that directly or indirectly leads other nations, without needing to conquer a single square kilometre of territory. For Fascism the tendency to Empire, that is to say, to the expansion of nations, is a manifestation of vitality; its opposite, staying at home, is a sign of decadence: peoples who rise or re-rise are imperialist, peoples who die are renunciatory. Fascism is the doctrine that is most fitted to represent the aims, the states of mind, of a people, like the Italian people, rising again after many centuries of abandonment or slavery to foreigners. But Empire calls for discipline, co-ordination of forces, duty and sacrifice; this explains many aspects of the practical working of the regime and the direction of many of the forces of the State and the necessary severity shown to those who would wish to oppose this spontaneous and destined impulse of the Italy of the twentieth century, to oppose it in the name of the superseded ideologies of the nineteenth, repudiated wherever great experiments of political and social transformation have been courageously attempted: especially where, as now, peoples thirst for authority, for leadership, for order. If every age has its own doctrine, it is apparent from a thousand signs that the doctrine of the present age is Fascism. That it is a doctrine of life is shown by the fact that it has resuscitated a faith. That this faith has conquered minds is proved by the fact that Fascism has had its dead and its martyrs.

Fascism henceforward has in the world the universality of all those doctrines which, by fulfilling themselves, have significance in the history of the human spirit.

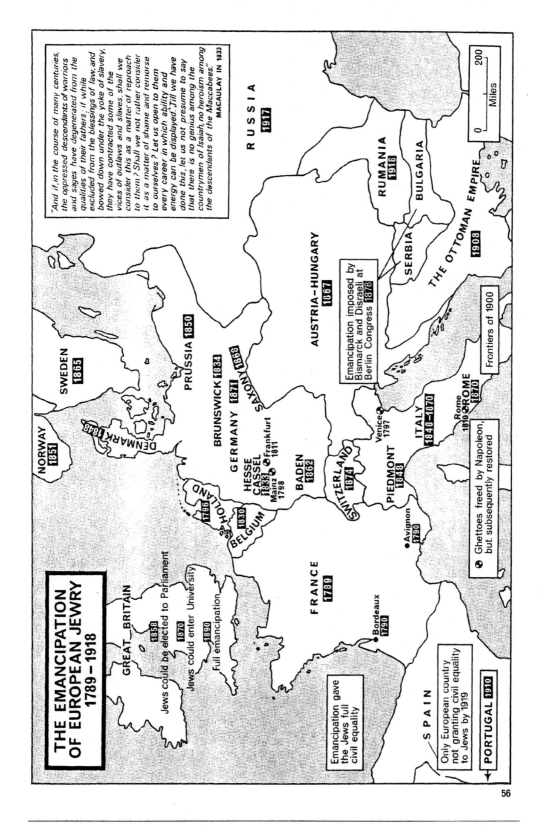

56

Map: "The Emancipation of European Jewry, 1789–1918" in *Jewish History Atlas* by Martin Gilbert (London, Macmillan Company) 1969.

20

Leni Yahil

THE HOLOCAUST: THE FATE OF EUROPEAN JEWRY, STATISTICAL CHART

TABLE E.1. *The extirpation of European Jewry by the military and police forces of Germany and its allies, 1939–1945*

	Initial Jewish population	Low estimate of Jewish population losses	%	High estimate of Jewish population losses	%
Austria[a]	185,000	50,000	27.0	50,000	27.0
Belgium	65,700	28,900	44.0	28,900	44.0
Bohemia and Moravia	118,310	78,150	66.1	78,150	66.1
Bulgaria[b]	61,000	11,000	18.0	11,000	18.0
Denmark[c]	7,800	60	0.12	60	0.12
Estonia	4,500	1,500	33.3	2,000	44.4
Finland	2,000	7	0.35	7	0.35
France[d]	350,000	77,320	22.1	77,320	22.1
Germany[e]	185,000	134,500	72.4	141,500	76.5
Greece[f]	66,380	49,000	73.8	56,000	84.4
Hungary[g]	825,000	550,000	66.7	569,000	69.0
Italy	44,500	7,680	17.3	7,680	17.3
Latvia[h]	91,500	70,000	76.5	71,500	78.1
Lithuania[i]	168,000	140,000	83.3	143,000	85.1
Luxembourg	3,500	1,950	55.7	1,950	55.7
Netherlands[j]	140,000	100,000	71.4	100,000	71.4
Norway	1,700	762	44.8	762	44.8
Poland[k]	3,300,000	2,900,000	87.9	3,000,000	90.9
Romania[l]	609,000	271,000	44.5	287,000	47.1
Slovakia[m]	88,950	68,000	76.4	71,000	79.8
USSR	3,020,000	1,000,000	33.1	1,100,000	36.4
Yugoslavia[n]	78,000	56,200	72.1	63,300	81.2
TOTAL	**9,415,840**	**5,596,029**	**59.4**	**5,860,129**	**62.2**

Leni Yahil, *The Holocaust: The Fate of European Jewry* (New York, Oxford University Press, 1990), Table E.1, 897–898.

Three-fifths of the civilian Jewish population of continental Europe[1] were done to death in the course of the Second World War by Germany and its allies. It was to be the solution for all time of what was conceived in Berlin as the Jewish Problem. Most victims were killed by firing squads or in gas chambers installed in camps dedicated to the purpose. The rest were finished off by massive ill treatment and starvation in the ghettos and concentration camps into which they had been corralled or by subjection to homicidally intense slave labour and forced marches. The military defeat of Germany occurred before the programme could be completed, but National Socialist hegemony over Europe lasted long enough for the result to fall very little short of the intention — which was to deal the Jewish people, notably in its great east European heartland, a blow from which recovery would be impossible.

Principal source: *Israel Gutman (ed.),* Ha-Enziklopediya shel ha-Sho'ah, *v (Tel Aviv, 1990), passim; but see Raul Hilberg,* The Destruction of the European Jews *(revised edn., New York 1985), appendix B, 1201–20. The discrepancy between Hilberg's figures and those of Gutman and his team owes a good deal to Hilberg not having had access to Russian sources.*

---

[a] 1938 figures.

[b] Inclusive of territories in Thrace and Macedonia annexed by Bulgaria in 1941.

[c] Inclusive of refugees from pre-war Germany, Austria, and Bohemia and Moravia.

[d] Inclusive of refugees from pre-war Germany, Austria, and Bohemia and Moravia.

[e] Exclusive of the some 65,000 ex-German Jews who were sent to their death from the countries in which they had found temporary asylum before the war.

[f] Exclusive of the Jewish inhabitants of Thrace and Macedonia ceded to Bulgaria in 1941.

[g] As enlarged by the annexation of Slovakian, Romanian, and Yugoslav territories in 1939, 1940, and 1941 respectively.

[h] Inclusive of refugees from pre-war Germany, Austria, and Bohemia and Moravia.

[i] Inclusive of refugees from pre-war Germany, Austria, and Bohemia and Moravia, but exclusive of the Vilna region annexed by Lithuania in October 1939.

[j] Inclusive of refugees from pre-war Germany, Austria, and Bohemia and Moravia.

[k] As of 31 Aug. 1939 and inclusive of Polish Jews who subsequently fled to the USSR but were caught up by the German war machine and liquidated.

[l] Exclusive of territory ceded to Hungary in 1940.

[m] Exclusive of territory ceded to Hungary in 1939.

[n] Exclusive of territory ceded to Hungary in 1941.

---

[1] Exclusive therefore of the moderately sized Jewish community of the undefeated and unoccupied United Kingdom and, for simplicity's sake, of the very small communities of the three neutral countries, Sweden, Switzerland, and the Irish Republic as well.

21

Michael Shermer

HOW WE KNOW THE HOLOCAUST HAPPENED: DEBUNKING THE DENIERS

The word *debunking* has negative connotations for most people, yet when you are presenting answers to claims of an extraordinary nature (and Holocaust denial surely qualifies), then debunking serves a useful purpose. There is, after all, a lot of bunk to be debunked. But I am attempting to do far more than this. In the process of debunking the deniers, I demonstrate how we know that the Holocaust happened, and that it happened in a particular way that most historians have agreed upon.

There is no immutable canon of truth about the Holocaust that can never be altered, as many deniers believe. When you get into the study of the Holocaust, and especially when you start attending conferences and lectures and tracking the debates among Holocaust historians, you discover that there is plenty of infighting about the major and minor points of the Holocaust. The brouhaha over Daniel Goldhagen's 1996 book, *Hitler's Willing Executioners*, in which he argued that "ordinary" Germans and not just Nazis participated in the Holocaust, is testimony to the fact that Holocaust historians are anything but settled on exactly what happened, when, why, and how. Nonetheless, an abyss lies between the points that Holocaust historians are debating and those that Holocaust deniers are promoting—their denial of intentional genocide based primarily on race, of programmatic use of gas chambers and crematoria for mass murder, and of the killing of five to six million Jews.

Methodology of Holocaust Denial

Before addressing the three main axes of Holocaust denial, let us look for a moment at the deniers' methodology, their modes of argument. Their fallacies of reasoning are eerily similar to those of other fringe groups, such as creationists.

Michael Shermer, "How We Know the Holocaust Happened: Debunking the Deniers," in *Why People Believe Weird Things: Pseudoscience, Superstition, and Other Confusions of Our Time* (New York, W. H. Freeman, 1997), chapter 14, 211–241.

1. They concentrate on their opponents' weak points, while rarely saying anything definitive about their own position. Deniers emphasize the inconsistencies between eyewitness accounts, for example.

2. They exploit errors made by scholars who are making opposing arguments, implying that because a few of their opponents' conclusions were wrong, *all* of their opponents' conclusions must be wrong. Deniers point to the human soap story, which has turned out to be a myth, and talk about "the incredible shrinking Holocaust" because historians have reduced the number killed at Auschwitz from four million to one million.

3. They use quotations, usually taken out of context, from prominent mainstream figures to buttress their own position. Deniers quote Yehuda Bauer, Raul Hilberg, Arno Mayer, and even leading Nazis.

4. They mistake genuine, honest debates between scholars about certain points within a field for a dispute about the existence of the entire field. Deniers take the intentionalist-functionalist debate about the development of the Holocaust as an argument about whether the Holocaust happened or not.

5. They focus on what is not known and ignore what is known, emphasize data that fit and discount data that do not fit. Deniers concentrate on what we do not know about the gas chambers and disregard all the eyewitness accounts and forensic tests that support the use of gas chambers for mass murder.

Because of the sheer quantity of evidence about the Holocaust—so many years and so much of the world involved, thousands of accounts and documents, millions of bits and pieces—there is enough evidence that some parts can be interpreted as supporting the deniers' views. The way that deniers treat testimony from the postwar Nuremberg trials of Nazis is typical of their handling of evidence. On the one hand, deniers dismiss the Nuremberg confessions as unreliable because it was a military tribunal run by the victors. The evidence, Mark Weber claims, "consists largely of extorted confessions, spurious testimonies, and fraudulent documents. The postwar Nuremberg trials were politically motivated proceedings meant more to discredit the leaders of a defeated regime than to establish truth" (1992, p. 201). Neither Weber nor anyone else has proven that most of the confessions were extorted, spurious, or fraudulent. But even if the deniers were able to prove that *some* of them were, this does not mean that they *all* were.

On the other hand, deniers cite Nuremberg trial testimony whenever it supports their arguments. For example, although deniers reject the testimony of Nazis who said there was a Holocaust and they participated in it, deniers accept the testimony of Nazis such as Albert Speer who said they knew nothing about it. But even here, deniers shy away from a deeper analysis. Speer indeed stated at the trials that he did not know about the extermination program. But his Spandau diary speaks volumes:

December 20, 1946. Everything comes down to this: Hitler always hated the Jews; he made no secret of that at any time. He was capable of tossing off quite calmly, between the soup and the vegetable course, "I want to annihilate the Jews in Europe. This war is the decisive confrontation between National Socialism and world Jewry. One or the other will bite the dust, and it certainly won't be us." So what I testified in court is true, that I had no knowledge of the killings of Jews; but it is true only in a superficial way. The question and my answer were the most difficult moment of my many hours on the witness stand. What I felt was not fear but shame that I as good as knew and still had not reacted; shame for my spiritless silence at the table, shame for my moral apathy, for so many acts of repression. (1976, p. 27)

In addition, Matthias Schmidt, in *Albert Speer: The End of a Myth*, details Speer's activities in support of the Final Solution. Among other things, Speer organized the confiscation of 23,765 apartments from Jews in Berlin in 1941; he knew of the deportation of more than 75,000 Jews to the east; he personally inspected the Mauthausen concentration camp, where he ordered a reduction of construction materials and redirected supplies that were needed elsewhere; and in 1977 he told a newspaper reporter, "I still see my guilt as residing chiefly in the approval of the persecution of the Jews and the murder of millions of them" (1984, pp. 181–198). Deniers cite Speer's Nuremberg testimony and ignore all Speer's elaborations about that testimony.

Convergence of Evidence

No matter what we wish to argue, we must bring to bear additional evidence from other sources that corroborates our conclusions. Historians know that the Holocaust happened by the same general method that scientists in such historical fields as archeology or paleontology use—through what William Whewell called a "consilience of inductions," or a convergence of evidence. Deniers seem to think that if they can just find one tiny crack in the Holocaust structure, the entire edifice will come tumbling down. This is the fundamental flaw in their reasoning. The Holocaust was not a single event. The Holocaust was thousands of events in tens of thousands of places, and is proved by millions of bits of data that converge on one conclusion. The Holocaust cannot be disproved by minor errors or inconsistencies here and there, for the simple reason that it was never proved by these lone bits of data in the first place.

Evolution, for example, is proved by the convergence of evidence from geology, paleontology, botany, zoology, herpetology, entomology, biogeography, anatomy, physiology, and comparative anatomy. No one piece of evidence from these diverse fields says "evolution" on it. A fossil is a snapshot. But when a fossil in a geological bed is studied along with other fossils of the same and different species, compared to species in other strata, contrasted to modern organisms, juxtaposed with species in other parts of the world, past and present, and so on, it turns from a snapshot into a motion picture. Evidence from each field lumps together to a grand conclusion—evolution. The process is no different in proving the Holocaust. Here is the convergence of proof:

Written documents: Hundreds of thousands of letters, memos, blueprints, orders, bills, speeches, articles, memoirs, and confessions.

Eyewitness testimony: Accounts from survivors, Kapos, Sonderkommandos, SS guards, commandants, local townspeople, and even upper-echelon Nazis who did not deny the Holocaust.

Photographs: Official military and press photographs and films, civilian photographs, secret photographs taken by prisoners, aerial photographs, and German and Allied film footage.

Physical evidence: Artifacts found at the sites of concentration camps, work camps, and death camps, many of which are still extant in varying degrees of originality and reconstruction.

Demographics: All those people who the deniers claim survived the Holocaust are missing.

Holocaust deniers ignore this convergence of evidence. They pick out what suits their theory and dismiss or avoid the rest. Historians and scientists do this too, but there is a difference. History and science have self-correcting mechanisms whereby one's errors are "revised" by one's colleagues in the true sense of the word. *Revision is the modification of a theory based on new evidence or a new interpretation of old evidence.* Revision should not be based on political ideology, religious conviction, or other human emotions. Historians are humans with emotions, of course, but they are the true revisionists because eventually the collective science of history separates the emotional chaff from the factual wheat.

Let us examine how the convergence of evidence works to prove the Holocaust, and how deniers select or twist the data to support their claims. We have an account by a survivor who says he heard about the gassing of Jews while he was at Auschwitz. The denier says that survivors exaggerate and that their memories are unsound. Another survivor tells another story different in details but with the core similarity that Jews were gassed at Auschwitz. The denier claims that rumors were floating throughout the camps and many survivors incorporated them into their memories. An SS guard confesses after the war that he actually saw people being gassed and cremated. The denier claims that these confessions were forced out of the Nazis by the Allies. But now a member of the Sonderkommando—a Jew who had helped the Nazis move dead bodies from the gas chambers and into the crematoria—says he not only heard about it and not only saw it happening, he had actually participated in the process. The denier explains this away by saying that the Sonderkommando accounts make no sense—their figures of numbers of bodies are exaggerated and their dates incorrect. What about the camp commandant, who confessed after the war that he not only heard, saw, and participated in the process but orchestrated it? He was tortured, says the denier. But what about his autobiography, written after his trial, conviction, and sentencing to death, when he had nothing to gain by lying? No one knows why people confess to ridiculous crimes, explains the denier, but they do.

No single testimony says "Holocaust" on it. But woven together they make a pattern, a story that holds together, while the deniers' story unravels. Instead of the historian having to present "just one proof," the denier must now disprove six pieces of historical data, with six different methods of disproof.

But there is more. We have blueprints of gas chambers and crematoria. Those were used strictly for delousing and body disposal, claims the denier; and thanks to the Allied war against Germany, the Germans were never given the opportunity to deport the Jews to their own homeland and instead had to put them into overcrowded camps where disease and lice were rampant. What about the huge orders for Zyklon-B gas? It was used strictly for delousing all those diseased inmates. What about those speeches by Adolf Hitler, Heinrich Himmler, Hans Frank, and Joseph Goebbels talking about the "extermination" of the Jews? Oh, they really meant "rooting out," as in deporting them out of the Reich. What about Adolf Eichmann's confession at his trial? He was coerced. Hasn't the German government confessed that the Nazis attempted to exterminate European Jewry? Yes, but they lied so they could rejoin the family of nations.

Now the denier must rationalize no less than fourteen different bits of evidence that converge to a specific conclusion. But the consilience continues. If six million Jews did not die, where did they go? They are in Siberia and Peoria, Israel and Los Angeles, says the denier. But why can't they find each other? They do—haven't you heard the stories of long-separated siblings making contact with one another after many decades? What about the photos and newsreels of the liberation of the camps with all those dead bodies and starving inmates? Those people were well taken care of until the end of the war when the Allies were mercilessly bombing German cities, factories, and supply lines, thus preventing food from reaching the camps; the Nazis tried valiantly to save their prisoners but the combined strength of the Allies was too much. But what about all the accounts by prisoners of the brutality of the Nazis—the random shootings and beatings, the deplorable conditions, the freezing temperatures, the death marches, and so on? That is the nature of war, replies the denier. The Americans interned Japanese-Americans and Japanese nationals in camps. The Japanese imprisoned Chinese. The Russians tortured Poles and Germans. War is hell. The Nazis were no different from anyone else.

We are now up to eighteen sets of evidence all converging toward one conclusion. The denier chips away at them all, determined not to give up his belief system. He is relying on what might be called *post hoc rationalization*—after-the-fact reasoning to justify contrary evidence—and then on demanding that the Holocaust historian disprove each of his rationalizations. But the convergence of positive evidence supporting the Holocaust means that the historian has already met the burden of proof, and when the denier demands that each piece of evidence independently prove the Holocaust he is ignoring the fact that no historian ever claimed that one piece of evidence proves the Holocaust or anything else. We must examine the evidence as part of a whole, and when we do so the Holocaust can be regarded as proven.

Intentionality

The first major axis of Holocaust denial is that genocide based primarily on race was not intended by Hitler and his followers.

Adolf Hitler

Deniers begin at the top, so I will too. In his 1977 *Hitler's War*, David Irving argued that Hitler did not know about the Holocaust. Shortly after, he put his money where his mouth is, promising to pay $1,000 to anyone who could produce documentary proof—specifically, a written document—that Hitler ordered the Holocaust. In a classic example of what I call the *snapshot fallacy*—taking a single frame out of a historical film—Irving reproduced, on page 505 of *Hitler's War*, Himmler's telephone notes of November 30, 1941, when the SS chief telephoned Reinhard Heydrich (deputy chief of the Reichssicherheitshaupamt [Head Office for Reich Security, or RSHA, of the SS]) "from Hitler's bunker at the Wolf's Lair, ordering that there was to be 'no liquidation' of Jews." From this, Irving concluded that "the Führer had ordered that the Jews were not to be liquidated" (1977, p. 504).

But we must see the snapshot in the context of the frames around it. As Raul Hilberg pointed out, in its entirety, the log entry says, "Jewish transport from Berlin. No liquidation." It was in reference to one particular transport, not all Jews. And, says Hilberg, "that transport *was* liquidated! That order was either ignored, or it was too late. The transport had already arrived in Riga [capital of Latvia] and they didn't know what to do with these thousand people so they shot them that very same evening" (1994). Moreover, for Hitler to veto an order for liquidation implies that liquidation was something that was ongoing. To that extent, David Irving's $1,000 challenge and Robert Faurisson's demand for "just one proof" are met. If Jews were not being exterminated, why would Hitler feel the need to halt the extermination of a particular transport? And this entry also proves that it was Hitler, and not Himmler or Goebbels, who ordered the Holocaust. As Speer observed regarding Hitler's role: "I don't suppose he had much to do with the technical aspects, but even the *decision* to proceed from shooting to gas chambers would have been his, for the simple reason, as I know only too well, that no major decisions could be made about *anything* without his approval" (in Sereny 1995, p. 362). As Yisrael Gutman noted, "Hitler interfered in all main decisions with regard to the Jews. All the people around Hitler came with their plans and initiatives because they knew that Hitler was interested [in solving the 'Jewish question'] and they wanted to please him and be the first to realize his intentions and his spirit" (1996).

Whether or not there was a specific order from Hitler for the extermination of the Jews does not matter, then, because it did not need to be spelled out. The Holocaust "was not so much a product of laws and commands as it was a matter of spirit, of shared comprehension, of consonance and synchronization" (Hilberg 1961, p. 55). This spirit was made plain in his speeches and writings. From his earliest political ramblings to the final Götterdämmerung of the end in his Berlin bunker, Hitler had it in for Jews. On April 12, 1922, in a speech given in Munich and later published in the newspaper *Völkischer Beobachter*, he told his audience, "The Jew is the ferment of the decomposition of people. This means that it is in the nature of the Jew to destroy, and he must destroy, because he lacks altogether any idea of working for the common good. He possesses certain characteristics given to him by nature and he never can rid himself of those characteristics. The Jew is harmful to us" (in Snyder 1981, p. 29). Thirty-three years later, with his world collapsing around him, Hitler said, "Against the Jews I fought open-eyed and in view of the whole world.... I made it plain that they, this parasitic vermin in Europe, will be finally exterminated" (February 13, 1945; in Jäckel 1993, p. 33), and "Above all I charge the leaders of the nation and those under them to scrupulous observance of the laws of race and to merciless opposition to the universal poisoner of all peoples, International Jewry" (April 29, 1945; in Snyder 1981, p. 521).

In between, Hitler made hundreds of similar statements. In a speech given January 30, 1939, for example, he said, "Today I want to be a prophet once more: If international finance Jewry inside and outside of Europe should succeed once more in plunging nations into another world war, the consequence will not be the Bolshevization of the earth and thereby the victory of Jewry, but the annihilation of the Jewish race in Europe" (in Jäckel 1989, p. 73). Hitler even told the Hungarian head of state, "In Poland this state of affairs has been...cleared up: if the Jews there did not *want* to work, they were shot. If they *could* not work, they were treated like tuberculosis bacilli with which a healthy body may become infected. This is not cruel if one remembers that even innocent creatures of nature, such as hares and deer when infected, have to be killed so that they cannot damage others. Why should the beasts who wanted to bring us Bolshevism be spared more than these innocents?" (in Sereny 1995, p. 420). How many more quotes do we need to prove that Hitler ordered the Holocaust—a hundred, a thousand, ten thousand?

Ausrotten *Among the Nazi Elite*

David Irving and other deniers make it sound like these speeches do not indicate a smoking gun, by playing a clever game of semantics with the word *ausrotten*, which according to modern dictionaries means "to exterminate, extirpate, or destroy." This word can be found in numerous Nazi speeches and documents referring to the Jews. But Irving insists that *ausrotten* really means "stamping or rooting out," arguing that "the word *ausrotten* means one thing now in 1994, but it meant something very different in the time Adolf Hitler uses it." Yet a check of historical dictionaries shows that *ausrotten* has always meant "to exterminate." Irving's rejoinder provides another example of *post hoc rationalization*:

> Different words mean different things when uttered by different people. What matters is what that word meant when uttered by Hitler. I would first draw attention to the famous memorandum on the Four-Year Plan of August 1936. In that Adolf Hitler says, "We are going to have to get our armed forces in a fighting state within four years so that we can go to war with the Soviet Union. If the Soviet Union should ever succeed in overrunning Germany it will lead to the *ausrotten* of the German people." There's that word. There is no way that

Hitler can mean the physical liquidation of 80 million Germans. What he means is that it will lead to the emasculation of the German people as a power factor. (1994)

I then pointed out that, at a December 1944 conference regarding the Ardennes attack against the Americans, Hitler ordered his generals "to *ausrotten* them division by division." Was Hitler giving the order to *transport* the Americans out of the Ardennes division by division? Irving countered:

Compare that with a speech he made in August 1939, in which he says, with regard to Poland, "we are going to destroy the living forces of the Polish Army." This is the job of any commander—you have to destroy the forces facing you. How you destroy them, how you "take them out" is probably a better phrase, is immaterial. If you take those pawns off the chess board they are gone. If you put the American forces in captivity they are equally neutralized whether they are in captivity or dead. And that's what the word *ausrotten* means there. (1994)

But what about Rudolf Brandt's use of the word? To SS Gruppenführer Dr. Grawitz of the SS Reichsarzt in Berlin, SS Sturmbannführer Brandt wrote concerning "the *Ausrottung* of tuberculosis as a disease affecting the nation." A year later, now an SS Obersturmbannführer, he wrote to Ernst Kaltenbrunner, Heydrich's successor as chief of RSHA, "I am sending you the outline of a press announcement concerning the accelerated *Ausrottung* of the Jews in occupied Europe." The same man is using the same word to discuss the same process for tuberculosis and Jews (see figure 20). What else could *ausrotten* have meant in these contexts except "extermination"?

And what about Hans Frank's use of the word? In a speech to a Nazi assembly held on October 7, 1940, Frank summed up his first year of effort as head of the Generalgouvernement of occupied Poland: "I could not *ausrotten* all lice and Jews in only one year. But in the course of time, and if you help me, this end will be attained" (Nuremberg Doc. 3363-PS, p. 891). On December 16, 1941, Frank addressed a government session at the office of the governor of Krakau in conjunction with the upcoming Wannsee Conference:

Currently there are in the Government Generalship approximately 2.5 million, and together with those who are kith and kin and connected in all kinds of ways, we now have 3.5 million Jews. We cannot shoot these 3.5 million Jews, nor can we poison them, yet we will have to take measures which will somehow lead to the goal of annihilation, and that will be done in connection with the great measures which are to be discussed together with the Reich. The territory of the General Government must be made free of Jews, as is the case in the Reich. Where and how this will happen is a matter of the means which must be used and created, and about whose effectiveness I will inform you in due time. (Original document and translation, National Archives, Washington, D.C., T922, PS 2233)

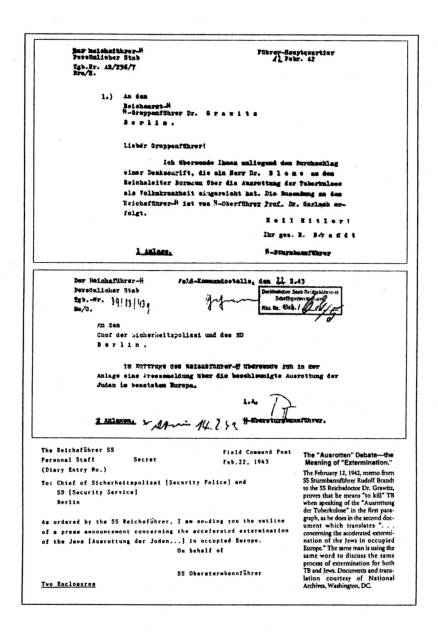

FIGURE 20: Rudolf Brandt writes about (*top*) "die Ausrottung die Tuberkulose" to SS Gruppenführer Dr. Grawitz of the SS Reichsarzt, February 12, 1942; and (*bottom*) "die beschleunigte Ausrottung der Juden" to Ernst Kaltenbrunner, chief of RSHA, February 22, 1943. *Ausrottung* means "extermination." [Documents and translation courtesy National Archives, Washington, D.C.]

If the Final Solution meant deportation out of the Reich, as Irving and other deniers claim, does this mean that Frank was planning to send lice out of Poland on trains? And why would Frank be making references to the extermination of Jews through means other than shooting or poisoning?

And then there are entries from the diary of Joseph Goebbels, Gauleiter (General) of Berlin, Reich Minister of Propaganda, and Reich Plenipotentiary for total war effort, such as these:

> *August 8, 1941*, concerning the spread of spotted typhus in the Warsaw ghetto: "The Jews have always been the carriers of infectious diseases. They should either be concentrated in a ghetto and left to themselves or be liquidated, for otherwise they will infect the populations of the civilized nations."

> *August 19, 1941*, after a visit to Hitler's headquarters: "The Führer is convinced his prophecy in the Reichstag is becoming a fact: that should Jewry succeed in again provoking a new war, this would end with their annihilation. It is coming true in these weeks and months with a certainty that appears almost sinister. In the East the Jews are paying the price, in Germany they have already paid in part and they will have to pay more in the future." (Broszat 1989, p. 143)

Himmler also talks about the *ausrotten* of the Jews, and again there is evidence that negates the deniers' definition of that word. For example, in a lecture on the history of Christianity given in January 1937, Himmler told his SS Gruppenführers, "I have the conviction that the Roman emperors, who exterminated [*ausrotteten*] the first Christians, did precisely what we are doing with the communists. These Christians were at that time the vilest scum, which the city accommodated, the vilest Jewish people, the vilest Bolsheviks there were" (Padfield 1990, p. 188). In June 1941, Himmler informed Rudolf Hoess, the commandant of Auschwitz, that Hitler had ordered the Final Solution (*Endlösung*) of the Jewish question, and that Hoess would play a major role at Auschwitz:

> It is a hard, tough task which demands the commitment of the whole person without regard to any difficulties that may arise. You will be given details by Sturmbannführer Eichmann of the RSHA who will come to see you in the near future. The department taking part will be informed at the appropriate time. You have to maintain the strictest silence about this order, even to your superiors. The Jews are the eternal enemies of the German people and must be exterminated. All Jews we can reach now, during the war, are to be exterminated without exception. If we do not succeed in destroying the biological basis of Jewry, some day the Jews will annihilate the German Volk [people]. (Padfield 1990, p. 334)

Himmler made many similarly damning speeches. One of the most notorious is the October 4, 1943, speech to the SS Gruppenführer in Poznan (Posen), which was recorded on a red oxide tape. Himmler was lecturing from notes, and early in the talk he stopped the tape recorder to make sure it was working. He then continued, knowing he was being recorded, and spoke for over three hours on a range of subjects, including the military and political situation, the Slavic peoples and racial blends, how the racial superiority of Germans would help them win the war, and the like. Two hours into the speech, Himmler began to talk about the bloody 1934 purges of traitors in the Nazi Party and "the extermination of the Jewish people."

I also want to refer here very frankly to a very difficult matter. We can now very openly talk about this among ourselves, and yet we will never discuss this publicly. Just as we did not hesitate on June 30, 1934, to perform our duty as ordered and put comrades who had failed up against the wall and execute them, we also never spoke about it, nor will we ever speak about it. Let us thank God that we had within us enough self-evident fortitude never to discuss it among us, and we never talked about it. Every one of us was horrified, and yet every one clearly understood that we would do it next time, when the order is given and when it becomes necessary.

I am now referring to the evacuation of the Jews, to the extermination of the Jewish people. This is something that is easily said: "The Jewish people will be exterminated," says every Party member, "this is very obvious, it is in our program—elimination of the Jews, extermination, will do." And then they turn up, the brave 80 million Germans, and each one has his decent Jew. It is of course obvious that the others are pigs, but this particular one is a splendid Jew. But of all those who talk this way, none had observed it, none had endured it. Most of you here know what it means when 100 corpses lie next to each other, when 500 lie there or when 1,000 are lined up. To have endured this and at the same time to have remained a decent person—with exceptions due to human weaknesses—has made us though. This is an honor roll in our history which has never been and never will be put in writing, because we know how difficult it would be for us if we still had Jews as secret saboteurs, agitators and rabble rousers in every city, what with the bombings, with the burden and with the hardships of the war. If the Jews were still part of the German nation, we would most likely arrive now at the state we were at in 1916/17. (Original document and translation, National Archives, Washington, D.C., PS Series 1919, pp. 64-67)

Irving's response to this quote was interesting:

Irving: I have a later speech he made on January 26, 1944, in which he is speaking to the same audience rather more bluntly about the *ausrotten* of Germany's Jews, when he announced that they had totally solved the Jewish problem. Most of the listeners sprang to their feet and applauded. "We were all there in Poznan," recalled a Rear Admiral, "when that man [Himmler] told us how he'd killed off the Jews. I can still recall precisely how he told us. 'If people ask me,' said Himmler, 'why did you have to kill the children, too then I can only say I am not such a coward that I leave for my children something I can do myself.'" Quite interesting—this is an Admiral afterwards recording this in British captivity without realizing he was being tape recorded, which is a very good summary of what Himmler actually said.

Shermer: That sounds to me like he means to kill Jews, not just transport them out of the Reich.

Irving: I agree, Himmler said that. He actually said, "We're wiping out the Jews. We're murdering them. We're killing them."

Shermer: What does that mean other than what it sounds like?

Irving: I agree, Himmler is admitting what I said happened to the 600,000. But, and this is the important point, nowhere does Himmler say "We are killing millions." Nowhere does he even say we are killing hundreds of thousands. He is talking about solving the Jewish problem, about having to kill off women and children too. (1994)

Irving, once again, has fallen into the fallacy of *ad hoc rationalization*. Since Himmler never exactly said millions, therefore he really meant thousands. But, please note, Himmler never said thousands either. Irving is inferring what he wants to infer. The actual numbers come from other sources, which, in conjunction with Himmler's speeches and many other pieces of evidence, converge on the conclusion that he meant millions would be killed. And millions were killed.

The Einsatzgruppen

Finally, there is telling evidence about the extermination of Jews from lower down in the ranks. The Einsatzgruppen were mobile SS and police units for special missions in occupied territories. Their mandate included rounding up and killing Jews and other unwanted persons in towns and villages prior to occupation by Germans. For the winter of 1941–1942, for example, Einsatzgruppe A reported 2,000 Jews killed in Estonia, 70,000 in Latvia, 136,421 in Lithuania, and 41,000 in Belorussia. On November 14, 1941, Einsatzgruppe B reported 45,467 shootings, and on July 31, 1942, the governor of Belorussia reported that 65,000 Jews were killed during the previous two months. Einsatzgruppe C estimated they had killed 95,000 by December 1941, and Einsatzgruppe D reported on April 8, 1942, a total of 92,000 killed. The grand total is 546,888 dead in less than one year.

Numerous eyewitness accounts from members of the Einsatzgruppen can be found in *"The Good Old Days": The Holocaust as Seen by Its Perpetrators and Bystanders* (Klee, Dressen, and Riess 1991). For example, on Sunday, September 27, 1942, SS Obersturmführer Karl Kretschmer wrote to "My dear Soska," his wife. He apologizes for not writing more, is feeling ill and in "low spirits" because "what you see here makes you either brutal or sentimental." His "gloomy mood," he explains, is caused by "the sight of the dead (including women and children)." Which dead? Dead Jews, who deserve to die: "As the war is in our opinion a Jewish war, the Jews are the first to feel it.

Here in Russia, wherever the German soldier is, no Jew remains. You can imagine that at first I needed some time to get to grips with this." In a subsequent letter, not dated, he explains to his wife that "there is no room for pity of any kind. You women and children back home could not expect any mercy or pity if the enemy got the upper hand. For that reason we are mopping up where necessary but otherwise the Russians are willing, simple and obedient. There are no Jews here any more." Finally, on October 19, 1942, in a letter signed "You deserve my best wishes and all my love, Your Papa," Kretschmer provides a paradigmatic example of what Hannah Arendt meant by the banality of evil:

> If it weren't for the stupid thoughts about what we are doing in this country, the Einsatz here would be wonderful, since it has put me in a position where I can support you all very well. Since, as I already wrote to you, I consider the last Einsatz to be justified and indeed approve of the consequences it had, the phrase "stupid thoughts" is not strictly accurate. Rather it is a weakness not to be able to stand the sight of dead people; the best way of overcoming it is to do it more often. Then it becomes a habit. (pp. 163–171)

There may not have been a written order, but the Nazi's intentionality of genocide primarily by race was not only clear but also known rather widely.

The Intentionalist-Functionalist Controversy

For several decades following the war, historians debated the "intentionalism" versus the "functionalism" of the Holocaust. Intentionalists argued that Hitler intended the mass extermination of the Jews from the early 1920s, that Nazi policy in the 1930s was programmed toward this end, and that the invasion of Russia and the quest for *Lebensraum* were directly planned and linked to the Final Solution of the Jewish question. Functionalists, by contrast, argued that the original plan for the Jews was expulsion and that the Final Solution evolved as a result of the failed war against Russia. Holocaust historian Raul Hilberg, however, feels that these are artificial distinctions: "In reality it is more complicated than either of these interpretations. I believe Hitler gave a plenary order, but that order was itself the end product of a process. He said many things along the way which encouraged the bureaucracy to think along certain lines and to take initiatives. But on the whole I would say that any kind of systematic shooting, particularly of young children or very old people, and any kind of gassing, required Hitler's order" (1994).

Under the weight of historical evidence, intentionalism has not survived the test of time. The immediate reason, as outlined by Ronald Headland, was dawning recognition of "the competitive, almost anarchical and decentralized quality of the National Socialist system, with its rivalries, its ubiquitous personality politics, and the ever-present pursuit of power among its agencies.... Perhaps the greatest merit of the functionalist approach has been the extent to which it has delineated the chaotic character of the Third Reich and the often great complexity of factors involved in the decision-making process" (1992, p. 194). But the ultimate reason for acceptance of the functionalist view is that events, especially an event as complicated and contingent as the Holocaust, rarely unfold as historical actors plan. Even the famous Wannsee Conference of January 1942, at which the Nazis confirmed the implementation of the Final Solution, has been shown by Holocaust scholar Yehuda Bauer to be just one more contingent step down the road from original expulsion to final extermination. This is backed up by the existence of a realistic plan to deport the Jews to the island of Madagascar and attempts to trade Jews for cash after the Wannsee Conference. Bauer quotes Himmler's note to himself of December 10, 1942: "I have asked the Führer with regard to letting Jews go in return for ransom. He gave me full powers to approve cases like that, if they really bring in foreign currency in appreciable quantities from abroad" (1994, p. 103).

Does this discount the intentionality of the Nazis to exterminate the Jews? No, says Bauer, but it demonstrates the complexity of history and the expediency of the moment:

> In prewar Germany, emigration suited the circumstances best, and when that was neither speedy enough or complete enough, expulsion—preferably to some "primitive" place, uninhabited by true Nordic Aryans, the Soviet Union or Madagascar—was the answer. When expulsion did not work either, and the prospect of controlling Europe and, through Europe, the world arose in late 1940 and early 1941, the murder policy was decided on, quite logically, on the basis of Nazi ideology. All these policies had the same aim: removal. (Bauer 1994, pp. 252–253)

The functional sequence went from eviction of the Jews from German life (including confiscation of most of their property and homes), to concentration and isolation (often under overcrowded and filthy conditions, leading to disease and death), to economic exploitation (unpaid forced labor that often involved overwork, starvation, and death), to extermination. Gutman agrees with this contingent interpretation: "The Final Solution was an operation that started from the bottom, from a local basis, with a kind of escalation from place to place, until it was a comprehensive event. I don't know if I would call it a plan. I say it was a blueprint. Physical destruction was the outcome of a series of steps and attacks against the Jews" (1996).

The Holocaust can be modeled as a feedback loop fed by the flow of information, intentions, and actions (figure 21). From the time the Nazis took power in 1933 and began passing legislation against Jews, to Kristallnacht and other acts of violence against Jews, to the deportation of Jews to ghettos and labor camps, to the extermination of Jews in labor and death camps, we can see at work such internal psychological components as xenophobia, racism, and violence, interacting with such external social components as a rigid hierarchical social structure, a strong central power, intolerance of diversity (religious, racial, ethnic, sexual, or political), built-in mechanisms of violence to handle dissenters, regular use of violence to enforce laws, and a low regard for civil liberties. Christopher Browning nicely summed up how this feedback loop worked in the Third Reich:

> In short, for Nazi bureaucrats already deeply involved in and committed to "solving the Jewish question," the final step to mass murder was incremental,

not a quantum leap. They had already committed themselves to a political movement, to a career, and to a task. They lived in an environment already permeated by mass murder. This included not only programs with which they were not directly involved, like the liquidation of the Polish intelligentsia, the gassing of the mentally ill and handicapped in Germany, and then on a more monumental scale the war of destruction in Russia. It also included wholesale killing and dying before their very eyes, the starvation in the ghetto of Lodz and the punitive expeditions and reprisal shooting in Serbia. By the very nature of their past activities, these men had articulated positions and developed career interests that inseparably and inexorably led to a similar murderous solution to the Jewish question. (1991, p. 143)

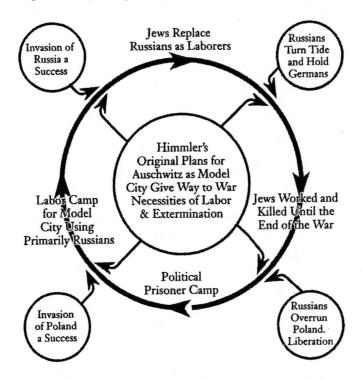

FIGURE 21: Holocaust feedback loop. Interaction of internal psychological states and external social conditions may produce a genocidal feedback loop.

History addresses the complexities of human acts, but within these complexities are simplicities of essences. Hitler, Himmler, Goebbels, Frank, and other Nazis were quite serious in their intention to solve the Jewish question, mainly because they were virulently antisemitic. They may have begun with resettlement, but they ended up at genocide because history's final pathways are determined by the functions of any given moment interacting with the intentions that came before. Hitler and his followers built out of their functions and intentions a road that led to camps, gas chambers and crematoria, and the extermination of millions.

Gas Chambers and Crematoria

The second major axis of Holocaust denial is that gas chambers and crematoria were not used for mass killings. How can anyone deny that the Nazis used gas chambers and crematoria? After all, these facilities still exist in many camps. To debunk the deniers can't you just go there and see for yourself? What about the evidence? In 1990, Arno Mayer noted in *Why Did the Heavens Not Darken?* that "sources for the study of the gas chambers are at once rare and unreliable." Deniers cite this sentence as vindication of their position. Mayer is a highly respected diplomatic historian at Princeton University, so one can see why deniers might be delighted by having him seemingly reinforce what they have always believed. But the entire paragraph reads:

> Sources for the study of the gas chambers are at once rare and unreliable. Even though Hitler and the Nazis made no secret of their war on the Jews, the SS operatives dutifully eliminated all traces of their murderous activities and instrument. No written orders for gassing have turned up thus far. The SS not only destroyed most camp records, which were in any case incomplete, but also razed nearly all killing and cremating installations well before the arrival of Soviet troops. Likewise, care was taken to dispose of the bones and ashes of the victims. (1990, p. 362)

Clearly, Mayer is not arguing that gas chambers were not used for mass extermination. Mayer's paragraph also neatly summarizes why the physical evidence for mass murder is not quite as overwhelmingly obvious as one might expect.

Deniers do not deny the use of gas chambers and crematoria, but they claim that gas chambers were used strictly for delousing clothing and blankets, and crematoria were used solely to dispose of bodies of people who died of "natural" causes in the camps. Before examining the evidence that the Nazis used gas chambers for mass murder in detail, consider in general the convergence of evidence from various sources:

Official Nazi documents: Orders for large quantities of Zyklon-B (the trade name of hydrocyanic acid gas), blueprints for gas chambers and crematoria, and orders for building materials for gas chambers and crematoria.

Eyewitness testimony: Survivor accounts, Jewish Sonderkommando diaries, and confessions of guards and commandants all tell of gas chambers and crematoria being used for mass murder.

Photographs: Photographs not only of the camps but also secret photographs of the burning of bodies at Auschwitz and Allied aerial reconnaissance photographs of prisoners being marched to the gas chambers at Auschwitz-Birkenau.

The camps themselves: Buildings and artifacts at the camps and the results of modern forensic tests that point to the use of both gas chambers and crematoria for killing large numbers of people.

No one source by itself proves that gas chambers and crematoria were used for genocide. It is the convergence of these sources that leads inexorably to this conclusion. For example, delivery of Zyklon-B to the camps in accordance with the written orders is corroborated by the remains of Zyklon-B canisters at the camps and by eyewitness accounts of the use of Zyklon-B in the gas chambers.

About the gassings themselves, deniers ask why no extermination victim has given an eyewitness account of an actual gassing (Butz 1976). This is like asking why no one from the killing fields of Cambodia or Stalin's purges came back to tell tales on their executioners. What we do have are hundreds of eyewitness accounts not only from SS men and Nazi doctors but from Sonderkommandos who dragged the bodies from the gas chambers and into the crematoria. In his *Eyewitness Auschwitz: Three Years in the Gas Chambers*, Filip Müller describes the deception and gassing process as follows:

> Two of the SS men took up positions on either side of the entrance door. Shouting and wielding their truncheons, like beaters at a hunt, the remaining SS men chased the naked men, women and children into the large room inside the crematorium. A few SS men were leaving the building and the last one locked the entrance door from the outside. Before long the increasing sound of coughing, screaming and shouting for help could be heard from behind the door. I was unable to make out individual words, for the shouts were drowned by knocking and banging against the door, intermingled with sobbing and crying. After some time the noise grew weaker, the screams stopped. Only now and then there was a moan, a rattle, or the sound of muffled knocking against the door. But soon even that ceased and in the sudden silence each one of us felt the horror of this terrible mass death. (1979, pp. 33–34)
>
> Once everything was quiet inside the crematorium, Unterscharführer Teuer, followed by Stark, appeared on the flat roof. Both had gas-masks dangling round their necks. They put down oblong boxes which looked like food tins; each tin was labeled with a death's head and marked Poison! What had been just a terrible notion, a suspicion, was now a certainty: the people inside the crematorium had been killed with poison gas. (p. 61)

We also have the confessions of guards. SS Unterscharführer Pery Broad was captured on May 6, 1945, by the British in their zone of occupation in Germany. Broad began work at Auschwitz in 1942 in the "Political Section" and stayed there until the liberation of the camp in January 1945. After his capture, while working as an interpreter for the British, he wrote a memoir that was passed on to the British Intelligence Service in July 1945. In December 1945, he declared under oath that what he wrote was true. On September 29, 1947, the document was translated into English and used at the Nuremberg trials regarding the gas chambers as mechanisms of mass murder. Later in 1947, he was released. When called to testify at a trial of Auschwitz SS men in April 1959, Broad acknowledged his authorship of the memoir, confirmed its validity, and retracted nothing.

I give this context for Broad's memoir because deniers dismiss damning Nazi confessions as either coerced or made up for bizarre psychological reasons (while accepting without hesitation confessions that support deniers' views). Broad was never tortured, and he had little to gain and everything to lose by confessing. When given the opportunity to recant, which he certainly could have in the later trial, he did not. Instead, he described in detail the gassing procedure, including the use of Zyklon-B, the early gassing experiments in Block 11 of Auschwitz, and the temporary chambers set up in the two abandoned farms at Birkenau (Auschwitz II), which he correctly called by their jargon name, "Bunkers I and II." He also recalled the construction of Kremas II, III, IV, and V at Birkenau, and accurately depicted (by comparison with blueprints) the design of the undressing room, gas chamber, and crematorium. Then Broad described the process of gassing in gruesome detail:

> The disinfectors are at work...with an iron rod and hammer they open a couple of harmless looking tin boxes, the directions read Cyclon [*sic*] Vermin Destroyer, Warning, Poisonous. The boxes are filled with small pellets which look like blue peas. As soon as the box is opened the contents are shaken out through an aperture in the roof. Then another box is emptied in the next aperture, and so on. After about two minutes the shrieks die down and change to a low moaning. Most of the men have already lost consciousness. After a further two minutes...it is all over. Deadly quiet reigns.... The corpses are piled together, their mouths stretched open.... It is difficult to heave the interlaced corpses out of the chamber as the gas is stiffening all their limbs. (in Shapiro 1990, p. 76)

Deniers point out that Broad's total of four minutes for the process is at odds with the statements of others, such as Commandant Hoess, who claim it was more like twenty minutes. Because of such discrepancies, deniers dismiss the account entirely. A dozen different accounts give a dozen different figures for time of death by gassing, so deniers believe no one was gassed at all. Does this make sense? Of course not. Obviously, the gassing process would take different amounts of time due to variations in conditions, including the temperature (the rate of hydrocyanic acid gas evaporation from the pellets depends on air temperature), the number of people in the room, the size of the room, and the amount of Zyklon-B poured into the room—not to mention that each observer would perceive time differently. If the time estimates were exactly the same, in fact, we would have to be suspicious that they were all taking their stories from a single account. In this case, discrepancy tends to support the veracity of the evidence.

Compare Broad's testimony with that of the camp physician, Dr. Johann Paul Kremer:

> *September 2, 1942.* Was present for first time at a special action at 3 A.M. By comparison Dante's Inferno seems almost a comedy. Auschwitz is justly called an extermination camp!

> *September 5, 1942.* At noon was present at a special action in the women's camp—the most horrible of all horrors. Hschf. Thilo, military surgeon, was right

when he said to me today that we are located here in the *anus mundi* [anus of the world]. (1994, p. 162)

Deniers seize upon the fact that Kremer says "special action," not "gassing," but at the trial of the Auschwitz camp garrison in Krakau in December 1947, Kremer specified what he meant by "special action":

> By September 2, 1942, at 3 A.M. I had already been assigned to take part in the action of gassing people. These mass murders took place in small cottages situated outside the Birkenau camp in a wood. The cottages were called "bunkers" in the SS-men's slang. All SS physicians on duty in the camp took turns to participate in the gassings, which were called *Sonderaktion* [special action]. My part as physician at the gassing consisted in remaining in readiness near the bunker. I was brought there by car. I sat in front with the driver and an SS hospital orderly sat in the back of the car with oxygen apparatus to revive SS-men, employed in the gassing, in case any of them should succumb to the poisonous fumes. When the transport with people who were destined to be gassed arrived at the railway ramp, the SS officers selected from among the new arrivals persons fit to work, while the rest—old people, all children, women with children in their arms and other persons not deemed fit to work—were loaded onto lorries' and driven to the gas chambers. There people were driven into the barrack huts where the victims undressed and then went naked to the gas chambers. Very often no incidents occurred, as the SS-men kept people quiet, maintaining that they were to bathe and be deloused. After driving all of them into the gas chamber the door was closed and an SS-man in a gas mask threw the contents of a Cyclon [*sic*] tin through an opening in the side wall. The shouting and screaming of the victims could be heard through that opening and it was clear that they were fighting for their lives. These shouts were heard for a very short while. (1994, p. 162n)

The convergence of Broad's and Kremer's accounts—and there are plenty more—provides evidence that the Nazis used gas chambers and crematoria for mass extermination.

We have hundreds of accounts of survivors describing the unloading and separation process of Jews at Auschwitz, and we have photographs of the process. We also have eyewitness accounts of the Nazis burning bodies in open pits after gassing (the crematoria often broke down), and we have a photograph of such a burning, taken secretly by a Greek Jew named Alex. Alter Fajnzylberg, a French Sonderkommando at Auschwitz, recalled how this photograph was obtained:

> On the day on which the pictures were taken we allocated tasks. Some of us were to guard the person taking the pictures. At last the moment came. We all gathered at the western entrance leading from the outside to the gas chamber of Crematorium V: we could not see any SS men in the watch-tower overlooking

the door from above the barbed wire, nor near the place where the pictures were to be taken. Alex, the Greek Jew, quickly took out his camera pointed it toward a heap of burning bodies, and pressed the shutter. This is why the photograph shows prisoners from the Sonderkommando working at the heap. (Swiebocka 1993, pp. 42–43)

Deniers also focus on the lack of photographic proof of gas chamber and crematoria activity in aerial reconnaissance photographs taken of the camps by the Allies. In 1992, denier John Ball actually published an entire book documenting this lack of evidence. The book is a high-quality, slick publication printed on glossy paper in order to hold the detail of the aerial photographs. Ball spent tens of thousands of dollars on the book, did all the layout and typesetting, and even printed the book himself. The project cost him more than just his savings. His wife gave him an ultimatum: her or the Holocaust. He chose the latter. Ball's book is a response to a 1979 CIA report on the aerial photographs—*The Holocaust Revisited: A Retrospective Analysis of the Auschwitz-Birkenau Extermination Complex*—in which the two authors, Dino A. Brugioni and Robert G. Poirier, present aerial photographs taken by the Allies that they claim prove extermination activities. According to Ball, the photographs were tampered with, marked, altered, faked. By whom? By the CIA itself, in order to match the story as depicted in the television mini-series *Holocaust*.

Figure 23: Aerial photograph of Krema II, August 25, 1944. Note the four staggered shadows on the gas chamber roof in this photograph and compare them to the four small structures visible on the roof of the gas chamber in figure 24. These photographs support eyewitness accounts of the Nazis pouring Zyklon-B pellets through the roof of the gas chamber—an example of how separate lines of evidence converge to a single conclusion. [Negative courtesy National Archives, Washington, D.C. (film 3185); enhancement courtesy Nevin Bryant.]

Thanks to Dr. Nevin Bryant, supervisor of cartographic applications and image processing applications at Caltech/NASA's Jet Propulsion Laboratory in Pasadena, California, I was able to get the CIA photographs properly analyzed by people who know what they are looking at from the air. Nevin and I analyzed the photographs using digital enhancement techniques not available to the CIA in 1979. We were able to prove that the photographs had not been tampered with, and we indeed found evidence of extermination activity. The aerial photographs were shot in sequence as the plane flew over the camp (on a bombing run toward its ultimate target—the IG Farben Industrial works). Since the photographs of the camp were taken a few seconds apart, stereoscopic viewing of two consecutive photographs shows movement of people and vehicles and provides better depth perception. The aerial photograph in figure 23 shows the distinctive features of Krema II. Note the long shadow from the crematorium chimney and, on the roof of the adjacent gas chamber at right angles to the crematorium building, note the four staggered shadows. Ball claims these shadows were drawn in, but four small structures that match the shadows are visible on the roof of the gas chamber in figure 24, a picture taken by an SS photographer of the back of Krema II (if you look directly below the chimney of Krema II, you will see two sides of the rectangular underground gas chamber structure protruding a few feet above the ground). This photographic evidence converges nicely with eyewitness accounts describing SS men pouring Zyklon-B pellets through openings in the roof of the gas chamber. The aerial photograph in figure 25 shows a group of prisoners being marched into Krema V for gassing. The gas chamber is at the end of the building, and the crematorium has double chimneys. From the camp's daily logs, it is clear that these are Hungarian Jews from an RSHA transport, some of whom were selected for work and the rest sent for extermination. (Additional photographs and detailed discussion appear in Shermer and Grobman 1997.)

FIGURE 25: Aerial photograph of prisoners being marched into Krema V, May 31, 1944. [Negative courtesy National Archives, Washington, D.C. (Film 3055); enhancement courtesy Nevin Bryant.]

For obvious reasons, there are no photographs recording an actual gassing, and the difficulty with photographic evidence is that any photograph of activity at a camp cannot by itself prove anything, even if it has not been tampered with. One photograph shows Nazis burning bodies at Auschwitz. So what, say deniers. Those are bodies of prisoners who died of natural causes, not of prisoners who were gassed. Several aerial photographs show the details of the Kremas at Birkenau and record prisoners being marched into them. So what, say deniers. The prisoners are going to work to clean up after bodies of people who died of natural causes were burned; or they are going for delousing. Again, it is context and convergence with other evidence that make such photographs telling—and the fact that none of the photographs records activities at variance with the accounts of life in the camps supports the Holocaust and the use of gas chambers and crematoria for mass murder.

How Many Jews Died?

The final major axis of Holocaust denial is the number of Jewish victims. Paul Rassinier concluded his *Debunking the Genocide Myth: A Study of the Nazi Concentration Camps and the Alleged Extermination of European Jewry* by claiming "a minimum of 4,419,908 Jews succeeded in leaving Europe between 1931 and 1945" (1978, p. x) and therefore far fewer than six million Jews died at the hands of the Nazis. Most Holocaust scholars, however, place the total number of Jewish victims between 5.1 and 6.3 million.

While estimates do vary, historians using different methods and different source materials independently arrive at five to six million Jewish victims of the Holocaust. The fact that the estimates vary actually adds credibility; that is, it would be more likely that the numbers were "cooked" if the estimates all came out the same. The fact that the estimates do not come out the same yet all are within a reasonable range of error variance means somewhere between five and six million Jews died in the Holocaust. Whether it is five or six million is irrelevant. It is a large number of people. And it was not just several hundred thousand or "only" one or two million, as some deniers suggest. More accurate estimates will be made in the future as new information arrives from Russia and former Soviet territories. The overall figure, however, is not likely to change by more than a few tens of thousands, and certainly not by hundreds of thousands or millions.

The table below presents estimated Jewish losses in the Holocaust by country. The figures were compiled by a number of scholars, each working in his or her own geographic area of specialty, and then combined by Yisrael Gutman and Robert Rozett for the *Encyclopedia of the Holocaust*. The figures were derived from population demographics, taking the number of Jews registered living in every village, town, and city in Europe, the number reported transported to camps, the number liberated from camps, the number killed in "special actions" by the Einsatzgruppen, and the number remaining alive after the war. The minimum and maximum loss figures represent the range of error variation.

Finally, one might ask the denier one simple question: If six million Jews did not die in the Holocaust, where did they all go? The denier will say they are living in Siberia and Kalamazoo, but for millions of Jews to suddenly appear out of the hinterlands of Russia or America or anywhere else is so unlikely as to be nonsensical. The Holocaust survivor who does turn up is a rare find indeed.

Conspiracies

There were many millions more killed by the Nazis, including Gypsies, homosexuals, mentally and physically handicapped persons, political prisoners, and especially Russians and Poles, but Holocaust deniers do not worry about the numbers of these dead. This fact has something to do with the widespread lack of attention to non-Jewish victims of the Holocaust, yet it also has something to do with the antisemitic core of Holocaust denial.

ESTIMATED LOSS OF JEWS IN THE HOLOCAUST

Country	Initial Jewish Population	Minimum Loss	Maximum Loss
Austria	185,000	50,000	50,000
Belgium	65,700	28,900	28,900
Bohemia and Moravia	118,310	78,150	78,150
Bulgaria	50,000	0	0
Denmark	7,800	60	60
Estonia	4,500	1,500	2,000
Finland	2,000	7	7
France	350,000	77,320	77,320
Germany	566,000	134,500	141,500
Greece	77,380	60,000	67,000
Hungary	825,000	550,000	569,000
Italy	44,500	7,680	7,680
Latvia	91,500	70,000	71,500
Lithuania	168,000	140,000	143,000
Luxembourg	3,500	1,950	1,950
Netherlands	140,000	100,000	100,000
Norway	1,700	762	762
Poland	3,300,000	2,900,000	3,000,000
Romania	609,000	271,000	287,000
Slovakia	88,950	68,000	71,000
Soviet Union	3,020,000	1,000,000	1,100,000
Total	**9,796,840**	**5,596,029**	**5,860,129**

SOURCE: *Encyclopedia of the Holocaust*, editor in chief Yisrael Gutman (New York: Macmillan, 1990), p. 1799.

Coupled with deniers' obsession with "the Jews" is an obsession with conspiracies. On the one hand, they deny that the Nazis had a plan (i.e., a conspiracy) to exterminate the Jews. They reinforce this argument by pointing out how extreme conspiratorial thinking can become (à la JFK conspiracy theories). They demand powerful evidence before historians can conclude that Hitler and his followers conspired to exterminate European Jewry (Weber 1994b). Fine. But they cannot then claim, on the other hand, that the idea of the Holocaust was a Zionist conspiracy to obtain reparations from Germany in order to fund the new State of Israel, without meeting their own demands for proof.

As a part this latter argument, deniers claim that if the Holocaust really happened as Holocaust historians say it did, then it would have been widely known during the war (Weber 1994b). It would be as obvious as, say, the D-day landing was. Plus, the Nazis would have discussed their murderous plans among themselves. Well, for obvious reasons, D-day was kept a secret and the D-day landing was not widely known until after it began. Likewise for the Holocaust. It was not something that was casually discussed even between fellow Nazis. Albert Speer, in fact, wrote about this in his Spandau diary:

> *December 9, 1946.* It would be wrong to imagine that the top men of the regime would have boasted of their crimes on the rare occasions when they met. At the trial we were compared to the heads of a Mafia. I recalled movies in which the bosses of legendary gangs sat around in evening dress chatting about murder and power, weaving intrigues, concocting coups. But this atmosphere of back room conspiracy was not at all the style of our leadership. In our personal dealings, nothing would ever be said about any sinister activities we might be up to. (1976, p. 27)

Speer's observation is corroborated by SS guard Theodor Malzmueller's description of his introduction to mass murder upon his arrival at the Kulmhof (Chelmno) extermination camp:

> When we arrived we had to report to the camp commandant, SS-Hauptsturmführer Bothmann. The SS-Hauptsturmführer addressed us in his living quarters, in the presence of SS-Untersturmführer Albert Plate. He explained that we had been dedicated to the Kulmhof extermination camp as guards and added that in this camp the plague boils of humanity, the Jews, were exterminated. We were to keep quiet about everything we saw or heard, otherwise we would have to reckon with our families' imprisonment and the death penalty. (Klee, Dressen, and Riess 1991, p. 217)

The answer to the deniers' overall contention that there was a conspiracy by Jews to concoct a Holocaust in order to finance the State of Israel (Rassinier 1978) is straightforward. The basic facts about the Holocaust were established before there was a State of Israel and before the United States or any other country gave it one cent. Moreover, when reparations were established, the amount Israel received from Germany was not based on numbers killed but on Israel's cost of absorbing and resettling the Jews who fled Germany and German-controlled countries before the war and the survivors of the Holocaust who came to Israel after the war. In March 1951, Israel requested from the Four Powers reparations, to be calculated on this basis.

> The government of Israel is not in a position to obtain and present a complete statement of all Jewish property taken or looted by the Germans, and said to total more than $6 thousand million. It can only compute its claim on the basis of total expenditures already made and the expenditure still needed for the integration of Jewish immigrants from Nazi-dominated countries. The number of these immigrants is estimated at some 500,000, which means a total expenditure of $1.5 thousand million. (Sagi 1980, p. 55)

Needless to say, if reparations were based on the total number of survivors, then any Zionist conspirators should have exaggerated not the number of Jews killed by the Nazis but the number of survivors. In fact, given the provisions of the reparation settlement, if the deniers are right and only a few hundred thousand Jews died, then Germany owes Israel far more in reparations, for where else could those five to six million survivors have gone? Deniers might argue that the Zionist conspirators traded reparation money from Germany for a greater prize: money and long-term sympathy from all over the world. But here we really go off the deep end. Why should the supposed conspirators have risked sure money for some uncertain future payoff? In reality, the State of Israel as the recipient of German money is a myth. Most of it went to individual survivors, not to the Israeli government.

Moral Equivalency

When all else fails, deniers shift from wrangling about intentionality, gassings and crematoria, and the number of Jews killed to arguing that the Nazi's treatment of the Jews is really no different from what other nations do to their perceived enemies. Deniers point out, for example, that the U.S. government obliterated with atomic weapons two entire Japanese cities filled with civilians (Irving 1994) and forced Japanese-Americans into camps, which is just what the Germans did to their perceived internal enemy—the Jews (Cole 1994).

The response to this is twofold. First, just because another country does evil does not make your own evil right. Second, there is a difference between war and the systematic state-organized killing of unarmed people within your own country, not in self-defense, not to gain more territory, raw materials, or wealth, but simply because they are perceived as a type of Satanic force and inferior race. At his trial in Jerusalem, Adolf Eichmann, SS Obersturmbannführer of the RSHA and one of the chief implementers of the Final Solution, tried to make the moral equivalence argument. But the judge didn't buy it, as this sequence from the trial transcript shows (Russell 1963, pp. 278-279):

> *Judge Benjamin Halevi to Eichmann:* You have often compared the extermination of the Jews with the bombing raids on German cities and you compared the murder of Jewish women and children with the death of German women in aerial bombardments. Surely it must be clear to you that there is a basic distinction between these two things. On the one hand the bombing is used as an instrument of forcing the enemy to surrender. Just as the Germans tried to force

the British to surrender by their bombing. In that case it is a war objective to bring an armed enemy to his knees.

On the other hand, when you take unarmed Jewish men, women, and children from their homes, hand them over to the Gestapo, and then send them to Auschwitz for extermination it is an entirely different thing, is it not?

Eichmann: The difference is enormous. But at that time these crimes had been legalized by the state and the responsibility, therefore, belongs to those who issued the orders.

Halevi: But you must know surely that there are internationally recognized Laws and Customs of War whereby the civilian population is protected from actions which are not essential for the prosecution of the war itself.

Eichmann: Yes, I'm aware of that.

Halevi: Did you never feel a conflict of loyalties between your duty and your conscience?

Eichmann: I suppose one could call it an internal split. It was a personal dilemma when one swayed from one extreme to the other.

Halevi: One had to overlook and forget one's conscience.

Eichmann: Yes, one could put it that way.

During his trial, Eichmann never denied the Holocaust. His argument was that "these crimes had been legalized by the state" and therefore the people that "issued the orders" are responsible. This was the classic defense used at the Nuremberg trials by most of the Nazis. Since the higher-ups all committed suicide—Hitler, Himmler, Goebbels, and Hermann Goring—they were off the hook, or so they thought.

We are not off the hook either. Like evolution denial, Holocaust denial is not simply going to go away and it is not benign or trivial. It has had and will have ugly and dire consequences, not only for Jews but for all of us and for future generations. We must provide answers to the claims of Holocaust deniers. We have the evidence and we must stand up and be heard.

22

Francis Fukuyama

THE END OF HISTORY?

In watching the flow of events over the past decade or so, it is hard to avoid the feeling that something very fundamental has happened in world history. The past year has seen a flood of articles commemorating the end of the Cold War, and the fact that "peace" seems to be breaking out in many regions of the world. Most of these analyses lack any larger conceptual framework for distinguishing between what is essential and what is contingent or accidental in world history, and are predictably superficial. If Mr. Gorbachev were ousted from the Kremlin or a new Ayatollah proclaimed the millennium from a desolate Middle Eastern capital, these same commentators would scramble to announce the rebirth of a new era of conflict.

And yet, all of these people sense dimly that there is some larger process at work, a process that gives coherence and order to the daily headlines. The twentieth century saw the developed world descend into a paroxysm of ideological violence, as liberalism contended first with the remnants of absolutism, then bolshevism and fascism, and finally an updated Marxism that threatened to lead to the ultimate apocalypse of nuclear war. But the century that began full of self-confidence in the ultimate triumph of Western liberal democracy seems at its close to be returning full circle to where it started: not to an "end of ideology" or a convergence between capitalism and socialism, as earlier predicted, but to an unabashed victory of economic and political liberalism.

The triumph of the West, of the Western *idea*, is evident first of all in the total exhaustion of viable systematic alternatives to Western liberalism. In the past decade, there have been unmistakable changes in the intellectual climate of the world's two largest communist countries, and the beginnings of significant reform movements in both. But this phenomenon extends beyond high politics and it can be seen also in the ineluctable spread of consumerist Western culture in such diverse contexts as the

Francis Fukuyama is deputy director of the State Department's policy planning staff and former analyst at the RAND Corporation. This article is based on a lecture presented at the University of Chicago's John M. Olin Center for Inquiry Into the Theory and Practice of Democracy. The author would like to pay special thanks to the Olin Center and to Nathan Tarcov and Allan Bloom for their support in this and many earlier endeavors. The opinions expressed in this article do not reflect those of the RAND Corporation or of any agency of the U.S. government.

Francis Fukuyama, "The End of History?" (1989) from *The National Interest*, 16 (Summer, 1989), 3–18.

peasants' markets and color television sets now omnipresent throughout China, the cooperative restaurants and clothing stores opened in the past year in Moscow, the Beethoven piped into Japanese department stores, and the rock music enjoyed alike in Prague, Rangoon, and Tehran.

What we may be witnessing is not just the end of the Cold War, or the passing of a particular period of postwar history, but the end of history as such: that is, the end point of mankind's ideological evolution and the universalization of Western liberal democracy as the final form of human government. This is not to say that there will no longer be events to fill the pages of *Foreign Affairs*'s yearly summaries of international relations, for the victory of liberalism has occurred primarily in the realm of ideas or consciousness and is as yet incomplete in the real or material world. But there are powerful reasons for believing that it is the ideal that will govern the material world *in the long run*. To understand how this is so, we must first consider some theoretical issues concerning the nature of historical change.

I

The notion of the end of history is not an original one. Its best known propagator was Karl Marx, who believed that the direction of historical development was a purposeful one determined by the interplay of material forces, and would come to an end only with the achievement of a communist utopia that would finally resolve all prior contradictions. But the concept of history as a dialectical process with a beginning, a middle, and an end was borrowed by Marx from his great German predecessor, Georg Wilhelm Friedrich Hegel.

For better or worse, much of Hegel's historicism has become part of our contemporary intellectual baggage. The notion that mankind has progressed through a series of primitive stages of consciousness on his path to the present, and that these stages corresponded to concrete forms of social organization, such as tribal, slave-owning, theocratic, and finally democratic-egalitarian societies, has become inseparable from the modern understanding of man. Hegel was the first philosopher to speak the language of modern social science, insofar as man for him was the product of his concrete historical and social environment and not, as earlier natural right theorists would have it, a collection of more or less fixed "natural" attributes. The mastery and transformation of man's natural environment through the application of science and technology was originally not a Marxist concept, but a Hegelian one. Unlike later historicists whose historical relativism degenerated into relativism *tout court*, however, Hegel believed that history culminated in an absolute moment—a moment in which a final, rational form of society and state became victorious.

It is Hegel's misfortune to be known now primarily as Marx's precursor, and it is our misfortune that few of us are familiar with Hegel's work from direct study, but only as it has been filtered through the distorting lens of Marxism. In France, however, there has been an effort to save Hegel from his Marxist interpreters and to resurrect him as the philosopher who most correctly speaks to our time. Among those modern French interpreters of Hegel, the greatest was certainly Alexandre Kojève, a brilliant Russian emigre who taught a highly influential series of seminars in Paris in the 1930s at the *Ecole Practique des Hautes Etudes*.[1] While largely unknown in the United States, Kojève had a major impact on the intellectual life of the continent. Among his students ranged such future luminaries as Jean-Paul Sartre on the Left and Raymond Aron on the Right; postwar existentialism borrowed many of its basic categories from Hegel via Kojève.

Kojève sought to resurrect the Hegel of the *Phenomenology of Mind*, the Hegel who proclaimed history to be at an end in 1806. For as early as this Hegel saw in Napoleon's defeat of the Prussian monarchy at the Battle of Jena the victory of the ideals of the French Revolution, and the imminent universalitization of the state incorporating the principles of liberty and equality. Kojève, far from rejecting Hegel in light of the turbulent events of the next century and a half, insisted that the latter had been essentially correct.[2] The Battle of Jena marked the end of history because it was at that point that the *vanguard* of humanity (a term quite familiar to Marxists) actualized the principles of the French Revolution. While there was considerable work to be done after 1806—abolishing slavery and the slave trade, extending the franchise to workers, women, blacks, and other racial minorities, etc.—the basic *principles* of the liberal democratic state could not be improved upon. The two world wars in this century and their attendant revolutions and upheavals simply had the effect of extending those principles spatially, such that the various provinces of human civilization were brought up to the level of its most advanced outposts, and of forcing those societies in Europe and North America at the vanguard of civilization to implement their liberalism more fully.

The state that emerges at the end of history is liberal insofar as it recognizes and protects through a system of law man's universal right to freedom, and democratic insofar as it exists only with the consent of the governed. For Kojève, this so-called "universal homogenous state" found real-life embodiment in the countries of postwar Western Europe—precisely those flabby, prosperous, self-satisfied, inward-looking, weak-willed states whose grandest project was nothing more heroic than the creation of the Common Market.[3] But this was only to be expected. For human history and the conflict that characterized it was based on the existence of "contradictions": primitive man's quest for mutual recognition, the dialectic of the master and slave, the transformation and mastery of nature, the struggle for the universal recognition of rights, and the dichotomy between proletarian and capitalist. But in the universal homogenous state, all prior contradictions are resolved and all human needs are satisfied. There is no struggle or conflict over "large" issues, and consequently no need

---

[1] Kojève's best-known work is his *Introduction à la lecture de Hegel* (Paris: Editions Gallimard, 1947), which is a transcript of the *Ecole Practique* lectures from the 1930s. This book is available in English entitled *Introduction to the Reading of Hegel* arranged by Raymond Queneau, edited by Allan Bloom, and translated by James Nichols (New York: Basic Books, 1969).

[2] In this respect Kojève stands in sharp contrast to contemporary German interpreters of Hegel like Herbert Marcuse who, being more sympathetic to Marx, regarded Hegel ultimately as an historically bound and incomplete philosopher.

[3] Kojève alternatively identified the end of history with the postwar "American way of life," toward which he thought the Soviet Union was moving as well.

for generals or statesmen; what remains is primarily economic activity. And indeed, Kojève's life was consistent with his teaching. Believing that there was no more work for philosophers as well, since Hegel (correctly understood) had already achieved absolute knowledge, Kojève left teaching after the war and spent the remainder of his life working as a bureaucrat in the European Economic Community, until his death in 1968.

To his contemporaries at mid-century, Kojève's proclamation of the end of history must have seemed like the typical eccentric solipsism of a French intellectual, coming as it did on the heels of World War II and at the very height of the Cold War. To comprehend how Kojève could have been so audacious as to assert that history has ended, we must first of all understand the meaning of Hegelian idealism.

II

For Hegel, the contradictions that drive history exist first of all in the realm of human consciousness, i.e. on the level of ideas[4]—not the trivial election year proposals of American politicians, but ideas in the sense of large unifying world views that might best be understood under the rubric of ideology. Ideology in this sense is not restricted to the secular and explicit political doctrines we usually associate with the term, but can include religion, culture, and the complex of moral values underlying any society as well.

Hegel's view of the relationship between the ideal and the real or material worlds was an extremely complicated one, beginning with the fact that for him the distinction between the two was only apparent.[5] He did not believe that the real world conformed or could be made to conform to ideological preconceptions of philosophy professors in any simpleminded way, or that the "material" world could not impinge on the ideal. Indeed, Hegel the professor was temporarily thrown out of work as a result of a very material event, the Battle of Jena. But while Hegel's writing and thinking could be stopped by a bullet from the material world, the hand on the trigger of the gun was motivated in turn by the ideas of liberty and equality that had driven the French Revolution.

For Hegel, all human behavior in the material world, and hence all human history, is rooted in a prior state of consciousness—an idea similar to the one expressed by John Maynard Keynes when he said that the views of men of affairs were usually derived from defunct economists and academic scribblers of earlier generations. This consciousness may not be explicit and self-aware, as are modern political doctrines, but may rather take the form of religion or simple cultural or moral habits. And yet this realm of consciousness *in the long run* necessarily becomes manifest in the material world, indeed creates the material world in its own image. Consciousness is cause and

---

[4] This notion was expressed in the famous aphorism from the preface to the *Philosophy of History* to the effect that "everything that is rational is real, and everything that is real is rational."

[5] Indeed, for Hegel the very dichotomy between the ideal and material worlds was itself only an apparent one that was ultimately overcome by the self-conscious subject; in his system, the material world is itself only an aspect of mind.

not effect, and can develop autonomously from the material world; hence the real subtext underlying the apparent jumble of current events is the history of ideology.

Hegel's idealism has fared poorly at the hands of later thinkers. Marx reversed the priority of the real and the ideal completely, relegating the entire realm of consciousness—religion, art, culture, philosophy itself—to a "superstructure" that was determined entirely by the prevailing material mode of production. Yet another unfortunate legacy of Marxism is our tendency to retreat into materialist or utilitarian explanations of political or historical phenomena, and our disinclination to believe in the autonomous power of ideas. A recent example of this is Paul Kennedy's hugely successful *The Rise and Fall of the Great Powers*, which ascribes the decline of great powers to simple economic overextension. Obviously, this is true on some level: an empire whose economy is barely above the level of subsistence cannot bankrupt its treasury indefinitely. But whether a highly productive modern industrial society chooses to spend 3 or 7 percent of its GNP on defense rather than consumption is entirely a matter of that society's political priorities, which are in turn determined in the realm of consciousness.

The materialist bias of modern thought is characteristic not only of people on the Left who may be sympathetic to Marxism, but of many passionate anti-Marxists as well. Indeed, there is on the Right what one might label the *Wall Street Journal* school of deterministic materialism that discounts the importance of ideology and culture and sees man as essentially a rational, profit-maximizing individual. It is precisely this kind of individual and his pursuit of material incentives that is posited as the basis for economic life as such in economic textbooks.[6] One small example will illustrate the problematic character of such materialist views.

Max Weber begins his famous book, *The Protestant Ethic and the Spirit of Capitalism*, by noting the different economic performance of Protestant and Catholic communities throughout Europe and America, summed up in the proverb that Protestants eat well while Catholics sleep well. Weber notes that according to any economic theory that posited man as a rational profit-maximizer, raising the piece-work rate should increase labor productivity. But in fact, in many traditional peasant communities, raising the piece-work rate actually had the opposite effect of *lowering* labor productivity: at the higher rate, a peasant accustomed to earning two and one-half marks per day found he could earn the same amount by working less, and did so because he valued leisure more than income. The choices of leisure over income, or of the militaristic life of the Spartan hoplite over the wealth of the Athenian trader, or even the ascetic life of the early capitalist entrepreneur over that of a traditional leisured aristocrat, cannot possibly be explained by the impersonal working of material forces, but come preeminently out of the sphere of consciousness—what we have labeled here broadly as ideology. And indeed, a central theme of Weber's work was to prove that contrary to Marx, the

---

[6] In fact, modern economists, recognizing that man does not always behave as a *profit*-maximizer, posit a "utility" function, utility being either income or some other good that can be maximized: leisure, sexual satisfaction, or the pleasure of philosophizing. That profit must be replaced with a value like utility indicates the cogency of the idealist perspective.

material mode of production, far from being the "base," was itself a "superstructure" with roots in religion and culture, and that to understand the emergence of modern capitalism and the profit motive one had to study their antecedents in the realm of the spirit.

As we look around the contemporary world, the poverty of materialist theories of economic development is all too apparent. The *Wall Street Journal* school of deterministic materialism habitually points to the stunning economic success of Asia in the past few decades as evidence of the viability of free market economics, with the implication that all societies would see similar development were they simply to allow their populations to pursue their material self-interest freely. Surely free markets and stable political systems are a necessary precondition to capitalist economic growth. But just as surely the cultural heritage of those Far Eastern societies, the ethic of work and saving and family, a religious heritage that does not, like Islam, place restrictions on certain forms of economic behavior, and other deeply ingrained moral qualities, are equally important in explaining their economic performance.[7] And yet the intellectual weight of materialism is such that not a single respectable contemporary theory of economic development addresses consciousness and culture seriously as the matrix within which economic behavior is formed.

Failure to understand that the roots of economic behavior lie in the realm of consciousness and culture leads to the common mistake of attributing material causes to phenomena that are essentially ideal in nature. For example, it is commonplace in the West to interpret the reform movements first in China and most recently in the Soviet Union as the victory of the material over the ideal—that is, a recognition that ideological incentives could not replace material ones in stimulating a highly productive modern economy, and that if one wanted to prosper one had to appeal to baser forms of self-interest. But the deep defects of socialist economies were evident thirty or forty years ago to anyone who chose to look. Why was it that these countries moved away from central planning only in the 1980s? The answer must be found in the consciousness of the elites and leaders ruling them, who decided to opt for the "Protestant" life of wealth and risk over the "Catholic" path of poverty and security.[8] That change was in no way made inevitable by the material conditions in which either country found itself on the

---

[7] One need look no further than the recent performance of Vietnamese immigrants in the U.S. school system when compared to their black or Hispanic classmates to realize that culture and consciousness are absolutely crucial to explain not only economic behavior but virtually every other important aspect of life as well.

[8] I understand that a full explanation of the origins of the reform movements in China and Russia is a good deal more complicated than this simple formula would suggest. The Soviet reform, for example, was motivated in good measure by Moscow's sense of *insecurity* in the technological-military realm. Nonetheless, neither country on the eve of its reforms was in such a state of *material* crisis that one could have predicted the surprising reform paths ultimately taken.

eve of the reform, but instead came about as the result of the victory of one idea over another.[9]

For Kojève, as for all good Hegelians, understanding the underlying processes of history requires understanding developments in the realm of consciousness or ideas, since consciousness will ultimately remake the material world in its own image. To say that history ended in 1806 meant that mankind's ideological evolution ended in the ideals of the French or American Revolutions: while particular regimes in the real world might not implement these ideals fully, their theoretical truth is absolute and could not be improved upon. Hence it did not matter to Kojève that the consciousness of the postwar generation of Europeans had not been universalized throughout the world; if ideological development had in fact ended, the homogenous state would eventually become victorious throughout the material world.

I have neither the space nor, frankly, the ability to defend in depth Hegel's radical idealist perspective. The issue is not whether Hegel's system was right, but whether his perspective might uncover the problematic nature of many materialist explanations we often take for granted. This is not to deny the role of material factors as such. To a literal-minded idealist, human society can be built around any arbitrary set of principles regardless of their relationship to the material world. And in fact men have proven themselves able to endure the most extreme material hardships in the name of ideas that exist in the realm of the spirit alone, be it the divinity of cows or the nature of the Holy Trinity.[10]

But while man's very perception of the material world is shaped by his historical consciousness of it, the material world can clearly affect in return the viability of a particular state of consciousness. In particular, the spectacular abundance of advanced liberal economies and the infinitely diverse consumer culture made possible by them seem to both foster and preserve liberalism in the political sphere. I want to avoid the materialist determinism that says that liberal economics inevitably produces liberal politics, because I believe that both economics and politics presuppose an autonomous prior state of consciousness that makes them possible. But that state of consciousness that permits the growth of liberalism seems to stabilize in the way one would expect at the end of history if it is underwritten by the abundance of a modern free market economy. We might summarize the content of the universal homogenous state as liberal democracy in the political sphere combined with easy access to VCRs and stereos in the economic.

---

[9] It is still not clear whether the Soviet peoples are as "Protestant" as Gorbachev and will follow him down that path.

[10] The internal politics of the Byzantine Empire at the time of Justinian revolved around a conflict between the so-called monophysites and monothelites, who believed that the unity of the Holy Trinity was alternatively one of nature or of will. This conflict corresponded to some extent to one between proponents of different racing teams in the Hippodrome in Byzantium and led to a not insignificant level of political violence. Modern historians would tend to seek the roots of such conflicts in antagonisms between social classes or some other modern economic category, being unwilling to believe that men would kill each other over the nature of the Trinity.

III

Have we in fact reached the end of history? Are there, in other words, any fundamental "contradictions" in human life that cannot be resolved in the context of modern liberalism, that would be resolvable by an alternative political-economic structure? If we accept the idealist premises laid out above, we must seek an answer to this question in the realm of ideology and consciousness. Our task is not to answer exhaustively the challenges to liberalism promoted by every crackpot messiah around the world, but only those that are embodied in important social or political forces and movements, and which are therefore part of world history. For our purposes, it matters very little what strange thoughts occur to people in Albania or Burkina Faso, for we are interested in what one could in some sense call the common ideological heritage of mankind.

In the past century, there have been two major challenges to liberalism, those of fascism and of communism. The former[11] saw the political weakness, materialism, anomie, and lack of community of the West as fundamental contradictions in liberal societies that could only be resolved by a strong state that forged a new "people" on the basis of national exclusiveness. Fascism was destroyed as a living ideology by World War II. This was a defeat, of course, on a very material level, but it amounted to a defeat of the idea as well. What destroyed fascism as an idea was not universal moral revulsion against it, since plenty of people were willing to endorse the idea as long as it seemed the wave of the future, but its lack of success. After the war, it seemed to most people that German fascism as well as its other European and Asian variants were bound to self-destruct. There was no material reason why new fascist movements could not have sprung up again after the war in other locales, but for the fact that expansionist ultranationalism, with its promise of unending conflict leading to disastrous military defeat, had completely lost its appeal. The ruins of the Reich chancellory as well as the atomic bombs dropped on Hiroshima and Nagasaki killed this ideology on the level of consciousness as well as materially, and all of the proto-fascist movements spawned by the German and Japanese examples like the Peronist movement in Argentina or Subhas Chandra Bose's Indian National Army withered after the war.

The ideological challenge mounted by the other great alternative to liberalism, communism, was far more serious. Marx, speaking Hegel's language, asserted that liberal society contained a fundamental contradiction that could not be resolved within its context, that between capital and labor, and this contradiction has constituted the chief accusation against liberalism ever since. But surely, the class issue has actually

---

[11] I am not using the term "fascism" here in its most precise sense, fully aware of the frequent misuse of this term to denounce anyone to the right of the user. "Fascism" here denotes any organized ultra-nationalist movement with universalistic pretensions—not universalistic with regard to its nationalism, of course, since the latter is exclusive by definition, but with regard to the movement's belief in its right to rule other people. Hence Imperial Japan would qualify as fascist while former strongman Stoessner's Paraguay or Pinochet's Chile would not. Obviously fascist ideologies cannot be universalistic in the sense of Marxism or liberalism, but the structure of the doctrine can be transferred from country to country.

been successfully resolved in the West. As Kojève (among others) noted, the egalitarianism of modern America represents the essential achievement of the classless society envisioned by Marx. This is not to say that there are not rich people and poor people in the United States, or that the gap between them has not grown in recent years. But the root causes of economic inequality do not have to do with the underlying legal and social structure of our society, which remains fundamentally egalitarian and moderately redistributionist, so much as with the cultural and social characteristics of the groups that make it up, which are in turn the historical legacy of premodern conditions. Thus black poverty in the United States is not the inherent product of liberalism, but is rather the "legacy of slavery and racism" which persisted long after the formal abolition of slavery.

As a result of the receding of the class issue, the appeal of communism in the developed Western world, it is safe to say, is lower today than any time since the end of the First World War. This can be measured in any number of ways: in the declining membership and electoral pull of the major European communist parties, and their overtly revisionist programs; in the corresponding electoral success of conservative parties from Britain and Germany to the United States and Japan, which are unabashedly pro-market and anti-statist; and in an intellectual climate whose most "advanced" members no longer believe that bourgeois society is something that ultimately needs to be overcome. This is not to say that the opinions of progressive intellectuals in Western countries are not deeply pathological in any number of ways. But those who believe that the future must inevitably be socialist tend to be very old, or very marginal to the real political discourse of their societies.

One may argue that the socialist alternative was never terribly plausible for the North Atlantic world, and was sustained for the last several decades primarily by its success outside of this region. But it is precisely in the non-European world that one is most struck by the occurrence of major ideological transformations. Surely the most remarkable changes have occurred in Asia. Due to the strength and adaptability of the indigenous cultures there, Asia became a battleground for a variety of imported Western ideologies early in this century. Liberalism in Asia was a very weak reed in the period after World War I; it is easy today to forget how gloomy Asia's political future looked as recently as ten or fifteen years ago. It is easy to forget as well how momentous the outcome of Asian ideological struggles seemed for world political development as a whole.

The first Asian alternative to liberalism to be decisively defeated was the fascist one represented by Imperial Japan. Japanese fascism (like its German version) was defeated by the force of American arms in the Pacific war, and liberal democracy was imposed on Japan by a victorious United States. Western capitalism and political liberalism when transplanted to Japan were adapted and transformed by the Japanese in such a way as to be scarcely recognizable.[12] Many Americans are now aware that Japanese industrial

---

[12] I use the example of Japan with some caution, since Kojève late in his life came to conclude that Japan, with its culture based on purely formal arts, proved that the universal homogenous state was

organization is very different from that prevailing in the United States or Europe, and it is questionable what relationship the factional maneuvering that takes place with the governing Liberal Democratic Party bears to democracy. Nonetheless, the very fact that the essential elements of economic and political liberalism have been so successfully grafted onto uniquely Japanese traditions and institutions guarantees their survival in the long run. More important is the contribution that Japan has made in turn to world history by following in the footsteps of the United States to create a truly universal consumer culture that has become both a symbol and an underpinning of the universal homogenous state. V.S. Naipaul travelling in Khomeini's Iran shortly after the revolution noted the omnipresent signs advertising the products of Sony, Hitachi, and JVC, whose appeal remained virtually irresistible and gave the lie to the regime's pretensions of restoring a state based on the rule of the *Shariah*. Desire for access to the consumer culture, created in large measure by Japan, has played a crucial role in fostering the spread of economic liberalism throughout Asia, and hence in promoting political liberalism as well.

The economic success of the other newly industrializing countries (NICs) in Asia following on the example of Japan is by now a familiar story. What is important from a Hegelian standpoint is that political liberalism has been following economic liberalism, more slowly than many had hoped but with seeming inevitability. Here again we see the victory of the idea of the universal homogenous state. South Korea had developed into a modern, urbanized society with an increasingly large and well-educated middle class that could not possibly be isolated from the larger democratic trends around them. Under these circumstances it seemed intolerable to a large part of this population that it should be ruled by an anachronistic military regime while Japan, only a decade or so ahead in economic terms, had parliamentary institutions for over forty years. Even the former socialist regime in Burma, which for so many decades existed in dismal isolation from the larger trends dominating Asia, was buffeted in the past year by pressures to liberalize both its economy and political system. It is said that unhappiness with strongman Ne Win began when a senior Burmese officer went to Singapore for medical treatment and broke down crying when he saw how far socialist Burma had been left behind by its ASEAN neighbors.

But the power of the liberal idea would seem much less impressive if it had not infected the largest and oldest culture in Asia, China. The simple existence of communist China created an alternative pole of ideological attraction, and as such constituted a threat to liberalism. But the past fifteen years have seen an almost total discrediting of Marxism-Leninism as an economic system. Beginning with the famous third plenum of the Tenth Central Committee in 1978, the Chinese Communist party set about decollectivizing agriculture for the 800 million Chinese who still lived in the countryside. The role of the state in agriculture was reduced to that of a tax collector, while production of consumer goods was sharply increased in order to give peasants a

not victorious and that history had perhaps not ended. See the long note at the end of the second edition of *Introduction à la Lecture de Hegel*, 462–3.

taste of the universal homogenous state and thereby an incentive to work. The reform doubled Chinese grain output in only five years, and in the process created for Deng Xiao-ping a solid political base from which he was able to extend the reform to other parts of the economy. Economic statistics do not begin to describe the dynamism, initiative, and openness evident in China since the reform began.

China could not now be described in any way as a liberal democracy. At present, no more than 20 percent of its economy has been marketized, and most importantly it continues to be ruled by a self-appointed Communist party which has given no hint of wanting to devolve power. Deng has made none of Gorbachev's promises regarding democratization of the political system and there is no Chinese equivalent of *glasnost*. The Chinese leadership has in fact been much more circumspect in criticizing Mao and Maoism than Gorbachev with respect to Brezhnev and Stalin, and the regime continues to pay lip service to Marxism-Leninism as its ideological underpinning. But anyone familiar with the outlook and behavior of the new technocratic elite now governing China knows that Marxism and ideological principle have become virtually irrelevant as guides to policy, and that bourgeois consumerism has a real meaning in that country for the first time since the revolution. The various slowdowns in the pace of reform, the campaigns against "spiritual pollution" and crackdowns on political dissent are more properly seen as tactical adjustments made in the process of managing what is an extraordinarily difficult political transition. By ducking the question of political reform while putting the economy on a new footing, Deng has managed to avoid the breakdown of authority that has accompanied Gorbachev's *perestroika*. Yet the pull of the liberal idea continues to be very strong as economic power devolves and the economy becomes more open to the outside world. There are currently over 20,000 Chinese students studying in the U.S. and other Western countries, almost all of them the children of the Chinese elite. It is hard to believe that when they return home to run the country they will be content for China to be the only country in Asia unaffected by the larger democratizing trend. The student demonstrations in Beijing that broke out first in December 1986 and recurred recently on the occasion of Hu Yao-bang's death were only the beginning of what will inevitably be mounting pressure for change in the political system as well.

What is important about China from the standpoint of world history is not the present state of the reform or even its future prospects. The central issue is the fact that the People's Republic of China can no longer act as a beacon for illiberal forces around the world, whether they be guerrillas in some Asian jungle or middle class students in Paris. Maoism, rather than being the pattern for Asia's future, became an anachronism, and it was the mainland Chinese who in fact were decisively influenced by the prosperity and dynamism of their overseas co-ethnics—the ironic ultimate victory of Taiwan.

Important as these changes in China have been, however, it is developments in the Soviet Union—the original "homeland of the world proletariat"—that have put the final nail in the coffin of the Marxist-Leninist alternative to liberal democracy. It should be clear that in terms of formal institutions, not much has changed in the four years since Gorbachev has come to power: free markets and the cooperative movement represent only a small part of the Soviet economy, which remains centrally planned; the political system is still dominated by the Communist party, which has only begun to democratize internally and to share power with other groups; the regime continues to assert that it is seeking only to modernize socialism and that its ideological basis remains Marxism-Leninism; and, finally, Gorbachev faces a potentially powerful conservative opposition that could undo many of the changes that have taken place to date. Moreover, it is hard to be too sanguine about the chances for success of Gorbachev's proposed reforms, either in the sphere of economics or politics. But my purpose here is not to analyze events in the short-term, or to make predictions for policy purposes, but to look at underlying trends in the sphere of ideology and consciousness. And in that respect, it is clear that an astounding transformation has occurred.

Emigres from the Soviet Union have been reporting for at least the last generation now that virtually nobody in that country truly believed in Marxism-Leninism any longer, and that this was nowhere more true than in the Soviet elite, which continued to mouth Marxist slogans out of sheer cynicism. The corruption and decadence of the late Brezhnev-era Soviet state seemed to matter little, however, for as long as the state itself refused to throw into question any of the fundamental principles underlying Soviet society, the system was capable of functioning adequately out of sheer inertia and could even muster some dynamism in the realm of foreign and defense policy. Marxism-Leninism was like a magical incantation which, however absurd and devoid of meaning, was the only common basis on which the elite could agree to rule Soviet society.

What has happened in the four years since Gorbachev's coming to power is a revolutionary assault on the most fundamental institutions and principles of Stalinism, and their replacement by other principles which do not amount to liberalism *per se* but whose only connecting thread is liberalism. This is most evident in the economic sphere, where the reform economists around Gorbachev have become steadily more radical in their support for free markets, to the point where some like Nikolai Shmelev do not mind being compared in public to Milton Friedman. There is a virtual consensus among the currently dominant school of Soviet economists now that central planning and the command system of allocation are the root cause of economic inefficiency, and that if the Soviet system is ever to heal itself, it must permit free and decentralized decision-making with respect to investment, labor, and prices. After a couple of initial years of ideological confusion, these principles have finally been incorporated into policy with the promulgation of new laws on enterprise autonomy, cooperatives, and finally in 1988 on lease arrangements and family farming. There are, of course, a number of fatal flaws in the current implementation of the reform, most notably the absence of a thoroughgoing price reform. But the problem is no longer a *conceptual* one: Gorbachev and his lieutenants seem to understand the economic logic of marketization well enough, but like the leaders of a Third World country facing the IMF, are afraid of the social consequences of ending consumer subsidies and other forms of dependence on the state sector.

In the political sphere, the proposed changes to the Soviet constitution, legal system, and party rules amount to much less than the establishment of a liberal state. Gorbachev has spoken of democratization primarily in the sphere of internal party affairs, and has shown little intention of ending the Communist party's monopoly of power; indeed, the political reform seeks to legitimize and therefore strengthen the CPSU's rule.[13] Nonetheless, the general principles underlying many of the reforms—that the "people" should be truly responsible for their own affairs, that higher political bodies should be answerable to lower ones, and not vice versa, that the rule of law should prevail over arbitrary police actions, with separation of powers and an independent judiciary, that there should be legal protection for property rights, the need for open discussion of public issues and the right of public dissent, the empowering of the Soviets as a forum in which the whole Soviet people can participate, and of a political culture that is more tolerant and pluralistic—come from a source fundamentally alien to the USSR's Marxist-Leninist tradition, even if they are incompletely articulated and poorly implemented in practice.

Gorbachev's repeated assertions that he is doing no more than trying to restore the original meaning of Leninism are themselves a kind of Orwellian doublespeak. Gorbachev and his allies have consistently maintained that intraparty democracy was somehow the essence of Leninism, and that the various liberal practices of open debate, secret ballot elections, and rule of law were all part of the Leninist heritage, corrupted only later by Stalin. While almost anyone would look good compared to Stalin, drawing so sharp a line between Lenin and his successor is questionable. The essence of Lenin's democratic centralism was centralsim, not democracy; that is, the absolutely rigid, monolithic, and disciplined dictatorship of a hierarchically organized vanguard Communist party, speaking in the name of the *demos*. All of Lenin's vicious polemics against Karl Kautsky, Rosa Luxemburg, and various other Menshevik and Social Democratic rivals, not to mention his contempt for "bourgeois legality" and freedoms, centered around his profound conviction that a revolution could not be successfully made by a democratically run organization.

Gorbachev's claim that he is seeking to return to the true Lenin is perfectly easy to understand: having fostered a thorough denunciation of Stalinism and Brezhnevism as the root of the USSR's present predicament, he needs some point in Soviet history on which to anchor the legitimacy of the CPSU's continued rule. But Gorbachev's tactical requirements should not blind us to the fact that the democratizing and decentralizing principles which he has enunciated in both the economic and political spheres are highly subversive of some of the most fundamental precepts of both Marxism and Leninism. Indeed, if the bulk of the present economic reform proposals were put into effect, it is hard to know how the Soviet economy would be more socialist than those of other Western countries with large public sectors.

The Soviet Union could in no way be described as a liberal or democratic country now, nor do I think that it is terribly likely that *perestroika* will succeed such that the

---

[13] This is not true in Poland and Hungary, however, whose Communist parties have taken moves toward true power-sharing and pluralism.

label will be thinkable any time in the near future. But at the end of history it is not necessary that all societies become successful liberal societies, merely that they end their ideological pretensions of representing different and higher forms of human society. And in this respect I believe that something very important has happened in the Soviet Union in the past few years: the criticisms of the Soviet system sanctioned by Gorbachev have been so thorough and devastating that there is very little chance of going back to either Stalinism or Brezhnevism in any simple way. Gorbachev has finally permitted people to say what they had privately understood for many years, namely, that the magical incantations of Marxism-Leninism were nonsense, that Soviet socialism was not superior to the West in any respect but was in fact a monumental failure. The conservative opposition in the USSR, consisting both of simple workers afraid of unemployment and inflation and of party officials fearful of losing their jobs and privileges, is outspoken and may be strong enough to force Gorbachev's ouster in the next few years. But what both groups desire is tradition, order, and authority; they manifest no deep commitment to Marxism-Leninism, except insofar as they have invested much of their own lives in it.[14] For authority to be restored in the Soviet Union after Gorbachev's demolition work, it must be on the basis of some new and vigorous ideology which has not yet appeared on the horizon.

If we admit for the moment that the fascist and communist challenges to liberalism are dead, are there any other ideological competitors left? Or put another way, are there contradictions in liberal society beyond that of class that are not resolvable? Two possibilities suggest themselves, those of religion and nationalism.

The rise of religious fundamentalism in recent years within the Christian, Jewish, and Muslim traditions has been widely noted. One is inclined to say that the revival of religion in some way attests to a broad unhappiness with the impersonality and spiritual vacuity of liberal consumerist societies. Yet while the emptiness at the core of liberalism is most certainly a defect in the ideology—indeed, a flaw that one does not need the perspective of religion to recognize[15]—it is not at all clear that it is remediable through politics. Modern liberalism itself was historically a consequence of the weakness of religiously-based societies which, failing to agree on the nature of the good life, could not provide even the minimal preconditions of peace and stability. In the contemporary world only Islam has offered a theocratic state as a political alternative to both liberalism and communism. But the doctrine has little appeal for non-Muslims, and it is hard to believe that the movement will take on any universal significance. Other less organized religious impulses have been successfully satisfied within the sphere of personal life that is permitted in liberal societies.

---

[14] This is particularly true of the leading Soviet conservative, former Second Secretary Yegor Ligachev, who has publicly recognized many of the deep defects of the Brezhnev period.

[15] I am thinking particularly of Rousseau and the Western philosophical tradition that flows from him that was highly critical of Lockean or Hobbesian liberalism, though one could criticize liberalism from the standpoint of classical political philosophy as well.

The other major "contradiction" potentially unresolvable by liberalism is the one posed by nationalism and other forms of racial and ethnic consciousness. It is certainly true that a very large degree of conflict since the Battle of Jena has had its roots in nationalism. Two cataclysmic world wars in this century have been spawned by the nationalism of the developed world in various guises, and if those passions have been muted to a certain extent in postwar Europe, they are still extremely powerful in the Third World. Nationalism has been a threat to liberalism historically in Germany, and continues to be one in isolated parts of "post-historical" Europe like Northern Ireland.

But it is not clear that nationalism represents an irreconcilable contradiction in the heart of liberalism. In the first place, nationalism is not one single phenomenon but several, ranging from mild cultural nostalgia to the highly organized and elaborately articulated doctrine of National Socialism. Only systematic nationalisms of the latter sort can qualify as a formal ideology on the level of liberalism or communism. The vast majority of the world's nationalist movements do not have a political program beyond the negative desire of independence *from* some other group or people, and do not offer anything like a comprehensive agenda for socio-economic organization. As such, they are compatible with doctrines and ideologies that do offer such agendas. While they may constitute a source of conflict for liberal societies, this conflict does not arise from liberalism itself so much as from the fact that the liberalism in question is incomplete. Certainly a great deal of the world's ethnic and nationalist tension can be explained in terms of peoples who are forced to live in unrepresentative political systems that they have not chosen.

While it is impossible to rule out the sudden appearance of new ideologies or previously unrecognized contradictions in liberal societies, then, the present world seems to confirm that the fundamental principles of socio-political organization have not advanced terribly far since 1806. Many of the wars and revolutions fought since that time have been undertaken in the name of ideologies which claimed to be more advanced than liberalism, but whose pretensions were ultimately unmasked by history. In the meantime, they have helped to spread the universal homogenous state to the point where it could have a significant effect on the overall character of international relations.

IV

What are the implications of the end of history for international relations? Clearly, the vast bulk of the Third World remains very much mired in history, and will be a terrain of conflict for many years to come. But let us focus for the time being on the larger and more developed states of the world who after all account for the greater part of world politics. Russia and China are not likely to join the developed nations of the West as liberal societies any time in the foreseeable future, but suppose for a moment that Marxism-Leninism ceases to be a factor driving the foreign policies of these states— a prospect which, if not yet here, the last few years have made a real possibility. How will the overall characteristics of a de-ideologized world differ from those of the one with which we are familiar at such a hypothetical juncture?

The most common answer is—not very much. For there is a very widespread belief among many observers of international relations that underneath the skin of ideology is a hard core of great power national interest that guarantees a fairly high level of competition and conflict between nations. Indeed, according to one academically popular school of international relations theory, conflict inheres in the international system as such, and to understand the prospects for conflict one must look at the shape of the system—for example, whether it is bipolar or multipolar—rather than at the specific character of the nations and regimes that constitute it. This school in effect applies a Hobbesian view of politics to international relations, and assumes that aggression and insecurity are universal characteristics of human societies rather than the product of specific historical circumstances.

Believers in this line of thought take the relations that existed between the participants in the classical nineteenth century European balance of power as a model for what a deideologized contemporary world would look like. Charles Krauthammer, for example, recently explained that if as a result of Gorbachev's reforms the USSR is shorn of Marxist-Leninist ideology, its behavior will revert to that of nineteenth century imperial Russia.[16] While he finds this more reassuring than the threat posed by a communist Russia, he implies that there will still be a substantial degree of competition and conflict in the international system, just as there was say between Russia and Britain or Wilhelmine Germany in the last century. This is, of course, a convenient point of view for people who want to admit that something major is changing in the Soviet Union, but do not want to accept responsibility for recommending the radical policy redirection implicit in such a view. But is it true?

In fact, the notion that ideology is a superstructure imposed on a substratum of permanent great power interest is a highly questionable proposition. For the way in which any state defines its national interest is not universal but rests on some kind of prior ideological basis, just as we saw that economic behavior is determined by a prior state of consciousness. In this century, states have adopted highly articulated doctrines with explicit foreign policy agendas legitimizing expansionism, like Marxism-Leninism or National Socialism.

The expansionist and competitive behavior of nineteenth-century European states rested on no less ideal a basis; it just so happened that the ideology driving it was less explicit than the doctrines of the twentieth century. For one thing, most "liberal" European societies were illiberal insofar as they believed in the legitimacy of imperialism, that is, the right of one nation to rule over other nations without regard for the wishes of the ruled. The justifications for imperialism varied from nation to nation, from a crude belief in the legitimacy of force, particularly when applied to non-Europeans, to the White Man's Burden and Europe's Christianizing mission, to the desire to give people of color access to the culture of Rabelais and Molière. But whatever the particular ideological basis, every "developed" country believed in the acceptability of higher civilizations ruling lower ones—including, incidentally, the United States with

---

[16] See his article, "Beyond the Cold War," *New Republic*, December 19, 1988.

regard to the Philippines. This led to a drive for pure territorial aggrandizement in the latter half of the century and played no small role in causing the Great War.

The radical and deformed outgrowth of nineteenth-century imperialism was German fascism, an ideology which justified Germany's right not only to rule over non-European peoples, but over *all* non-German ones. But in retrospect it seems that Hitler represented a diseased bypath in the general course of European development, and since his fiery defeat, the legitimacy of any kind of territorial aggrandizement has been thoroughly discredited.[17] Since the Second World War, European nationalism has been defanged and shorn of any real relevance to foreign policy, with the consequence that the nineteenth-century model of great power behavior has become a serious anachronism. The most extreme form of nationalism that any Western European state has mustered since 1945 has been Gaullism, whose self-assertion has been confined largely to the realm of nuisance politics and culture. International life for the part of the world that has reached the end of history is far more preoccupied with economics than with politics or strategy.

The developed states of the West do maintain defense establishments and in the postwar period have competed vigorously for influence to meet a worldwide communist threat. This behavior has been driven, however, by an external threat from states that possess overtly expansionist ideologies, and would not exist in their absence. To take the "neo-realist" theory seriously, one would have to believe that "natural" competitive behavior would reassert itself among the OECD states were Russia and China to disappear from the face of the earth. That is, West Germany and France would arm themselves against each other as they did in the 1930s, Australia and New Zealand would send military advisers to block each others' advances in Africa, and the U.S.-Canadian border would become fortified. Such a prospect is, of course, ludicrous: minus Marxist-Leninist ideology, we are far more likely to see the "Common Marketization" of world politics than the disintegration of the EEC into nineteenth-century competitiveness. Indeed, as our experience in dealing with Europe on matters such as terrorism or Libya prove, they are much further gone than we down the road that denies the legitimacy of the use of force in international politics, even in self-defense.

The automatic assumption that Russia shorn of its expansionist communist ideology should pick up where the czars left off just prior to the Bolshevik Revolution is therefore a curious one. It assumes that the evolution of human consciousness has stood still in the meantime, and that the Soviets, while picking up currently fashionable ideas in the realm of economics, will return to foreign policy views a century out of date in the rest of Europe. This is certainly not what happened to China after it began its reform process. Chinese competitiveness and expansionism on the world scene have virtually disappeared: Beijing no longer sponsors Maoist insurgencies or tries to cultivate influence in distant African countries as it did in the 1960s. This is not to say that there are not troublesome aspects to contemporary Chinese foreign policy, such as the

---

[17] It took European colonial powers like France several years after the war to admit the illegitimacy of their empires, but decolonialization was an inevitable consequence of the Allied victory which had been based on the promise of a restoration of democratic freedoms.

reckless sale of ballistic missile technology in the Middle East; and the PRC continues to manifest traditional great power behavior in its sponsorship of the Khmer Rouge against Vietnam. But the former is explained by commercial motives and the latter is a vestige of earlier ideologically-based rivalries. The new China far more resembles Gaullist France than pre-World War I Germany.

The real question for the future, however, is the degree to which Soviet elites have assimilated the consciousness of the universal homogenous state that is post-Hitler Europe. From their writings and from my own personal contacts with them, there is no question in my mind that the liberal Soviet intelligentsia rallying around Gorbachev has arrived at the end-of-history view in a remarkably short time, due in no small measure to the contacts they have had since the Brezhnev era with the larger European civilization around them. "New political thinking," the general rubric for their views, describes a world dominated by economic concerns, in which there are no ideological grounds for major conflict between nations, and in which, consequently, the use of military force becomes less legitimate. As Foreign Minister Shevardnadze put it in mid-1988:

> The struggle between two opposing systems is no longer a determining tendency of the present-day era. At the modern stage, the ability to build up material wealth at an accelerated rate on the basis of front-ranking science and high-level techniques and technology, and to distribute it fairly, and through joint efforts to restore and protect the resources necessary for mankind's survival acquires decisive importance.[18]

The post-historical consciousness represented by "new thinking" is only one possible future for the Soviet Union, however. There has always been a very strong current of great Russian chauvinism in the Soviet Union, which has found freer expression since the advent of *glasnost*. It may be possible to return to traditional Marxism-Leninism for a while as a simple rallying point for those who want to restore the authority that Gorbachev has dissipated. But as in Poland, Marxism-Leninism is dead as a mobilizing ideology: under its banner people cannot be made to work harder, and its adherents have lost confidence in themselves. Unlike the propagators of traditional Marxism-Leninism, however, ultranationalists in the USSR believe in their Slavophile cause passionately, and one gets the sense that the fascist alternative is not one that has played itself out entirely there.

The Soviet Union, then, is at a fork in the road: it can start down the path that was staked out by Western Europe forty-five years ago, a path that most of Asia has followed, or it can realize its own uniqueness and remain stuck in history. The choice it makes will be highly important for us, given the Soviet Union's size and military strength, for that power will continue to preoccupy us and slow our realization that we have already emerged on the other side of history.

---

[18] *Vestnik Ministerstva Inostrannikh Del SSSR* no. 15 (August 1988), 27–46. "New thinking" does of course serve a propagandistic purpose in persuading Western audiences of Soviet good intentions. But the fact that it is good propaganda does not mean that its formulators do not take many of its ideas seriously.

V

The passing of Marxism-Leninism first from China and then from the Soviet Union will mean its death as a living ideology of world historical significance. For while there may be some isolated true believers left in places like Managua, Pyongyang, or Cambridge, Massachusetts, the fact that there is not a single large state in which it is a going concern undermines completely its pretensions to being in the vanguard of human history. And the death of this ideology means the growing "Common Marketization" of international relations, and the diminution of the likelihood of large-scale conflict between states.

This does not by any means imply the end of international conflict *per se*. For the world at that point would be divided between a part that was historical and a part that was post-historical. Conflict between states still in history, and between those states and those at the end of history, would still be possible. There would still be a high and perhaps rising level of ethnic and nationalist violence, since those are impulses incompletely played out, even in parts of the post-historical world. Palestinians and Kurds, Sikhs and Tamils, Irish Catholics and Walloons, Armenians and Azeris, will continue to have their unresolved grievances. This implies that terrorism and wars of national liberation will continue to be an important item on the international agenda. But large-scale conflict must involve large states still caught in the grip of history and they are what appear to be passing from the scene.

The end of history will be a very sad time. The struggle for recognition, the willingness to risk one's life for a purely abstract goal, the worldwide ideological struggle that called forth daring, courage, imagination, and idealism, will be replaced by economic calculation, the endless solving of technical problems, environmental concerns, and the satisfaction of sophisticated consumer demands. In the post-historical period there will be neither art nor philosophy, just the perpetual caretaking of the museum of human history. I can feel in myself, and see in others around me, a powerful nostalgia for the time when history existed. Such nostalgia, in fact will continue to fuel competition and conflict even in the post-historical world for some time to come. Even though I recognize its inevitability, I have the most ambivalent feelings for the civilization that has been created in Europe since 1945, with its north Atlantic and Asian offshoots. Perhaps this very prospect of centuries of boredom at the end of history will serve to get history started once again.

Aleksandr I. Solzhenitsyn

A WORLD SPLIT APART

I am sincerely happy to be here with you on the occasion of the 327th commencement of this old and illustrious university. My congratulations and best wishes to all of today's graduates.

Harvard's motto is "Veritas." Many of you have already found out and others will find out in the course of their lives that truth eludes us as soon as our concentration begins to flag, all the while leaving the illusion that we are continuing to pursue it. This is the source of much discord. Also, truth seldom is sweet; it is almost invariably bitter. A measure of bitter truth is included in my speech today, but I offer it as a friend, not as an adversary.

Three years ago in the United States I said certain things that were rejected and appeared unacceptable. Today, however, many people agree with what I then said....

The split in today's world is perceptible even to a hasty glance. Any of our contemporaries readily identifies two world powers, each of them already capable of utterly destroying the other. However, the understanding of the split too often is limited to this political conception: the illusion according to which danger may be abolished through successful diplomatic negotiations or by achieving a balance of armed forces. The truth is that the split is both more profound and more alienating, that the rifts are more numerous than one can see at first glance. The deep manifold splits bear the danger of equally manifold disaster for all of us, in accordance with the ancient truth that a kingdom—in this case, our Earth—divided against itself cannot stand.

Contemporary Worlds

There is the concept of the Third World: thus, we already have three worlds. Undoubtedly, however, the number is even greater; we are just too far away to see. Every ancient and deeply rooted self-contained culture, especially if it is spread over a wide part of the earth's surface, constitutes a self-contained world, full of riddles and surprises to Western thinking. As a minimum, we must include in this category China, India, the Muslim world, and Africa, if indeed we accept the approximation of viewing

Aleksandr Solzhenitsyn, "A World Split Apart" (1978) from *Solzhenitsyn at Harvard: The Address, Twelve Early Responses, and Six Later Reflections* (Ethics and Public Policy Center, Washington, D. C., 1978) 3–20.

the latter two as uniform. For one thousand years Russia belonged to such a category, although Western thinking systematically committed the mistake of denying its special character and therefore never understood it, just as today the West does not understand Russia in Communist captivity. And while it may be that in past years Japan has increasingly become, in effect, a Far West, drawing ever closer to Western ways (I am no judge here), Israel, I think, should not be reckoned as part of the West, if only because of the decisive circumstance that its state system is fundamentally linked to religion.

How short a time ago, relatively, the small world of modern Europe was easily seizing colonies all over the globe, not only without anticipating any real resistance, but usually with contempt for any possible values in the conquered peoples' approach to life. It all seemed an overwhelming success, with no geographic limits. Western society expanded in a triumph of human independence and power. And all of a sudden the twentieth century brought the clear realization of this society's fragility. We now see that the conquests proved to be short-lived and precarious (and this, in turn, points to defects in the Western view of the world which led to these conquests). Relations with the former colonial world now have switched to the opposite extreme and the Western world often exhibits an excess of obsequiousness, but it is difficult yet to estimate the size of the bill which former colonial countries will present to the West and it is difficult to predict whether the surrender not only of its last colonies, but of everything it owns, will be sufficient for the West to clear this account.

Convergence

But the persisting blindness of superiority continues to hold the belief that all the vast regions of our planet should develop and mature to the level of contemporary Western systems, the best in theory and the most attractive in practice; that all those other worlds are but temporarily prevented (by wicked leaders or by severe crises or by their own barbarity and incomprehension) from pursuing Western pluralistic democracy and adopting the Western way of life. Countries are judged on the merit of their progress in that direction. But in fact such a conception is a fruit of Western incomprehension of the essence of other worlds, a result of mistakenly measuring them all with a Western yardstick. The real picture of our planet's development bears little resemblance to all this.

The anguish of a divided world gave birth to the theory of convergence between the leading Western countries and the Soviet Union. It is a soothing theory which overlooks the fact that these worlds are not at all evolving toward each other and that neither one can be transformed into the other without violence. Besides, convergence inevitably means acceptance of the other side's defects, too, and this can hardly suit anyone.

If I were today addressing an audience in my country, in my examination of the overall pattern of the world's rifts I would have concentrated on the calamities of the East. But since my forced exile in the West has now lasted four years and since my audience is a Western one, I think it may be of greater interest to concentrate on certain aspects of the contemporary West, such as I see them.

A Decline in Courage

A decline in courage may be the most striking feature that an outside observer notices in the West today. The Western world has lost its civic courage, both as a whole and separately, in each country, in each government, in each political party, and of course, in the United Nations. Such a decline in courage is particularly noticeable among the ruling and intellectual elites, causing an impression of a loss of courage by the entire society. There remain many courageous individuals, but they have no determining influence on public life. Political and intellectual functionaries exhibit this depression, passivity, and perplexity in their actions and in their statements, and even more so in their self-serving rationales as to how realistic, reasonable, and intellectually and even morally justified it is to base state policies on weakness and cowardice. And the decline in courage, at times attaining what could be termed a lack of manhood, is ironically emphasized by occasional outbursts of boldness and inflexibility on the part of those same functionaries when dealing with weak governments and with countries that lack support, or with doomed currents which clearly cannot offer any resistance. But they get tongue-tied and paralyzed when they deal with powerful governments and threatening forces, with aggressors and international terrorists.

Must one point out that from ancient times a decline in courage has been considered the first symptom of the end?

Well-Being

When the modern Western states were being formed, it was proclaimed as a principle that governments are meant to serve man and that man lives in order to be free and pursue happiness. (See, for example, the American Declaration of Independence.) Now at last during past decades technical and social progress has permitted the realization of such aspirations: the welfare state. Every citizen has been granted the desired freedom and material goods In such quantity and of such quality as to guarantee in theory the achievement of happiness, in the debased sense of the word which has come into being during those same decades. (In the process, however, one psychological detail has been overlooked: the constant desire to have still more things and a still better life and the struggle to this end imprint many Western faces with worry and even depression, though it is customary to carefully conceal such feelings. This active and tense competition comes to dominate all human thought and does not in the least open a way to free spiritual development.) The individual's independence from many types of state pressure has been guaranteed; the majority of the people have been granted well-being to an extent their fathers and grandfathers could not even dream about; it has become possible to raise young people according to these ideals, preparing them for and summoning them toward physical bloom, happiness, the possession of material goods, money, and leisure, toward an almost unlimited freedom in the choice of pleasures. So who should now renounce all this, why and for the sake of what should one risk one's precious life in defense of the common good and particularly in the nebulous case when the security of one's nation must be defended in an as yet distant land?

Even biology tells us that a high degree of habitual well-being is not advantageous to a living organism. Today, well-being in the life of Western society has begun to take off its pernicious mask.

Legalistic Life

Western society has chosen for itself the organization best suited to its purposes and one I might call legalistic. The limits of human rights and rightness are determined by a system of laws; such limits are very broad. People in the West have acquired considerable skill in using, interpreting, and manipulating law (though laws tend to be too complicated for an average person to understand without the help of an expert). Every conflict is solved according to the letter of the law and this is considered to be the ultimate solution. If one is right from a legal point of view, nothing more is required, nobody may mention that one could still not be entirely right, and urge self-restraint or a renunciation of these rights, call for sacrifice and selfless risk: this would simply sound absurd. Voluntary self-restraint is almost unheard of: everybody strives toward further expansion to the extreme limit of the legal frames. (An oil company is legally blameless when it buys up an invention of a new type of energy in order to prevent its use. A food product manufacturer is legally blameless when he poisons his produce to make it last longer: after all, people are free not to purchase it.)

I have spent all my life under a Communist regime and I will tell you that a society without any objective legal scale is a terrible one indeed. But a society with no other scale but the legal one is also less than worthy of man. A society based on the letter of the law and never reaching any higher fails to take advantage of the full range of human possibilities. The letter of the law is too cold and formal to have a beneficial influence on society. Whenever the tissue of life is woven of legalistic relationships, this creates an atmosphere of spiritual mediocrity that paralyzes man's noblest impulses.

And it will be simply impossible to bear up to the trials of this threatening century with nothing but the supports of a legalistic structure.

The Direction of Freedom

Today's Western society has revealed the inequality between the freedom for good deeds and the freedom for evil deeds. A statesman who wants to achieve something important and highly constructive for his country has to move cautiously and even timidly; thousands of hasty (and irresponsible) critics cling to him at all times; he is constantly rebuffed by parliament and the press. He has to prove that his every step is well-founded and absolutely flawless. Indeed, an outstanding, truly great person who has unusual and unexpected initiatives in mind does not get any chance to assert himself; dozens of traps will be set for him from the beginning. Thus mediocrity triumphs under the guise of democratic restraints.

It is feasible and easy everywhere to undermine administrative power and it has in fact been drastically weakened in all Western countries. The defense of individual rights has reached such extremes as to make society as a whole defenseless against certain individuals. It is time, in the West, to defend not so much human rights as human obligations.

On the other hand, destructive and irresponsible freedom has been granted boundless space. Society has turned out to have scarce defense against the abyss of human decadence, for example against the misuse of liberty for moral violence against young people, such as motion pictures full of pornography, crime, and horror. This is all considered to be part of freedom and to be counterbalanced, in theory, by the young people's right not to look and not to accept. Life organized legalistically has thus shown its inability to defend itself against the corrosion of evil.

And what shall we say about the dark realms of overt criminality? Legal limits (especially in the United States) are broad enough to encourage not only individual freedom but also some misuse of such freedom. The culprit can go unpunished or obtain undeserved leniency—all with the support of thousands of defenders in the society. When a government earnestly undertakes to root out terrorism, public opinion immediately accuses it of violating the terrorists' civil rights. There is quite a number of such cases.

This tilt of freedom toward evil has come about gradually, but it evidently stems from a humanistic and benevolent concept according to which man—the master of this world—does not bear any evil within himself, and all the defects of life are caused by misguided social systems, which must therefore be corrected. Yet strangely enough, though the best social conditions have been achieved in the West, there still remains a great deal of crime; there even is considerably more of it than in the destitute and lawless Soviety society. (There is a multitude of prisoners in our camps who are termed criminals, but most of them never committed any crime; they merely tried to defend themselves against a lawless state by resorting to means outside the legal framework.)

The Direction of the Press

The press, too, of course, enjoys the widest freedom. (I shall be using the word "press" to include all the media.) But what use does it make of it?

Here again, the overriding concern is not to infringe the letter of the law. There is no true moral responsibility for distortion or disproportion. What sort of responsibility does a journalist or a newspaper have to the readership or to history? If they have misled public opinion by inaccurate information or wrong conclusions, even if they have contributed to mistakes on a state level, do we know of any case of open regret voiced by the same journalist or the same newspaper? No; this would damage sales. A nation may be the worse for such a mistake, but the journalist always gets away with it. It is most likely that he will start writing the exact opposite to his previous statements with renewed aplomb.

Because instant and credible information is required, it becomes necessary to resort to guesswork, rumors, and suppositions to fill in the voids, and none of them will ever be refuted; they settle into the readers' memory. How many hasty, immature, superficial, and misleading judgments are expressed every day, confusing readers, and are then left hanging? The press can act the role of public opinion or miseducate it. Thus we may see terrorists heroized, or secret matters pertaining to the nation's defense publicly revealed, or we may witness shameless intrusion into the privacy of well-known people according to the slogan "Everyone is entitled to know everything." (But this is a false slogan of a false era; far greater in value is the forfeited right of people *not to know*, not to have their divine souls stuffed with gossip, nonsense, vain talk. A person who works and leads a meaningful life has no need for this excessive and burdening flow of information.)

Hastiness and superficiality — these are the psychic diseases of the twentieth century and more than anywhere else this is manifested in the press. In-depth analysis of a problem is anathema to the press; it is contrary to its nature. The press merely picks out sensational formulas.

Such as it is, however, the press has become the greatest power within the Western countries, exceeding that of the legislature, the executive, and the judiciary. Yet one would like to ask: According to what law has it been elected and to whom is it responsible? In the Communist East, a journalist is frankly appointed as a state official. But who has voted Western journalists into their positions of power, for how long, and with what prerogatives?

There is yet another surprise for someone coming from the totalitarian East with its rigorously unified press: One discovers a common trend of preferences within the Western press as a whole (the spirit of the time), generally accepted patterns of judgment, and maybe common corporate interests, the sum effect being not competition but unification. Unrestrained freedom exists for the press, but not for the readership, because newspapers mostly transmit in a forceful and emphatic way those opinions which do not too openly contradict their own and that general trend.

A Fashion in Thinking

Without any censorship in the West, fashionable trends of thought and ideas are fastidiously separated from those that are not fashionable, and the latter, without ever being forbidden, have little chance of finding their way into periodicals or books or being heard in colleges. Your scholars are free in the legal sense, but they are hemmed in by the idols of the prevailing fad. There is no open violence, as in the East; however, a selection dictated by fashion and the need to accommodate mass standards frequently prevents the most independent-minded persons from contributing to public life and gives rise to dangerous herd instincts that block successful development. In America, I have received letters from highly intelligent persons — maybe a teacher in a faraway small college who could do much for the renewal and salvation of his country, but the country cannot hear him because the media will not provide him with a forum. This gives birth to strong mass prejudices, to a blindness which is perilous in our dynamic era. An example is the self-deluding interpretation of the state of affairs in the contemporary world that functions as a sort of a petrified armor around people's minds, to such a degree that human voices from seventeen countries of Eastern Europe and Eastern Asia cannot pierce it. It will be broken only by the inexorable crowbar of events.

I have mentioned a few traits of Western life which surprise and shock a new arrival to this world. The purpose and scope of this speech will not allow me to continue such a survey, in particular to look into the impact of these characteristics on important aspects of a nation's life, such as elementary education, advanced education in the humanities, and art.

Socialism

It is almost universally recognized that the West shows all the world the way to successful economic development, even though in past years it has been sharply offset by chaotic inflation. However, many people living in the West are dissatisfied with their own society. They despise it or accuse it of no longer being up to the level of maturity attained by mankind. And this causes many to sway toward socialism, which is a false and dangerous current.

I hope that no one present will suspect me of expressing my partial criticism of the Western system in order to suggest socialism as an alternative. No; with the experience of a country where socialism has been realized, I shall certainly not speak for such an alternative. The mathematician Igor Shafarevich, a member of the Soviet Academy of Science, has written a brilliantly argued book entitled *Socialism*; this is a penetrating historical analysis demonstrating that socialism of any type and shade leads to a total destruction of the human spirit and to a leveling of mankind into death. Shafarevich's book was published in France almost two years ago and so far no one has been found to refute it. It will shortly be published in English in the United States.

Not a Model

But should I he asked, instead, whether I would propose the West, such as it is today, as a model to my country, I would frankly have to answer negatively. No, I could not recommend your society as an ideal for the transformation of ours. Through deep suffering, people in our country have now achieved a spiritual development of such intensity that the Western system in its present state of spiritual exhaustion does not look attractive. Even those characteristics of your life which I have just enumerated are extremely saddening.

A fact which cannot be disputed is the weakening of human personality in the West while in the East it has become firmer and stronger. Six decades for our people and three decades for the people of Eastern Europe; during that time we have been through a spiritual training far in advance of Western experience. The complex and deadly crush of life has produced stronger, deeper, and more interesting personalities than those generated by standardized Western well-being. Therefore, if our society were to be transformed into yours, it would mean an improvement in certain aspects, but also a change for the worse on some particularly significant points. Of course, a society cannot remain in an abyss of lawlessness, as is the case in our country. But it is also demeaning for it to stay on such a soulless and smooth plane of legalism, as is the case in yours. After the suffering of decades of violence and oppression, the human soul longs for things higher, warmer, and purer than those offered by today's mass living habits, introduced as by a calling card by the revolting invasion of commercial advertising, by TV stupor, and by intolerable music.

All this is visible to numerous observers from all the worlds of our planet. The Western way of life is less and less likely to become the leading model.

There are telltale symptoms by which history gives warning to a threatened or perishing society. Such are, for instance, a decline of the arts or a lack of great statesmen. Indeed, sometimes the warnings are quite explicit and concrete. The center of your democracy and of your culture is left without electric power for a few hours only, and all of a sudden crowds of American citizens start looting and creating havoc. The smooth surface film must be very thin, then, the social system quite unstable and unhealthy.

But the fight for our planet, physical and spiritual, a fight of cosmic proportions, is not a vague matter of the future; it has already started. The forces of Evil have begun their decisive offensive. You can feel their pressure, yet your screens and publications are full of prescribed smiles and raised glasses. What is the joy about?

Short-sightedness

Very well known representatives of your society, such as George Kennan, say: "We cannot apply moral criteria to politics." Thus we mix good and evil, right and wrong, and make space for the absolute triumph of absolute evil in the world. Only moral criteria can help the West against communism's well-planned world strategy. There are no other criteria. Practical or occasional considerations of any kind will inevitably be swept away by strategy. After a certain level of the problem has been reached, legalistic thinking induces paralysis; it prevents one from seeing the scale and the meaning of events.

In spite of the abundance of information, or maybe partly because of it, the West has great difficulty in finding its bearings amid contemporary events. There have been naïve predictions by some American experts who believed that Angola would become the Soviet Union's Vietnam or that the impudent Cuban expeditions in Africa would best be stopped by special U.S. courtesy to Cuba. Kennan's advice to his own country—to begin unilateral disarmament—belongs to the same category. If you only knew how the youngest of the officials in Moscow's Old Square[1] roar with laughter at your political wizards! As to Fidel Castro, he openly scorns the United States, boldly sending his troops to distant adventures from his country right next to yours.

However, the most cruel mistake occurred with the failure to understand the Vietnam war. Some people sincerely wanted all wars to stop just as soon as possible; others believed that the way should be left open for national, or Communist, self-

---

[1] The Old Square in Moscow (*Staraya Ploshchad*) is the place where the headquarters of the Central Committee of the CPSU are located; it is the real name of what in the West is conventionally referred to as the Kremlin.

determination in Vietnam (or in Cambodia, as we see today with particular clarity). But in fact, members of the U.S. antiwar movement became accomplices in the betrayal of Far Eastern nations, in the genocide and the suffering today imposed on thirty million people there. Do these convinced pacifists now hear the moans coming from there? Do they understand their responsibility today? Or do they prefer not to hear? The American intelligentsia lost its nerve and as a consequence the danger has come much closer to the United States. But there is no awareness of this. Your short-sighted politician who signed the hasty Vietnam capitulation seemingly gave America a carefree breathing pause; however, a hundredfold Vietnam now looms over you. Small Vietnam had been a warning and an occasion to mobilize the nation's courage. But if the full might of America suffered a full-fledged defeat at the hands of a small Communist half-country, how can the West hope to stand firm in the future?

I have said on another occasion that in the twentieth century Western democracy has not won any major war by itself; each time it shielded itself with an ally possessing a powerful land army, whose philosophy it did not question. In World War II against Hitler, instead of winning the conflict with its own forces, which would certainly have been sufficient, Western democracy raised up another enemy, one that would prove worse and more powerful, since Hitler had neither the resources nor the people, nor the ideas with broad appeal, nor such a large number of supporters in the West—a fifth column—as the Soviet Union possessed. Some Western voices already have spoken of the need of a protective screen against hostile forces in the next world conflict; in this case, the shield would be China. But I would not wish such an outcome to any country in the world. First of all, it is again a doomed alliance with evil; it would grant the United States a respite, but when at a later date China with its billion people would turn around armed with American weapons, America itself would fall victim to a Cambodia-style genocide.

Loss of Will

And yet, no weapons, no matter how powerful, can help the West until it overcomes its loss of will power. In a state of psychological weakness, weapons even become a burden for the capitulating side. To defend oneself, one must also be ready to die; there is little such readiness in a society raised in the cult of material well-being. Nothing is left, in this case, but concessions, attempts to gain time, and betrayal. Thus at the shameful Belgrade conference, free Western diplomats in their weakness surrendered the line of defense for which enslaved members of the Helsinki Watch Groups are sacrificing their lives.

Western thinking has become conservative: the world situation must stay as it is at any cost; there must be no changes. This debilitating dream of a status quo is the symptom of a society that has ceased to develop. But one must be blind in order not to see that the oceans no longer belong to the West, while the land under its domination keeps shrinking. The two so-called world wars (they were by far not on a world scale, not yet) constituted the internal self-destruction of the small progressive West which has thus prepared its own end. The next war (which does not have to be an atomic one; I do not believe it will be) may well bury Western civilization forever.

In the face of such danger, with such historical values in your past, with such a high level of attained freedom and, apparently, a devotion to it, how is it possible to lose to such an extent the will to defend oneself?

Humanism and Its Consequences

How has this unfavorable relation of forces come about? How did the West decline from its triumphal march to its present debility? Have there been fatal turns and losses of direction in its development? It does not seem so. The West kept advancing steadily in accordance with its proclaimed social intentions, hand in hand with a dazzling progress in technology. And all of a sudden it found itself in its present state of weakness.

This means that the mistake must be at the root, at the very foundation of thought in modern times. I refer to the prevailing Western view of the world which was born in the Renaissance and has found political expression since the Age of Enlightenment. It became the basis for political and social doctrine and could be called rationalistic humanism or humanistic autonomy: the proclaimed and practiced autonomy of man from any higher force above him. It could also be called anthropocentricity, with man seen as the center of all.

The turn introduced by the Renaissance was probably inevitable historically: the Middle Ages had come to a natural end by exhaustion, having become an intolerable despotic repression of man's physical nature in favor of the spiritual one. But then we recoiled from the spirit and embraced all that is material, excessively and incommensurately. The humanistic way of thinking, which has proclaimed itself our guide, did not admit the existence of intrinsic evil in man, nor did it see any task higher than the attainment of happiness on earth. It started modern Western civilization on the dangerous trend of worshiping man and his material needs. Everything beyond physical well-being and the accumulation of material goods, all other human requirements and characteristics of a subtler and higher nature, were left outside the area of attention of state and social systems, as if human life did not have any higher meaning. Thus gaps were left open for evil, and its drafts blow freely today. Mere freedom per se does not in the least solve all the problems of human life and even adds a number of new ones.

And yet in early democracies, as in American democracy at the time of its birth, all individual human rights were granted on the ground that man is God's creature. That is, freedom was given to the individual conditionally, in the assumption of his constant religious responsibility. Such was the heritage of the preceding one thousand years. Two hundred or even fifty years ago, it would have seemed quite impossible, in America, that an individual be granted boundless freedom with no purpose, simply for the satisfaction of his whims. Subsequently, however, all such limitations were eroded everywhere in the West; a total emancipation occurred from the moral heritage of Christian centuries with their great reserves of mercy and sacrifice. State systems were becoming ever more materialistic. The West has finally achieved the rights of man, and even to excess, but man's sense of responsibility to God and society has grown dimmer and dimmer. In the past decades, the legalistic selfishness of the Western approach to the world has reached its peak and the world has found itself in a harsh spiritual crisis and a political impasse. All the celebrated technological achievements of progress, including the conquest of outer space, do not redeem the twentieth century's moral poverty, which no one could have imagined even as late as the nineteenth century.

An Unexpected Kinship

As humanism in its development was becoming more and more materialistic, it also increasingly allowed its concepts to be used first by socialism and then by communism. So that Karl Marx was able to say, in 1844, that "communism is naturalized humanism."

This statement has proved to be not entirely unreasonable. One does see the same stones in the foundations of an eroded humanism and of any type of socialism: boundless materialism; freedom from religion and religious responsibility (which under Communist regimes attains the stage of antireligious dictatorship); concentration on social structures with an allegedly scientific approach. (This last is typical of both the Age of Enlightenment and of Marxism.) It is no accident that all of communism's rhetorical vows resolve around Man (with a capital *M*) and his earthly happiness. At first glance it seems an ugly parallel: common traits in the thinking and way of life of today's West and today's East? But such is the logic of materialistic development.

The interrelationship is such, moreover, that the current of materialism which is farthest to the left, and is hence the most consistent, always proves to be stronger, more attractive, and victorious. Humanism which has lost its Christian heritage cannot prevail in this competition. Thus during the past centuries and especially in recent decades, as the process became more acute, the alignment of forces was as follows: Liberalism was inevitably pushed aside by radicalism, radicalism had to surrender to socialism, and socialism could not stand up to communism. The Communist regime in the East could endure and grow due to the enthusiastic support from an enormous number of Western intellectuals who (feeling the kinship!) refused to see communism's crimes, and when they no longer could do so, they tried to justify these crimes. The problem persists: In our Eastern countries, communism has suffered a complete ideological defeat; it is zero and less than zero. And yet Western intellectuals still look at it with considerable interest and empathy, and this is precisely what makes it so immensely difficult for the West to withstand the East.

Before the Turn

I am not examining the case of a disaster brought on by a world war and the changes which it would produce in society. But as long as we wake up every morning under a peaceful sun, we must lead an everyday life. Yet there is a disaster which is already very much with us. I am referring to the calamity of an autonomous, irreligious humanistic consciousness.

It has made man the measure of all things on earth—imperfect man, who is never free of pride, self-interest, envy, vanity, and dozens of other defects. We are now paying for the mistakes which were not properly appraised at the beginning of the journey. On the way from the Renaissance to our days we have enriched our experience, but we have lost the concept of a Supreme Complete Entity which used to restrain our passions and our irresponsibility. We have placed too much hope in politics and social reforms, only to find out that we were being deprived of our most precious possession: our spiritual life. It is trampled by the party mob in the East, by the commercial one in the West. This is the essence of the crisis: the split in the world is less terrifying than the similarity of the disease afflicting its main sections.

If, as claimed by humanism, man were born only to be happy, he would not be born to die. Since his body is doomed to death, his task on earth evidently must be more spiritual: not a total engrossment in everyday life, not the search for the best ways to obtain material goods and then their carefree consumption. It has to be the fulfillment of a permanent, earnest duty so that one's life journey may become above all an experience of moral growth: to leave life a better human being than one started it. It is imperative to reappraise the scale of the usual human values; its present incorrectness is astounding. It is not possible that assessment of the President's performance should be reduced to the question of how much money one makes or to the availability of gasoline. Only by the voluntary nurturing in ourselves of freely accepted and serene self-restraint can mankind rise above the world stream of materialism.

Today it would be retrogressive to hold on to the ossified formulas of the Enlightenment. Such social dogmatism leaves us helpless before the trials of our times.

Even if we are spared destruction by war, life will have to change in order not to perish on its own. We cannot avoid reassessing the fundamental definitions of human life and human society. Is it true that man is above everything? Is there no Superior Spirit above him? Is it right that man's life and society's activities should be ruled by material expansion above all? Is it permissible to promote such expansion to the detriment of our integral spiritual life?

If the world has not approached its end, it has reached a major watershed in history, equal in importance to the turn from the Middle Ages to the Renaissance. It will demand from us a spiritual blaze; we shall have to rise to a new height of vision, to a new level of life, where our physical nature will not be cursed, as in the Middle Ages, but even more importantly, our spiritual being will not be trampled upon, as in the Modern Era.

This ascension is similar to climbing onto the next anthropological stage. No one on earth has any other way left but—upward.